The Future of
the Christian
Tradition

The Future of the Christian Tradition

Robert J. Miller, editor

POLEBRIDGE PRESS
Santa Rosa, California

Cover and interior design by Robaire Ream

Library of Congress Cataloging-in-Publication Data

The future of the Christian tradition / edited by Robert J. Miller.
    p. cm.
  ISBN 978-1-59815-000-1 (alk. paper)
 1. Christianity--21st century. 2. Jesus Seminar. I. Miller, Robert J. (Robert Joseph), 1954-
  BR121.3.F88 2007
  230--dc22

                            2007017539

Contents

Contributors

Joe Bessler-Northcutt is Associate Professor of Theology at Phillips Theological Seminary in Tulsa, Oklahoma.

Don Cupitt is a Life Fellow and former Dean of Emmanuel College, Cambridge.

Arthur J. Dewey is Professor of Theology at Xavier University in Cincinnati, Ohio.

Robert W. Funk retired as Professor of Religious Studies, University of Montana. He was founder of the Jesus Seminar and Director of the Westar Institute.

Lloyd Geering is Emeritus Professor of Religious Studies at Victoria University, Wellington, New Zealand.

Jack A. Hill is Associate Professor of Religion at Texas Christian University in Fort Worth, Texas.

Richard Holloway is Bishop of Edinburgh and Primus of the Scottish Episcopal Church, Retired.

Roy W. Hoover is Weyerhaeuser Professor of Biblical Literature and Professor of Religion Emeritus at Whitman College in Walla Walla, Washington.

John C. Kelly is Emeritus Professor of Philosophy at the University of Nevada, Reno.

Robert J. Miller is Professor of Religious Studies at Juniata College in Huntingdon, Pennsylvania.

Darren J. N. Middleton is Associate Professor of Religion at Texas Christian University in Fort Worth, Texas.

Stephen J. Patterson is Professor of New Testament at Eden Theological Seminary in St. Louis, Missouri.

Robert M. Price is Professor of Theology and Scriptural Studies at Johnnie Colemon Theological Seminary in Florida.

Anne Primavesi is a Fellow of the Centre for the Interdisciplinary Study of Religion, Birkbeck College, University of London.

Daryl Schmidt was John F. Weatherly Professor of New Testament at Texas Christian University in Fort Worth, Texas.

Eugenie C. Scott is Executive Director of the National Center for Science Education in Oakland, California.

John Shelby Spong is Episcopal Bishop Emeritus of Newark, New Jersey.

Introduction

Robert J. Miller

I n 2004 the Westar Institute moved its spring meeting from Santa Rosa in California to Times Square in New York City. For this extraordinary meeting the Institute suspended its ongoing seminars on the Historical Jesus and other historical and biblical projects in order that all the attending Fellows and Associates could come together to consider a special and timely topic: the future of the Christian tradition in the Second Axial Age. The scholarly work of the various Westar seminars is predominately historical in its focus and is therefore usually oriented to the Christian past. In 2004, nearly twenty years after the inauguration of Westar's first and best-known project, the Jesus Seminar, the time was right to pause in order to assess the present condition of the Christian tradition in light of what we have learned about its past and to articulate our hopes and fears for the future life of the Christian tradition as it confronts the challenges and opportunities of the global age and the new millennium.

On the term "Axial Age." The period from 800 to 200 BCE is referred to by many historians as the Axial Age because it was a time of seismic transformations in human consciousness. During this period philosophers, sages, and prophets from Greece, Israel, Persia, India, and China brought revolutionary insights and revelations that have permanently stamped the way we think about the spiritual, moral, and religious dimensions of human life. A small but increasing number of scholars believe that humanity has entered another period of transformation in consciousness as far-reaching and world-changing as the Axial Age—hence the term "Second Axial Age." There is no unanimity as to when this second age began and many believe that it is still in its early stages. Some of the phenomena that are part cause and part effect of the ongoing transformation in how we humans look at ourselves and our world are the rapid advances in science, the increasing ease of telecommunications (especially the Internet), the globalization of the economy and culture, and a burgeoning environmental awareness.

1

The Essays

Contributions to the spring 2004 conference were invited in four areas. (1) *An Authentic Contemporary Faith*. What elements of a traditional Christian faith can be carried forward as ingredients in an authentic contemporary faith? Elements of the old cosmology? A non-theistic deity? The Bible as sacred scripture? Life after death? Sin and guilt? (2) *Wisdom for the Global Age*. What kind of wisdom is needed in the Second Axial Age and how does it relate to conventional or traditional wisdom(s)? (3) *Religion, Science, and the Future of Life on Earth*. We have begun to see that humankind was included by God within the general evolutionary processes that formed the Earth's life support systems. The future of human life depends on the health of those systems. How do we make this earth-centered vision the heart of a faith commensurate with the Second Axial Age? (4) *The Moral Imperative: Sources and Sanctions*. The moral landscape has changed dramatically in the last half century. What new moral guidance is required for the Second Axial Age?

Contributors were free to choose their topics and the essays were written independently of one another. The grouping of the essays in this volume under the four categories is strictly for convenience; several essays could justifiably be placed in more than one category.

Part 1
An Authentic
Contemporary Faith

Robert Funk's opening address to the conference, "An Enlightened Faith for an Enlightened Age," first sketches the wisdom of the historical Jesus and some revolutionary insights of the Second Axial Age (which Funk sees beginning around 1600) and then expresses hope for a Christianity that can meet the challenges of the "second enlightenment." Jesus glimpsed an alternative reality (the "divine domain") which contrasted with the paramount reality of the everyday world. Jesus described that domain with a counterintuitive wisdom crystallized in such expressions as loving your enemies, hating your parents, and saving your life by forfeiting it. The Second Axial Age has reshaped our understanding of reality in ways that "contravene the paramount reality we inherited from our ancestors" and the intuitions grounded in our everyday experience. The circumnavigation of the globe alerted Europeans to more continents than they imagined; the Copernican revolution displaced humans from the center of the universe; the Enlightenment encouraged the rise of the secular state, the middle class, and modern democracy; Darwin showed us our intrinsic relatedness to all life forms; Einstein demonstrated that the physical universe follows laws that are profoundly counterintuitive; String Theory asks us to imagine ten dimensions and multiple universes beyond our sight. "The imagined worlds of the great sages of the First Axial Age begin to look quite tame alongside the fantasies we are now expected to endorse on the authority of the sciences." Funk believes that Christianity is in the midst of a "second enlightenment" during which the new knowledge of the Second Axial Age has put the God of theism into terminal decline and in which we humans must absorb the lesson that we are not at the center of things. Funk hopes for a new liberal spirit in Christianity, "a neo-liberalism with fresh intellectual vigor, immaculate honesty, and moral muscle" that will empower the radical rethinking of Christian symbols, beliefs, and practices, which is the only way Christianity can be reinvigorated for our times. It comes down to an "old choice: we can let the old time religion encumber us with a new dark ages or we can embrace the second enlightenment and continue our spiritual odyssey."

John Shelby Spong's, "Beyond Theism but not Beyond God: Beyond Incarnation but not Beyond Christ," is centered on his conviction that "if my Christianity cannot live inside the thought forms of the twenty-first century, then I do not believe it can live at all." He points out that "Christianity has never been static or stable." It has changed profoundly over the centuries as it adapted itself to the different ways of thinking in different ages. Spong argues that for Christianity to thrive in the twenty-first century, it must abandon two principles commonly considered to be its core: theism (the belief in God as a supreme Being external to the world and periodically intervening in it) and "the concept of Jesus as the Incarnation of this theistic deity." "Once this theistic God is dismissed the entire superstructure of traditional Christianity collapses. A twenty-first-century Christian must have the courage to let that happen." Spong then turns "to sketch a vision of what twenty-first-century Christianity might look like," focusing on the two principles just mentioned. (1) On the question of the reality of God, Spong avoids both theological realism and non-realism. The word "God" names not a Being outside the world, but a "dimension of our humanity that calls us beyond our normal limits." God is the source of life, "part of who I am, but more than what I am." Spong identifies God with the "life force, present in the universe, quite physical and real." The term "love" is entirely appropriate for it. (2) "The deepest truth that people experienced in Jesus was the experience of love," an experience which led them to profess that they had encountered God in the life of Jesus. Christianity is therefore not about doctrines or miracles or formulations of truth; it is "about entering the transcendent depth of life, love, and being in a human experience with a man named Jesus of Nazareth and calling that experience God." Spong concludes with a personal affirmation of how he believes he has experienced God and of how that experience shapes his life as a Christian.

In "Facing Up to Hard Questions: Christian Faith for a New Age," **Joe Bessler-Northcutt** confronts three "hard questions" which he believes Christianity will have to face if it is to "be taken seriously on intellectual and moral grounds." (1) Can Christians articulate an approach to God that is credible to our contemporary understanding of language and reality? (2) Can Christians articulate a Christology that rejects the logic of supercessionism and the imperial logic of Christian metaphysics? (3) Can Christians articulate an approach to life that respects and learns from both other intellectual disciplines and other religious traditions?"

Most of Bessler-Northcutt's essay is devoted to answering the first question. Building on the recognition that the word "God" is "a symbol or metaphor within the web of language" rather than a pointer to an external and objective reality, Bessler-Northcutt suggests that "the word 'God' attempts to name the mysterious power at work in the vastness of human freedom and history," a phenomenon that Hannah Arendt called "natality." Bessler-Northcutt analyzes and develops Arendt's meditation on natality to argue that God should be understood "not as an external power controlling events but as the felt power of newness and renewal at work in the ambiguity and unpredictability of history and human freedom." Arendt sees the power of natality most authentically expressed when it empowers humans to fulfill their obligation to risk themselves in public life. For Bessler-Northcutt, Christian faith is the acceptance of that obligation and the commitment to fulfill it, for example, "by standing with those who are in need, by listening to the voices, needs, and insights of strangers." The Christian appropriation of the idiom of natality also obliges Christians to face hard questions about the destructive effects of Christianity's past and present claims to possess exclusive authority.

In grappling with his second question, Bessler-Northcutt calls for a Christology grounded in the historical Jesus: "Jesus' Christological significance is not in himself, as such, but in the public capacity for newness and rebirth that he pointed to and embodied in parable and presence." Bessler-Northcutt briefly responds to his third question by emphasizing the necessity of the virtue of humility as the church faces the future.

Arthur Dewey's "Ecclesial Tectonics: *Non Est Extra*" is not an essay, but a series of numbered theses, more aphoristic than discursive, divided into eleven parts. Dewey's aim is to "focus the future of the church through the lead metaphors found in tectonics." Part 1, "A Linguistic Foothold," defines Ecclesial Tectonics as "a critical understanding of the artisanship that has historically constructed ecclesial communities." Parts 2 and 3, "Jesus as Peasant Artisan" and "Exposure of the Domination System," are brief sketches of the historical Jesus, his teaching of the Empire of God, and the meaning of his death. Parts 4 and 5, "Diversity from the Outset" and "The Fourth-Century Watershed," reflect on Eusebius's construction of early church history in the interests of imperial power. Part 6, "Heretical Tectonics," traces the historical development of the concept of "heresy" and freedom of conscience up to the present. Dewey emphasizes that language describing heresy is the "victory speech of the winners" and warns of contemporary temptations to fall into that language. Part 7, "Looking for Weapons of Mass Construction," reviews the early twentieth-century Modernist controversy during which officials of the Catholic Church refused to acknowledge that the church is historically (and thus humanly) constructed, a refusal which remains to this day, even though nearly everything the popes condemned in Modernism is now taught in Catholic universities. In Parts 8 and 9, "Colonial Aftershocks" and "Degrees of Complexity," Dewey argues that the demographic shift in Christianity toward South America, Africa, and Asia, can be the occasion for Christian theology, art, and sacraments to actualize their potential for embracing the complexity of life, which is always life together in history. Parts 10 and 11, "*Non est extra*" and "*Credo in unam, sanctam, catholicam ecclesiam*," express Dewey's vision for a future church which can redefine its creedal affirmations of being "one, holy, catholic, and apostolic" so as to embrace the diversity and complexity of the global reality of our life together on our fragile planet.

"Killing Jesus" by **Stephen J. Patterson**, outlines the diverse ways that Jesus' early followers interpreted his death: he was a victim of Roman power, a martyr for the Empire of God, a sacrifice that bound together a new community. Patterson shows that with each of those interpretations "Jesus' followers were in fact drawing attention to his *life*. His death mattered to them because his life had mattered to them." By understanding his death as the fitting end to his particular life, his followers "reaffirmed their own commitment to the values and visions stamped into his life by his words and deeds." Over time Christians no longer understood Jesus' death in the context of his life and Jesus became another of Antiquity's dying-rising savior gods. Eventually he became the most powerful god and his cross became a logo of a political empire and a "symbol of merciless power."

For most Christians today Jesus' death has lost all connection to his life. His death "has become for us a mythic event connected to the universal problem of death and the mysterious and frightening end of human life," concerns which eclipse the historical Jesus' words and deeds and render them functionally irrelevant to how Christian live. Jesus' earliest followers dared to believe that his death had not neutralized his life and teachings; on the contrary, the cross symbolized their truth and empowered his followers to live by them. Patterson warns that in our age in which Christians treat Jesus as a personal savior even while ignoring what he lived for, contemporary Christians are doing what the cross could not do: "We are killing Jesus."

Robert J. Miller begins "Literal Incarnation or Universal Love?" by showing how the doctrine of the literal incarnation (that is, "Jesus is the Son of God, fully divine and fully human, one person with two distinct natures") undergirds both Christianity's sense of its superiority to all other religions and Christians' confidence in their own salvation. However, the orthodox concept of a literal incarnation is not philosophically viable. "Every attempt at explaining, as opposed to restating, the orthodox doctrine has resulted in heresy." The concept that Christ is one person with two natures is an intellectual artifact that is both incoherent philosophically and a failure doctrinally in that it cannot be explained in a religiously acceptable way. However, since "the religious value of a belief has little to do with its philosophical coherence," Miller goes on to assess whether the literal incarnation is religiously helpful by weighing both its cost and its benefits. While the belief is certainly attractive, even beautiful, it comes with two high costs, the first of which is the intolerance inherent in Christian exclusivism. The second cost is the "scandal of limited access." If the incarnation is an act of love, why has there been only one incarnation that has affected only a minority of humanity? Miller argues that there is no way to affirm "both that there is an important advantage to being Christian *and* that Christians are not favored in a way that is unjust to the majority." Therefore, "Christian theology must make a choice: either a literal incarnation or a God of limitless and universal love." Although exclusivist forms of Christianity cannot relinquish a literal incarnation, Miller maintains that Christianity is better served by taking the incarnation metaphorically and offers a brief and simple creed expressing that belief.

"Tradition and Faith in a New Era" by **Roy Hoover** notes that our Second Axial Age has its roots in the scientific breakthroughs of Copernicus and Galileo, discoveries which were "world-destroying and world-constituting" and which marked "*the* epochal shift of the modern age." Whereas the church at that time opposed this new knowledge, the later churches have mostly ignored it, maintaining "the traditional forms of their faith and religious understanding as if nothing much had happened." Hoover traces the contemporary churches' crisis of credibility to this "holy narcolepsy" and recommends a cure: reorienting the churches' theological task away from defending orthodoxy toward a commitment to "veracity," the willingness and ability "to see things exactly as they are." Hoover probes the thought of two theologians who maintain that for Christian faith to be authentic it must resist adjusting its traditional affirmations in the light of new knowledge about the way things really are. For those theologians, authentic faith requires a stalwart defense of Christian affirmations that have been "believed everywhere, always, and by all" as revealed truth with the authority to judge all other (merely) human claims to truth. Hoover decries such a retreat as a refusal to ask whether the faith it affirms corresponds with reality, "but only whether 'faithful' Christian have always believed it." Hoover argues that to defend an orthodoxy that rejects new knowledge is to deprive the Judeo-Christian tradition of its credibility for the modern mind and that "a faith that has lost its credibility has lost its meaning." "To continue to recite traditional expressions of faith that have lost their meaning is to deprive people of a spiritual life." What our present situation demands of us is not an updated creed, "but something prior: an unconditional commitment to veracity."

The aim of **Richard Holloway**'s "The Church Organist and the Jazz Pianist" is to analyze the emerging cultural changes of the Second Axial Age as an example of a cultural and religious paradigm shift. Holloway explains the utility of paradigm theory, which began with the work of Thomas Kuhn in the history of science, for studying changes and developments within human culture. Holloway draws on insights from Marx and Nietzsche to understand what causes a paradigm shift in religion. Like all cultural systems, religions are, in part, power systems. Since all power creates victims, power systems (including religions) inevitably create victims who revolt against them. People in charge of religions, just as inevitably, use their power to oppose that challenge. Structural change begins when some of those within the power system turn against it and ally with its victims. Holloway then turns to describing four emergent characteristics of "the new evolutionary social paradigm:" (1) "a radical suspicion of power and authority," as opposed to the respect for authority that characterized the previous paradigm; (2) the principle of consent: "We expect to be asked, not told, in every area that concerns our own welfare." (3) "Pleasure is considered to be a good that need not always be delayed." (4) Ethical plurality is welcomed because it serves to prevent abuses of power. In closing, Holloway warns that the emergent paradigm shift will bring losses as well as gains, argues that it needs conservatives as well as liberals, and urges us to face the future by learning the art of adaptive improvisation, or "ethical jazz."

Part 2
Wisdom for
the Global Age

The starting point for **Daryl Schmidt**'s "VERITAS: The Truth of the Matter about Religion" is Marcus Borg's theory of religion. For Borg, belief in the reality of God can be grounded in religious experience; religions are human constructions built in response to experiences of the sacred. Schmidt points out that defenders of religion have often appealed to religious experience as a kind of empirical (and thus scientifically respectable) basis for religion, but also as a self-validating experience that cannot be explained (away) by scientific investigation. Schmidt wants to think critically about the nature and role of religious experience, and does so by turning to the theological work of C. David Grant. Grant frames religious experience as part of the "common human consciousness of the need for meaning." Meaning is not something we experience; rather, it is what we make out of our experience. For Grant, religious experience is an experience of our own need for transcendent meaning and religion is a worldview responding to that need.

Schmidt explains Grant's analysis of the Christian religion as a meaning-world centered on "grace," a meaning through which we regard life as a gift, and which awakens our gratitude for that gift and the desire to share it. We affirm grace by committing ourselves to live by it, to act graciously even in the face of evil in a world of imperfect justice. To live that way requires faith, understood as trust. Schmidt explores biblical corollaries to Grant's analyses of grace and faith and connects these to some fundamental findings of Westar's seminars on Jesus and Paul.

In "Beginning All Over Again," **Don Cupitt** argues that traditional religion focused on a world beyond this one is in terminal decline in the West. Against that backdrop Cupitt offers his own personal Creed, in five articles. Explicating his Creed, Cupitt professes that true religion is centered on a full affirmation of our contingent existence in this world and that it abjures any claims about the supernatural. We must claim our full ownership over our own lives and assume the responsibility for running them, committing ourselves to "productive value-realising action in the public world." In this religion, faith is letting go of certainties and the anxieties that come with them. Cupitt is convinced that such a religion is emerging on its own among common people, that "we in the modern West are finally abandoning the old 'dogmatic' vision of the world, and are moving over to a new outlook," which he calls "empty radical humanism." As evidence for this popular shift away from traditional religion, Cupitt cites the example of the growing interest in spirituality. However, the material found in bookstores in the spirituality section is "an avalanche of terminally self-indulgent tosh" that avoids the "cool recognition of the facts of the human condition: we are alone, everything passes away, we'll die, and there is no magic formula or specially-provided way out of all this." Cupitt entertains the possibility that Christianity can play a vital role in the new emergent religion—"those themes in Christianity which are most precious may yet have a future"—but only if it undergoes another Reformation in which it gives up "the old politics of truth" and is willing to sacrifice "its own identity and its own privileged status."

In the brief tribute, "On Behalf of John Robinson," **Don Cupitt** remembers his bishop mentor, who died in 1983, and the great controversy that swirled around his *Honest to God* in the 1960s. Cupitt explains the intellectual and cultural context for Robinson's thinking and argues that "Robinson was completely misunderstood, especially by the Church." Cupitt sketches the controversy over whether Robinson was an atheist, a charge Robinson denied, but which nonetheless led to the premature termination of his ecclesial and teaching career.

John Kelly's "Anti-Realism and Religious Belief" is a critical analysis of Don Cupitt's non-realist interpretation of religion. Kelly argues that Cupitt's philosophical non-realism combines Kantian skepticism ("we cannot know the nature of things in themselves, but only things as they appear to us") with an expansive view of the power of language to shape our thinking, a view, rooted in nineteenth-century Romanticism, that "we make our worlds through our various vocabularies." According to Kelly, "Cupitt's skepticism and Romanticism are deeply at odds with one another." Anti-realism undercuts its own claim to know that reality exceeds our ability to capture it in language. Kelly goes on to explore "the pragmatic implications of adopting Cupitt's non-realist interpretation of religious belief." The vast majority of Christians (including most theologians, conservative and liberal) would reject Cupitt's account of their faith, not out of unthinking rejection of a perceived threat, but because traditional Christian language is so deeply rooted in realism that it could not function as a vital expression of Christian life if reinterpreted by Cupitt's non-realism. To put it pointedly, "the concept of Christian non-realism is an oxymoron." Kelly also analyzes Cupitt's more recent departure from Christian anti-realism to his new embrace of a "religion of everyday life" (as articulated in Cupitt's *Life, Life*). Here too Cupitt's skepticism and philosophy of language are in fundamental tension with each other. Kelly argues that one cannot wholeheartedly embrace a worldview, not even the one entailed by the religion of everyday life, while harboring systemic doubts about its truth.

Darren Middleton begins his "Relational Theology in the Second Axial Age: A Response to Don Cupitt's Religious Theory" by summarizing Don Cupitt's description of the religious worldview emerging among ordinary people in the Second Axial Age, a worldview which "there is no ready-made, Real World out there, separate from life's shimmering flux and mutability." Rather, humans create our world out of emptiness through language. Because nothing is stable or fixed, Cupitt argues that we should embrace our own radical contingency and acknowledge that we construct our own humanity rather than receive it from an external Creator. Middleton expresses serious qualms over the incongruity between Cupitt's claim to be describing the Second Axial Age that is being shaped by ordinary people and the statistical data that show that most people (and a huge majority of Christians) do not share the worldview Cupitt describes. Middleton worries that Cupitt is prescribing a worldview that he believes people should embrace rather than describing one they actually do. However, Middleton maintains that Cupitt's own theory shows how to remedy this problem. Since language, which according to Cupitt is our means for creating our world, is social, it binds us to others in dialogue. Therefore, Middleton argues, the future of faith in the Second Axial Age must be worked out in "a dialogue characterized by constant movement between differences, the ceaseless to and fro of cultural perspectives, the endless back and forth of ideological nuances, and a conversation that does not fear life's messy verities." Of paramount importance is that Western academics take seriously the stories and values of other peoples and see their own Western liberal values as important contributions to the global dialogue, rather than as a universal standard by which to measure people from the non-Western world.

Lloyd Geering is convinced that "humankind faces a common future or no future at all." "A Path of Faith in the Global Future" sketches some salient features of the Judeo-Christian tradition in the Second Axial Age and explains their continuities with and departures from features of the First Axial Age. Geering emphasizes that the coming global culture will be a secular ("'this worldly and natural' as opposed to 'other-worldly and supernatural'"). He also insists that "secular" does not mean "non-religious" because religion is "the depth dimension of every culture." Geering maintains that "the emerging secular and humanistic world is not Christian in the way pre-modern Christendom was. But neither is it anti-Christian. It is best described as post-Christian, for it still reflects the values and customs of the tradition that gave it birth." Geering compares the evolution of modern secular culture out of Christian culture to the evolution of Christianity out of Judaism. During each of those transitions the tensions between old and new were obvious; "only when viewed from a distance does the continuity become apparent." A central example in both transitions is the concept of divinity. In the First Axial Age the traditional gods were rejected as the products of human imagination and replaced by one God; in the Second Axial Age "the God of classical monotheism has lost reality as a divine person and has come to be seen as a humanly created symbol, referring to a cluster of supreme values." A major aspect of the continuity of the post-Christian Second Axial Age with the First is that "the values most highly prized in the secular world are the continuation and expansion of values in the Judeo-Christian tradition. These values, such as love, justice, and freedom, convince us by their own inherent authority. They do not need the support of divine authority. The authority their worth exerts over us has replaced that of the now departing deity." Geering illustrates his thesis about continuity-in-discontinuity with three themes from the Bible: faith, hope, and love. These values "are basic to the Judeo-Christian tradition, and yet universal to the human condition." Freed from their connections to the theism of the past, faith, hope, and love remain vital to the religious and moral dimensions of life in the secular, global world.

Part 3
Religion, Science, and
the Future of Life on Earth

In "Evolution, Creationism, and the Myths of Nature," **Eugenie Scott** assesses the potential for both creationism and evolution to be sources for myth. In describing evolution Scott distinguishes its "Big Idea" (living things have common ancestors) from its processes (random mutation and natural selection) and its pattern (the taxonomy of life forms). Scott defines myths as "symbolic representations of values or cultural motifs that are central to the culture." Scott then discusses two forms of creationism, Young-Earth Creationism and Intelligent Design Creationism. The former, rooted in biblical literalism, rejects not only evolution, but also the results of modern physics, astronomy, geology, biology, and anthropology. Because Young-Earth Creationism is incoherent with modern knowledge, it cannot be a source for myth. Intelligent Design Creationism is not based on the Bible and does not make claims about past events. Nor does it aim to produce new knowledge about living things. Its primary aim is to demonstrate that certain features of living things cannot have evolved and so must have been directly created by God. "Intelligent Design Creationism stakes out such a minimalist position that there is scarcely anything to base a mythology on." Can evolution ground a myth of nature? Scott argues that it cannot. Nothing about the patterns of evolution is the stuff of myth. The processes of evolution have been and are the substratum of several irreconcilable ideologies and so fail as a source of myth. Evolution's Big Idea (common descent) has some potential for mythmaking, but it can just as easily be the basis for a myth of human superiority to all other life forms as it can for a myth of human solidarity with other life. Scott emphasizes, "Evolution *allows* but does not *compel* any particular religious or philosophical view." Moreover, because science constantly changes with the accumulation of new knowledge, it cannot provide the continuity necessary for myth to sustain a culture. Science just "makes lousy myth."

In "The Age of Ecology" **Anne Primavesi** maintains that the Age of Ecology should not be considered an age within human history, "for without what we now call 'ecology' there would have been no human history to divide into 'Ages.'" Primavesi believes that framing human history as a part of the Age of Ecology is radically subversive because such a framing undermines the assumption that human progress has freed us from dependence on the natural world and has allowed us to manage it for our own ends. Primavesi argues that humans' experience of living in cities makes it all too easy to ignore our utter dependence on natural systems. Primavesi explores the etymology of the term "ecology:" the "eco" derives from the Greek *oikos* ("household") and connotes a system of interdependent supply and consumption, as in the word "economy" (*oikonomia*). That term is used theologically in the early Christian tradition to refer to "the mystery of the relationships of love within God, and of God to the world, but also to divine government of the natural world." Unfortunately, the Greek concept of "divine economy" was translated into English (via Latin) with such terms as "dispensation" and "stewardship," terms with their own connotations that "cut the mystery of the divine economy down to human size" and enabled us to see ourselves as possessing the divine authority to manage the Earth solely for our own benefit. "The religious vision of Nature's economy as God's gift to the whole household of life had been reduced to one of ourselves as its stewards." Primavesi argues that an ecological paradigm can help us to escape that narrow vision and to counter the theological arrogance of assuming that God's interactions with the world are centered solely on us humans.

Part 4
The Moral Imperative:
Sources and Sanctions

"Can We Still Teach Biblical Moral Values?" by **Robert Price** explores the contemporary relevance of biblical teachings on sexual morality. On first consideration the Bible would seem to have little to say to us today. Sexual mores in the Bible changed over time, confounding any conservative attempt to look to the Bible for eternal truths. What is more important, "biblical sexual norms are based on quite different assumptions than the bases of our moral reasoning, whether we are fundamentalists or liberals," in three areas. (1) The Bible treats female chastity as a matter of male property rights. (2) Sexual mores in the Bible are often more a matter of purity (i.e., fitness for ritual participation) than of morality. (3) "Biblical sexual laws have more to do with honor and shame than with good and evil." The Bible's evaluation of sexual behavior within the three frameworks of property rights, purity, and honor also produced a blatant double standard which restricted women far more than men. Price concludes that the Bible "is not really talking about sexual morality in our sense at all." Nevertheless, Price argues that the notions of sexual property, purity, and honor can provide meaningful ethical guidance today if we apply them creatively and repudiate the Bible's gender bias. Teaching young women that their sexuality

is their own property can help them value it. Teaching young men
to behave with honor—by not dishonoring women—can motivate
them positively. Price makes the case that regarding premarital
sex—which the Bible never explicitly condemns as immoral—as a
transgression against ritual purity rather than as morally wrong can,
if treated with the appropriate nuance, inculcate "an appropriate and
honest conscience" about sex between unmarried persons.

In "The Boy Scout and the Mafia Boss," **Jack A. Hill** isolates and
analyzes two "polar moral identifications" that "reflect deep-seated
tensions in the American psyche." The Boy Scout is the ideal of
"the reliable and self-disciplined young man who is always prepared to take care of himself and to help people in need." On the
other end of our moral imagination is the mafia boss, a figure with
whom Americans are fascinated, who "bends people to his will"
and "is like a god unto himself . . . acting above the law to achieve
his own sense of justice." Hill demonstrates how these two models
"recapitulate core moral traditions in the American experience" by
correlating them with four basic "narratives" in American culture:
"the Biblical covenant, the mission of America, the Enlightenment
vision of progress, and the human potential movement." The belief
of the Pilgrims that they were a new Israel called to build a kingdom
of God in America and the belief that America has a God-given
mission to spread freedom and democracy, by force if necessary, to
all peoples match up to virtues of the Boy Scout. The other two
American stories, the rags-to-riches myth of the "self-made man"
and the quest to "find oneself" and achieve personal well-being cor-
relate, in some respects, to the image of the mafia boss who values
"individualism, private property, the accumulation of wealth, and
competition." Hill then considers the moral import of the historical Jesus (using the gospel material identified by the Jesus Seminar
as authentic) in the light of the mafia boss and the Boy Scout. By
reading the well-known teachings of Jesus against the moral norms
implicit in the models of the Boy Scout and the mafia boss, Hill
shows that some of the most familiar of Jesus teachings work in
ways that confound bedrock American expectations. Hill makes
the case that "on close examination, Jesus begins to look less and
less like a Boy Scout." And although the moral consciousness that
Jesus advocates is quite unlike that of the mafia boss, that model
can help us make sense out of some of the more enigmatic and
disturbing parables (such as the Talents, the Dishonest Manager,
the Unforgiving Servant, the Widow and the Judge, and the Great
Dinner), Hill concludes with reflections on how Jesus' vision of the
moral life can speak to Americans today.

Part I

An Authentic Contemporary Faith

An Enlightened Faith for an Enlightened Age

Robert W. Funk

A lmost twenty-five years ago, the Fellows and Friends of the Jesus Seminar embarked on a collective spiritual odyssey. The defining moment of our odyssey was the divorce of the historical Jesus from the mythical matrix in which the early Jesus movement had cradled him.

The underlying figure turned out to be a sage informed by the wisdom of Israel and the insights of the First Axial Age. The First Axial Age represents what was perhaps the first major transition in human history, during which all of the world's living religions were born. Jesus comes relatively late in the period that begins ca. 800 BCE. Yet in his insights we catch glimpses of things that are to come, indeed, that have not yet fully come. He drew on the insights of his precursors, the great prophets of Israel, and perhaps the Cynic philosophers.

For some reason, in the West, developments came to a halt about 200 CE. That was about the time both Jewish and Christian canons of scripture were closed. It seems the spirit had departed from both Israel and the Church. In the fourth century, the church encased Jesus in the creed and the dark ages set in. For 1400 years, the human imagination in the West appeared to lie dormant. And, then, suddenly around 1600, the heavens opened and visionaries began to dream new dreams. New worlds opened up and what is now coming to be thought of as the Second Axial Age was inaugurated.

We were barely four hundred years into this new age when the Global Age arrived. It arrived dramatically on 9/11 2001. Lloyd Geering has wisely proposed that we begin counting from 2001 as the first year of the new age. It is now clear that we live in a single global community. The advent of the global age has put additional new strains on the adjustments have we been trying to make in the first four centuries of the Second Axial Age.

We live between the times, as Nietzsche and the poet Hölderlin observed a century ago. We are in transition from one paramount reality to another. And the stresses and strains on our ability to adjust have grown exponentially. The tension is enormous as we attempt to navigate the passage from the old, pre-modern worldview to the new reality sense that is only now emerging in the common consciousness. It is both modern and post-modern as well as global: the triple assault is producing a massive cultural earthquake.

Human beings live perpetually out of one reality sense into another. A new reality is always under construction. Strong "poets' and prophets catch glimpses of who we are and where we are as one world is being dismantled and another assembled. A strong "poet," according to Harold Bloom, is not simply a writer of verse, but one whose glimpse of things above and beyond we cannot completely assimilate. The insights of strong poets live on as troublesome reminders of our tendency to settle for the conventional.

We are here at this conference to ask ourselves whether the Judeo-Christian tradition has anything to offer in the Second Axial Age. Will any part of that tradition survive the transition? I intend to focus this evening on the prospects of the Christian strand of that tradition.

I intend to do so, first, by sketching the insights of Jesus of Nazareth that are worth pondering in the new age. A second part of my essay will sketch, in barest outline, the revolutionary insights of the first four centuries of the Second Axial Age. The third part of my essay will be devoted to a handful of insights I believe to be pertinent to the Global Age.

Halford Luccock, professor of Homiletics at Yale for many years, was once asked how many points a sermon should have. His laconic reply: "At least one." My sole point is that the three religions stemming from Abraham are being put to the test; whether they survive and whether they will contribute to our collective futures, depends on whether they can not only adjust to the new reality requirements of the Second Axial Age but are able to move beyond them.

The Wisdom of Jesus & the First Axial Age

The Ecstatic Condition

At some point in his career, Jesus went down to the Jordan and was baptized by John the Baptist. As he came up out of the water, we are told by the gospel writer, the heavens opened and the spirit descended on him like a dove. According to Marcus Borg, at that moment Jesus achieved the "ecstatic state of consciousness." In Borg's words, Jesus momentarily got a peek into another world, as though through a door or "tear."[1] I can also agree with Borg that true visions are *noetic*. They have some cognitive content and are not just mountain top experiences with no particular intelligence. Glimpses of other worlds are not uncommon among poets and prophets. In Buddhism such a vision is called enlightenment. Other names for them are epiphanies or revelations.

In his book, *Omens of Millennium*, Harold Bloom asserts that transcendence that cannot be articulated is an incoherence. Authentic transcendence, he says, is communicated by the mastery of language, by metaphor, which is a kind of carrying-across from one kind of experience to another.[2] Jesus appears to have articulated his vision in metaphors carried across from the everyday to what he called the kingdom of God.

While I agree that Jesus had a vision, I do not think the baptismal scene depicted in the Gospel of Mark tells us anything about its content. The voice from heaven announcing that Jesus is God's favorite son is the gospel writer's own message to his listeners or readers. It is the beginning of the process of turning the Jewish sage into the son of God.

The Divine Domain

According to the Synoptic Gospels, Jesus caught a glimpse of something he called the kingdom of God. He expressed that glimpse in his aphorisms and parables.

Three preliminary observations about his language will help us understand his words.

1. Jesus focused exclusively on things and events in the everyday world. He does not speak of things in the world above, or the world below, or a future world. His parables and aphorisms consist of pointed observations on ordinary things and events.

Of course, he speaks of demons and Satan, but those were part and parcel of his lived world. But he was no theologian. He does not use abstract language. He would not have thought to say, "All men have sinned and fallen short of the glory of God." It would not even have occurred to him to say, "God is love." He certainly would not have announced that God is the ground of being.

2. These vignettes and metaphors drawn from the world at hand are actually facets or fragments of the vision of an alternative reality forming in his mind. That alternative reality he named the divine domain. (I have elected to translate "kingdom of God" as *divine domain* to avoid both "kingdom" and "God.")

3. The third observation is crucial: The alternative reality Jesus sees contrasts with the paramount reality of the everyday world. His wisdom is counterintuitive. Jesus' vision contravenes received wisdom, habituated experience. In the divine domain, things are not what they seem. The divine domain lies through the door, so to speak, to another reality.

But that other reality is not in another place, or off in some indeterminate future; it is right there in the interstices of the everyday, in the crossroads and junctions of the ordinary. Under the influence of the Platonic worldview we have come to assume that the domain of God lies in another dimension, or another time, inaccessible to us here and now. For Jesus the divine domain is as near as the neighbor, as close as someone pounding on your door at midnight asking for a loaf of bread, as imminent as a beggar with an extended hand.

The Ten Words of Jesus

What are the contours of the divine domain as Jesus sees them? I have attempted to summarize them in ten words.

I am tempted to call these the new ten words, as the Ten Commandments are called. But they are not commandments and I do not recommend them as a monument for courthouse lobbies.

1. *The divine domain belongs to the poor.*

In the first beatitude, the poor learn, to their surprise, that the divine domain belongs to them. That contravenes appearances.

2. *Love your enemies.*

The admonition to love enemies is an invitation to transcend tribal boundaries.

3. *Hate your father and mother.*

Jesus tells potential followers that they must abandon their primary structures of socialization if they want to be his disciples.

4. *Whoever tries to hang on to life will forfeit it, but whoever forfeits life will preserve it.*

In the divine domain, according to Jesus, to seek to preserve life is to lose life. To have life we must give it away.

5. *Forgive and you'll be forgiven.*

This assurance is an oblique rejection of the brokerage system. He advises his followers to function as their own priests.

6. *No prophet is welcome on his home turf.*

Jesus was an outsider and outcast. He was unwelcome in his hometown, like other prophets.

> 7. *If someone sues you for your coat, give him the shirt off your back to go with it.*

In a two-garment society, that would have produced gales of laughter. Humor has a way of undermining the domination structures.

Thus far I have spoken only of the alterations to the human social world. Jesus also has some hints about the cosmic context that differ from the received worldview.

> 8. *According to Jesus, there is no room for demons in the divine domain.*

The fall of Satan is the first huge step in sweeping the heavens clear of gods and demons.

> 9. *Consider the lilies and the sparrows.*

The divine domain extends even to the flowers and the birds.

> 10. *God sends the rain on both the good and the bad, and causes the sun to shine on both the just and unjust.*

The cosmos is indifferent to human projects and goals.

The Narrow Door

Now imagine a world in which these particulars hold true. As a vision, it is always outstanding. That is because there is always some neighbor to be helped, always someone in need, always a barrier to be broken, always some horizon to be pushed back. Faith is perpetually subversive of the status quo. The door to this reality is narrow and few find it.

Paul of Tarsus

Paul of Tarsus grasped the contrast. The account of Paul's vision on the Damascus road parallels the baptismal scene for Jesus. In Galatians, Paul labels that vision "the truth of the gospel" and sums it up in the dictum that in the divine domain there is neither Jew nor Greek, neither slave nor free, neither male nor female; all have the same status. Paul contrasts the wisdom of the world—the paramount reality—and the foolishness of the gospel—the new reality—in First Corinthians. In Second Corinthians, in reflecting on his own disposition Paul becomes painfully aware of how this feature of the new reality robs him of his arrogance, of his tendency to brag, to impose his views on everyone and everything. As Jack Spong has wisely said, the gospel runs counter to the habits of mind and instincts we acquired in our long, slow evolution from earlier life forms.

The Second Axial Age

The Second Axial Age, which began around 1600, is turning the earth on its axis: reality has taken on a new cast. The new age is driven by new glimpses of things that contravene habituated human experience and received wisdom. Brian Greene, the author of the best selling *The Elegant Universe,* sums up what he and many other contemporary physicists think function as roadblocks to new perceptions of the physical universe:

> Like believing the earth flat or that man was created on the sixth day, our willingness to place unjustified faith in immediate perceptions of received wisdom leads us to an inaccurate and starkly limited vision of reality.[3]

The two items—flat earth and creation on the sixth day—are part of a symbolic universe that once held together as a cohesive myth. That mythic constellation served to legitimize all the parts—geocentric solar system, homocentric life world, patricentric social structures—by integrating them into a believable whole. Once in place, the tenacity of that myth has been remarkable.

The old symbolic universe has served to block new perceptions of reality. But the Second Axial Age is a period in which our notions of ultimate reality are rapidly changing, almost on a daily basis.

Richard Lewontin, a biologist, puts the matter this way:

> Virtually the entire body of modern science is an attempt to explain phenomena that cannot be experienced directly by human beings, by reference to forces and processes that we cannot directly perceive because they are too small, like molecules, or too vast, like the entire known universe, or the result of forces that our senses cannot detect like electromagnetism, or the outcome of extremely complex interactions, like the coming into being of an individual organism from its conception as a fertilized egg.[4]

Beginning with the invention of the telescope, and later the microscope, human beings began to investigate consequences that lay out of sight, or contradicted the self-evident. Howard Margolis puts the contrast this way: "Suppose that what was discovered by classical science was essentially what could be noticed without violating some intuition strongly supported by experience."[5] Suppose, further, that beginning about 1600, science began a new kind of boldness and persistence in pushing received intuitions up against closer observation and rigorous analysis. This process, according to E. O. Wilson, released us from the cognitive prison in which limited sight and hearing had held us captive. Now, suddenly, we began to 'see' much larger worlds, well beyond the natural limits of human observation. I put 'see' always in inverted commas to remind us that we do not actually see particles unimaginably small or universes unbelievably big, or black holes so incredibly powerful that nothing, not even light, can escape.

As a consequence of these advances in 'seeing,' an alternative reality began to emerge, and that reality contravened the paramount reality we inherited from our ancestors.

The Circumnavigation of the Globe

You will recall that Gutenberg invented the printing press around 1440. That did not change our perceptions of reality, but it did promote the dissemination of information. Then in 1517 Luther launched the Reformation, which, John Dillenberger tells me, lasted only about thirty years. That brings us to the Council of Trent in 1545, when the church again tried to put a lid on developments.

The story of the sciences in the Second Axial Age is that adventurers started out looking for one thing and in the process discovered something startlingly new.

In 1492 Columbus went looking for another way to spice-rich China and stumbled on the new world. Columbus died in 1506 thinking he had reached some islands off the west coast of China. In 1507, a German cartographer, Waldseemuller, produced a new map of the world that featured another continent on the opposite side of the earth from the three known landmasses. Ferdinand Magellan set sail for the Pacific in 1519 and discovered how formidable that new continent was.

Up until that time, it was standard wisdom to believe the earth was the center of a nested world: As the center of the earth, Jerusalem was surrounded by three landmasses, Asia, Africa, and Europe. The sun and planets orbited the earth, whose position was fixed. The fixed stars lay beyond in the vault of heaven.

The insight that there was another continent on the far side of the globe may have prompted Copernicus to perceive the earth as another planet. One around-the-corner, in this case, around-the-globe, insight led to another.

The Copernican Revolution

Then, in 1543, Copernicus published his view of the heavens, in which he replaced the earth with the sun as the center of the solar system. He set out to account for those strange loops the planets appeared to make in their orbits. What he discovered turned the Ptolemaic scheme propagated 1400 years earlier inside out. Copernicus was not the first, of course, to propose a heliocentric solar system That honor goes to Aristarchus 1800 years earlier. But Copernicus finally saw that it made sense to have Venus and Mars orbit the sun, and thus to see that the earth did the same. Copernicus' radical idea transformed the status of the earth: it was no longer sublunar; it became a heavenly body.

Copernicus' move countered common sense. It is hard to believe that the earth orbits the sun while turning on its axis as it whirls through space. Copernicus' challenge to common sense opened up a new phase of scientific observation.

The problem Copernicus, Galileo, and Kepler posed was that the whole scheme involving the earth and the entire heavens had to be rethought from a totally new perspective. A tightly knit set of insights produced a new comprehensive vision of the world. A new symbolic universe was coming into being in the imagination.

Galileo walked with his telescope through the door opened by Copernicus, and Kepler confirmed the results. Later in that fabulous century, Newton formulated the law of gravity with a mathematical precision that was used to put Neil Armstrong on the moon in 1969 and the two rovers on Mars in 2004. The Newtonian universe was a mathematically precise affair that lent itself to deism, the view that, like a great watchmaker, God created the world and then went off to let it tick on its own.

Enlightenment

To the third of these remarkable transitions we give the name Enlightenment. The Enlightenment represents the shift from the Middle Ages to the modern period.

I use the term Enlightenment here to include the scientific revolution that began with Copernicus, but also to include radical thinkers like René Descartes, Baruch Spinoza, John Locke, and David Hume, all of whom were innovators.

The liberal spirit was the chief product of the Enlightenment. Enlightenment thinkers rejected external authority in favor of observation, hypothesis, and experiment. Reason replaced revelation as the arbiter of knowledge. Accordingly, the liberal spirit has always been the champion of learning and freedom of inquiry.

The Thirty Years War (1618–1648) wiped out half the population of Germany and gave rise to the secular state. The secular state was created to keep one parochialism from imposing its will on all others.

The Enlightenment encouraged the rise of a merchant class. Monastic asceticism was replaced by the work ethic, which permitted the formation of a middle class. A strong middle class is the foundation of all modern democracies.

The Enlightenment promoted humanitarian motives in modern Western societies. The liberal spirit was a cry for justice and the rule of law. It was and is an optimistic spirit. The great thinkers and scientists of the Enlightenment were essentially propagandists—they wrote for the general reader.

We have learned, of course, that some excesses of the Enlightenment are no longer desirable. An absolute reliance on reason was moderated by the Romantic movement of the nineteenth century. The Industrial Revolution brought many improvements in daily life for the average person, but it also ultimately led to the abuse of workers, and the rise of a corporate culture and global capitalism, both of which are not without their evils.

The reign of reason came to an abrupt end in the French reign of terror, but it crossed the Atlantic and gave birth to the Declaration of Independence and the Bill of Rights. "We hold these truths to be self-evident . . ." is a declaration of the Enlightenment through Franklin and Jefferson.

(I need to add that the British anticipated all this with the Magna Carta, signed by King John in 1215, which guaranteed certain liberties. But the Magna Carta came a little early in the transition and left royalty and the class system to be dissolved more slowly over a longer period of time.)

Darwin

Two hundred years after Newton, in *On the Origin of Species by Means of Natural Selection*, 1859, Darwin proposed what became the theory of evolution. It became obvious at once that Homo sapiens was a late arrival on planet earth and had developed from earlier life forms. The quest for the origin of species led to a second unanticipated conclusion. Some theologians saw immediately that the Genesis account of creation must be a fiction that awards human beings the crowning position in the grand scheme of things. The biblical scholars and theologians who espoused the new views at the end of the nineteenth century were charged with heresy and many lost their pulpits and academic posts. The sciences alone, it seems, have had to drag the churches and synagogues kicking and screaming into the twenty-first century.

Einstein and Relativity

Three hundred years after Newton, Einstein formulated the theory of special relativity, which he later modified into the theory of general relativity. Einstein taught us that there are no absolutes; everything is relative to the location and motion of the perceiver. A clock in motion ticks more slowly than a clock at rest. The one exception, of course, is the speed of light. No matter how we perceive light, it always travels at the same speed, 186,000 miles a second. Space and time are interwoven and relative. There is now only spacetime (one word). Also interwoven are energy and mass. If we know the mass of a thing, we can calculate its energy and vice versa. The result is the famous formula $E = mc^2$. The letter c stands for the speed of light and that is a huge number. The application of this formula to a small amount of uranium produced the explosion at Hiroshima.

Brian Greene sums up the real problem we face in the attempt to absorb these advances:

> The meta-lesson of both relativity and quantum mechanics is that when we deeply probe the fundamental workings of the universe we may come upon aspects that are vastly different from our expectations. The boldness of asking deep questions may require unforeseen flexibility if we are to accept the answers.[6]

The basic feature of all these insights is that they are essentially counterintuitive.

Einstein's work concerned the universe on the largest of scales. Quantum mechanics examines the universe on the smallest of scales. Quantum theory holds that we cannot predict the behavior of particles when observed at the atomic and subatomic level. This development, too, was disturbingly counterintuitive.

String Theory: The Theory of Everything

Our need to adjust is just in its infancy, however. In the 1980s, just as the Jesus Seminar was getting underway, physicists and mathematicians were propounding a new theory, called string theory. We are now supposed to believe, again against our senses and our common sense, that there are at least ten dimensions to space, in addition to time, which itself may have more than one dimension. It turns out that atoms are not the most fundamental building blocks of the universe. By the early 1930s, scientists had established that atoms consist of a nucleus made up of neutrons and protons, around which electrons swarm. In 1968, we learned that each proton and neutron consists of quarks, which themselves come in two varieties, up-quarks and down-quarks. Indirect evidence since then has led to the identification of even more exotic particles called neutrinos, muons, taus, and more kinds of quarks.

The new microcosm is made of something much smaller, called strings, both open ended and looped. A typical string loop is about a hundred billion billion (10^{20}) times smaller than an atomic nucleus. It now appears that on this planet we live on a brane (a membrane) of limited dimensions, but there are many other worlds invisible to our eyes.

The physicists have now announced they are working on a theory of everything (T.O.E. for short). They refer to it as the new Holy Grail, the object of the ultimate quest. More than one physicist has exclaimed that we will get to the fundamental building block of reality and then we will know the mind of God. One of them has said: "It took the abstractions of the sciences to undo the obvious." The obvious was what we all thought to be the case.

The imagined worlds of the great sages of the First Axial Age begin to look quite tame alongside the fantasies we are now expected to endorse on the authority of the sciences. The essential features of both sets of glimpses were fundamentally counterintuitive.

Ecology: Apocalypse Now

The bloated appetites of the human species are threatening the viability of our life together on this planet.

Overpopulation and unrestrained demand for a better life are depleting our natural resources at a devastating rate. The world population is now passing six billion. The critical mass is eight billion. The current birth rate is 2.6 children per woman and declining. Even if it declines to 2.2, the world's population will reach 12.5 billion by 2050, only forty-six years away. And most of the growth will take place in developing countries, which are already stressed and economically impoverished. That is an apocalypse in the making. We will not be able to feed, house, and clothe our offspring beyond that point.

The sad thing is that we are making it even harder on ourselves by the ruthless and avaricious destruction of portions of the ecosystem that help support us in the first place. Why this piece of wisdom, this salient insight has come so late is, I suppose, part of the human inability to transcend its own previous concept of itself as the crown of creation. We have come late to the realization that our well being depends on the well being of all life forms in the biosphere. The loss of the ozone, the pollution of lakes and rivers, the wanton destruction of rain forests, the insatiable need for oil from the ground and fish from the sea, are robbing us of any tenable future. We needn't wait for the big crunch a few billion years hence to end it all; we are creating the big crunch for ourselves here and now.

The Second Enlightenment

A second Enlightenment took place in the decade of the 1960s. It was called a reawakening by Robert Ellwood. A counterculture was born. The Civil Rights Movement took wings. John XXIII convened Vatican II (1962–1965). Haight-Ashbury became the center of the new cult. JFK and Martin Luther King were assassinated. The sexual revolution reached its peak. Tom Wolfe popularized the drug culture in his *The Electric Kool-Aid Acid Test* (1968). Harvey Cox gave us the *Secular City* (1965). The decade formed a decisive watershed in modern cultural history.

The Demise of the Theistic God

It was during this same period that the death of God movement got underway.

John A. T. Robinson published his prescient book *Honest to God* in 1963. In his book, Robinson summed up the impact of new knowledge of the universe by saying that we can no more convince people of a "God out there" than we can persuade them that the gods of Olympus are "up there." That, he went on to say, is because most moderns are "secularists." By that he meant they put their faith in reason & the sciences rather than in the church.

For Robinson: the question of God is the question of transcendence—self-transcendence, species transcendence, and world transcendence. Dietrich Bonhoeffer, a precursor of Robinson, attempted to salvage the transcendence of God by saying "God is the 'beyond' in our midst."

The God of theism has suffered terminal decline under the impact of the sciences and the humanities since the beginning of the Second Axial Age. The God concept may, of course, continue to serve as a symbol of transcendence. I would define that symbol this way: There is a "beyond" to everything we know or can know. There will always be something smaller, or larger, or older, or newer, or just beyond view, or just around the perceptual corner to pique our curiosity. A theory of everything will fall short and we will go on searching for the ultimate explanation. The earth is curved, we are told, so we can't see too far ahead. This is a limitation that actually opens up unlimited possibilities for the future. For those who are enamored of the idea of God, we could say that God is the oncoming future. God is the fund of possibilities the future lays on the present. That is a precious gift. It is probably the gift that makes us human.

The Displacement of Homo Sapiens

In the New York Times, 11 January 2004, William J. Broad wrote:

> The story of astronomy is one long, slow assault on our [human] sense of self-importance. The ancients knew they were at the center of things. Their eyes told them that the sun and stars moved around them day and night, eternally circling their snug homes.

One of the most profound insights of the Second Axial Age is the story of the slow displacement of human beings from the center of everything.

What we have learned in the Second Axial Age has prompted us to shrink God down to size to fit in a new mythical universe. We should also have learned, but probably haven't as yet, that human beings have yet to shrink down to their proportional size in the grand scheme of things.

Because we are at the top of the food chain, have language, and can achieve the "ecstatic condition," we think we have the right to dominate the earth and all that's in it. Developments in the Second Axial Age have been a steady assault on that self-understanding.

When the universe ceased to be geocentric, it also ceased to be homocentric, as Anne Primavesi puts it. As the universe grew in size and complexity, humans grew smaller and less significant by comparison. Then Darwin added to the painful shrinkage by making humans a belated addition to the earth's higher mammals. The mapping of the human genome has recently put another dent in human pride. As it turns out, we are quite closely related to other life forms.

The human capacity for self-transcendence is to be highly prized. At the same time, that gift has a downside. Humans also have the innate, infinite capacity to deceive themselves. There is nothing we cannot sublimate, rationalize, or justify. This defect is perhaps the last vestige of what we used to call original sin. The antidote to the downside is genuine self-transcendence, nurtured in carefully structured human communities, and liberal applications of humor.

We need Bill Maher as our master of ceremonies.

The Rise and Fall of Mythical Worlds

In the period beginning about 1960, we also learned that mythical worlds are a social product with a history (Peter Berger and

Thomas Luckman, *The Social Construction of Reality,* 1966). We can trace the history of their rise, for example, in ancient Israel and in early Christian communities. Both borrowed foundational elements from still older Near Eastern mythologies. We can also trace their modification and decline. The Western versions came to their widely recognized demise in the 60s.

Because symbols and myths are social products, we cannot adopt or abandon them arbitrarily. They are created collectively and can only be abandoned collectively. But we can track their trajectories. It is worth knowing where we are in the life cycle of a symbol system. And we know these larger trends will eventually take all of us with them. They have the power of glaciers as they mould and modify our cultural landscape. However, we also know that we can deflect or modify the direction of their rise, development, and decline by exerting concentrated, focused cultural pressure. Christianity did just that when it borrowed the tribal traditions of Israel and turned them into transethnic symbols and eventually into cosmic myths. In our case, we are faced with a more formidable challenge: we shall have to replace the old symbols and myths with new ones appropriate to the global age we are now entering. New symbols will include the earth seen from space as a unitary biosphere, the telescope, the microscope, and the round table at the center of new communities of faith. That is a Herculean task, one might even say, a task for the gods.

The Decline of the Liberal Spirit

We need a rebirth of the Liberal Spirit. We require a neo-liberalism with fresh intellectual rigor, immaculate honesty, and moral muscle, circumspectly informed by the sciences, and awash in toe-tapping cadences inspired by the need to sing and dance. The new spirit will wither if not allied with the arts.

We must begin by leaving old-fashioned liberalism behind. The old version in the political arena is probably beyond repair, and the edition once alive and well in the churches and synagogues has suffered terminal decline.

The old religious liberalism has gone to seed in political correctness and post-modern cynicism. The ethical muscle of the old social gospel evaporated in formulas, quotas, and labels. The privatization of all opinion has robbed liberals of their ability to act collectively. Liberalism has become a spectator sport.

The liberal churches have largely abandoned their commitment to scholarship, the sciences, and candor. They divorced their scholars in order to patronize a shrinking clientele. The scholars, for their part, retreated into their library carrels and took up equally esoteric pursuits of interest only to themselves. As a consequence, that scholarship lost its public base.

To recover that public and contribute to an elevated literacy level, we must reconnect with the churches from the bottom up. Our Jesus Seminar On-the-Road programs are designed for that purpose.

Yet the Seminar has yet to deal with key issues that block real progress. Those issues: the Bible as Word of God; the Sunday Morning Experience; and the cross as the primary Christian symbol.

The Bible

We have yet to explore seriously whether the formation of the Christian canon of scripture was a "tragic mistake," as some have alleged, or whether we can surround the Bible with enough critical lore to maintain its selective credibility. Because the Bible has become, in the U.S., a cultural artifact, the malady is culture wide; it is not restricted to the churches.

My own conviction is that we need a thorough revision of the canon of scriptures, in more than one recension. It is important to have multiple collections of sacred texts that appear in the "Bible" sections of bookstores.

Sunday Morning Experience

The Sunday Morning Experience is an excursion into a virtual reality that wilts under the demands of the Monday Morning reality check. The emerging paramount reality, dictated largely by the sciences, physical, social, and psychological, is at war with the premodern mind set. The latter is in decline and will eventually fade away. If we do not reform the Sunday Morning experience, or create an equivalent, Christianity will fade away with it.

The Christian Symbols

As human beings, we invent symbols in which we invest passion and authority, as James Carroll reminds us, quoting Joyce Carol Oates. The pre-eminent Christian symbol has come to be the cross. It was not always so. That investment began in earnest with Constantine in the fourth century and was renewed with interest in the Crusades. It haunts the relation of Christians to Jews. Mel Gibson has set Christianity back about four hundred years with his passion play on film by focusing exclusively on the cross in its bloodiest form as the symbol of Christianity. The film is deeply anti-Jewish, just as the gospels, especially John, are anti-Jewish. I see no way to eradicate this blemish on the Christian conscience other than to revise the gospels and replace the cross as the primary symbol.

The New Faith Community

In the process of searching for the historical Jesus, we discovered, by chance, that what we have in common is more important than what divides us. That was a discovery of epic proportions for academics who live and die by their differences. It was the epitome of our spiritual journey.

In our pluralistic age, diversity is seriously overvalued. It is not simply all right for everyone to go his or her own way. The late Senator Daniel Patrick Moynihan used to say, "Everyone is entitled to their own opinion, but no one is entitled to their own facts." We were searching for the facts in the Seminar, for what we had in common. That was the basis of our decision making. In searching for the facts, we discovered that we shared a new symbolic universe, one that deviated markedly from the biblical world we had inherited. It was a transforming experience.

But we also discovered that having one's own opinion is also overrated. Merely having an opinion obscures, or tends to obscure, the larger frame of reference within which we live and move and have our social being. In the Seminar, we were in danger, at first, of missing the fact that the old mythical world of the Bible had crumbled more or less unnoticed. So long as we continued to use that symbolic world as the framework of the quest, we were stymied, just as the churches are stymied.

In the divine domain, mythical worlds are irrelevant. As Rudolf Bultmann observed, there is nothing particularly Christian about the old mythical worldview. As Jesus perceived in concert with the First Axial Age, in the divine domain, community transcends tribal culture and transgresses social boundaries. What humans have in common exceeds the parameters of ethnicity. What we have in common is larger than sexual differences, male and female, heterosexual and homosexual. We now know we have much in common with all other life forms on planet earth, and we know that our well being depends on the total health of the biosphere that is our home. We must all subscribe to that insight if we are to survive on this planet.

To return briefly to the Judeo-Christian Tradition:

The divine domain is an unreachable destination. It is a perpetual journey. Like Moses, we are not permitted to cross over and settle down in the promised land. We catch sight of it from a distance, across the water. Or, to put it differently, we are allowed to cross over repeatedly, only to find that we inevitably adopt the ways of the Canaanites, who symbolize our inclination to settle for the received tradition, the conventional, the old wisdom. When we wake up from our slumbers, we make a new pilgrimage into the wilderness, catch sight of some promised land anew, and the process starts all over again.

We have before us the old choice: we can let the old time religion encumber us with a new dark ages, or we can embrace the second enlightenment and continue our spiritual odyssey. I much prefer the latter.

Beyond Theism but not beyond God

John Shelby Spong

I live my life inside the tension created by two deeply held commitments. These commitments stand today in such stark contrast one to the other, that there are many who believe them to be mutually contradictory. For me, however, they are the stretching, rigorous polarities inside which my faith must be defined and my life lived out.

My first commitment is to being a Christian. I am a disciple of Jesus whom I call the Christ. I do not mean by this that I simply give intellectual assent to a particular religious system. I mean that I am a deeply convinced, believing Christian. Jesus stands at the center of all I do and say and this shapes the way I think. I cannot recall a time when this Christ was not at the heart of my life. I was baptized as an infant; nurtured in this faith through church school, confirmed as a young adolescent, participated actively in my youth group as a teenager, and in the Campus Christian Ministry as a university student. I do not remember ever wanting to be anything but a priest.

I studied for that vocation in one of my church's theological centers. I served as deacon and priest for twenty-one years and then was elected by my church to the office of bishop at the ripe old age of 44. I served in that office for twenty-four years and was, when I retired, the senior sitting bishop of the Episcopal Church in the United States.

On every level the life of the Christian Church has been woven through the very fabric of my life. When I think of the special transitional moments in my life of both joy and sorrow, I note that all of them were observed liturgically before the altars of my church. I cannot imagine stepping outside this faith that has nurtured me for a lifetime. It is my witness that I meet the reality I call God in the person of Jesus. I, therefore, have no difficulty in echoing St. Paul's ecstatic proclamation that somehow, in some way, through some means God was in Christ. Jesus is my window into the holy, my doorway into God. It would be to speak under false pretenses if I did not acknowledge that I stand before you today as a practicing Christian.

My second commitment is equally real and equally central to all that I do and say and am. It also shapes the way I think. It must, therefore be stated with equal power and conviction. I am a child of the twenty-first century. I cannot be what some people call a first-century, Bible-believing Christian. I cannot be what others call an orthodox fourth-century, creed-reciting Christian. I cannot be a thirteenth-century liturgically-worshipping Christian. I cannot even be a sixteenth-century renaissance Christian. I have to be, I must be and I am a twenty-first-century Christian. If my Christianity cannot live inside the thought forms of the twenty-first century, then I do not believe it can live at all. It is not that I believe the twenty-first century has finally captured all truth or that its insights are somehow eternal and unchanging. Nothing could be further away from my understanding than that. It does mean, however, that because the twenty-first century is my time, it is the only frame of reference that I can finally have and I cannot pretend that a faith system bound to any other period of history is still capable of speaking to my world or to my moment in time.

My study of history has led me to the conclusion that Christianity has never been static or stable. There is for me no body of beliefs that have ever constituted what the Epistle of Jude calls "the faith once delivered to the saints." The Christianity in which I live has always been a churning, ever changing dialogue between the experience of God as a real presence and the thought forms of the world in which that experience is being articulated. Christianity was born in a powerful God experience in first-century Judaism. That experience finally could not be contained within the established boundaries of its birthing womb, so in time, the Christian movement leaped its Jewish boundaries and began the process of translating itself into a wider, Mediterranean, Greek thinking, gentile world. That was a world that did not know Joseph, to say nothing of Abraham or Moses. It was rather a world that had been shaped by the thinking of the great philosopher Plato and his spiritual children. Inevitably this growing Christian Faith had to be totally recast inside the platonic thought forms of this new world. This was accomplished primarily through the efforts of a fourth-century Christian theologian named Augustine. Christianity could never have lived in this platonic world had this radical recasting of its message not occurred. Augustine's work was so thorough and so powerful that it lasted for almost a thousand

years, causing many people to think that eternal truth had indeed
finally been captured for all time in the forms that Christianity
assumed in Augustine's day. But as the poet James Russell Lowell
once remarked with a sense of inevitability, the passage of time
"makes all ancient good uncouth." So Christianity moved on to
its next incarnation.

That occurred when a new emerging world-view forced a reformulation of this faith tradition, this time in terms of the thought
of the philosopher named Aristotle. That came in the thirteenth
century and was primarily the work of Thomas Aquinas. No one can
finally contemplate God except in the thought forms that shape his
or her own perception of reality.

Christianity was reformulated once again in the Reformation of
the sixteenth century, this time, as a result of Renaissance thinking
with its fresh, brilliant insights that ushered in the modern world.
Slowly the lesson began to be learned that truth is always tempered
by the way in which reality is perceived in the movement of history,
so every articulation of truth cannot escape being relative, subjective
and bound by the time in which the articulator of that truth lives.
Eternal truth never assumes a human form.

Today my vocation as a Christian is to assist in the process of
recasting this faith tradition in which I live into the thought forms
and world-view of the twenty-first century. I cannot, therefore be
defensive or fearful when the assumed truth of the Christian past
begins to die. Christianity is a faith tradition that has always been
in process. It has never been settled. It must, therefore be reformulated in every generation or it will die. There is no other alternative.
As I live in the twenty-first century I see two principles that most
people think of as the core of Christianity that must, I believe, now
be abandoned. They are, first, the concept of 'theism', as a way
of speaking about God, and second the concept of Jesus as the
Incarnation of this theistic deity. I must seek a God beyond theism
and a Christ beyond Incarnation.

Theism, defined as the belief in God as a Being, sometimes called
'the supreme Being', who is supernatural in power, dwelling somewhere external to this world and who periodically invades this world
to accomplish the divine will or to answer prayers, has in my opinion
died. I cannot pretend, as a citizen of today's world, that the earth is
at the center of the universe and that God dwells somewhere above
the sky. I embrace a universe that ancient believers could not even
have imagined. Living in the twenty-first century on the far side of
Copernicus and Galileo, I have to face the fact that the skies are
empty and apply that insight to the way I perceive my faith. At that
moment the radical reformulation of the Christian story begins.

There was no wandering star that led the wise man. There was no ascension by Jesus into the skies. There is no guilt producing heavenly Judge who looks down on this world in order to keep the divine record books up to date, controlling our behavior with the promise of reward or the threat of punishment. There is no intervening, supernatural, miracle-working deity and I, as a Christian in the twenty-first century must stop pretending that there is. The God I worship does not heal the sick, answer our prayers or split the Red Sea. There is no God who stands ready to fight our enemies, justify our wars or bless our nation at the call of every politician. On the most crass of levels there is no God who helps any athletic team defeat its opponent, though one would not know that from listening to athletes talk after a close victory in a championship game. How embarrassing is this popular but unbelievable theistic god-talk. A Christian faith built on the ignorance of yesterday will not live in the twenty-first century.

If God continues to be defined theistically as a miracle working, invasive deity, then Christianity becomes little more than a dying superstition. The question remains, however, as to whether theism is so deeply part of this faith tradition that removing it would prove to be fatal. Once this theistic God is dismissed then the entire superstructure of traditional Christianity collapses. A twenty-first-century Christian must have the courage to let that happen and so we continue this journey.

There was also no good and perfect creation like the biblical story suggests. There is rather an ongoing, unfinished creative process of which we are all a part. There was no fall from the perfection of creation and no original sin. There is only emerging, unfinished life in an endless struggle for advantage so that the battle for survival can be won. There was for Jesus no virgin birth nor physical resuscitation in the tomb, nor was he in Charles Wesley's words, a god figure who was simply "veiled in flesh" and sent to accomplish the task of rescuing fallen sinners by paying the price of their sin on the cross of Calvary in an orgy of divine child abuse, carried out by a sado-masochistic father god! To say it in language that every evangelical can understand, "Jesus did not die for your sins." These myths are no longer even good metaphors to help us understand the nature of our humanity; they are neither accurate nor healthy. Yet these ideas, wrapped around the central Christian doctrine of the atonement are so deeply at the core of Christian self understanding that they are the crucial lynchpin that when pulled causes the whole enterprise to crumble. I am not discussing peripheral matters.

Baptism, designed to wash away the stain of the fall becomes irrelevant. The Eucharist or The Mass created to reenact the victory over sin that Jesus purchased with his "precious blood" on the cross becomes little more than a tale of sick unreality. The idea that I can be rescued from a fall that never happened in order to be restored to a status that I have never possessed becomes pre-Darwinian mythology and post-Darwinian nonsense. That song will not sing, or as we used to say in the South, "that dog will not hunt" in the twenty-first century.

As a child of my generation I must now look at so many elements of my faith story through eyes shaped by the great minds that helped to create the twenty-first century. I think of Sigmund Freud, who suggested that one function of traditional religion was to perpetuate immaturity, by encouraging childlike dependency. A disciple of Jesus in my day must be able to identify this neurotic mentality. The traditional plea so often heard in the Church that "you must be born again" is one manifestation of a childlike dependency. Perhaps we have not noticed that the idea of being born again merely extends our childhood and perpetuates childlike dependency. Today's Christian does not need to be born again. Today's Christian needs to grow up, to celebrate maturity.

The quest for maturity begins when believers give up certainty, sacrifice security and embrace reality. The call of Christ in the twenty-first century is a call to embrace insecurity and uncertainty as the marks of our humanity that no religion can ever be allowed to remove. I do not covet something the Church once called peace of mind. I covet rather the courage to live creatively in the radical uncertainty of my humanity. So the twenty-first-century Christian must abandon all authority claims aimed at the creation of certainty. There is no ultimate truth that anyone can either possess or reduce to a prepositional statement. There is no true church, no true religion, no infallible Pope, no inerrant Bible. All of these are the spiritual constructs of frightened, dependent, childlike people of the past, but they have become impediments to maturity, and to human development. They cannot be part of the Christianity of the twenty-first century.

The pace of challenge continues relentlessly. There are no ethical norms, written on tablets of stone or otherwise enshrined in the words of scripture to which one can appeal to govern human behavior for all time. Those are also nothing but the pious claims left over from the childhood of our faith tradition. Quoting the Bible to determine attitudes and ethical norms has had a disastrous history that does not merit any further life. One has only to ask the scientists like Bruno or Galileo, who were persecuted by the Church when their truth challenged ecclesiastical perceptions. One has only to ask those people who were first enslaved and then segregated with the Church's blessing, or the women who were denied equality by the scripture-quoting Church, or the gay and lesbian people of the world who have not only been denied the Church's blessing, but with the Church's active participation have been oppressed and even murdered. For anyone to cling to any of these attitudes today, in the name of an idol called "the unity of the Church," is to doom the Christian faith to being an irrelevance that will ultimately disappear, lost in the antiquity of another time in history.

This litany of the things that must be sacrificed if Christianity is to live in our day is clearly not complete, but it should be enough to pose the problems present when one insists on being a Christian in the twenty-first century. When traditional believers hear these things stated so overtly their fears inevitably rise; their sense of threat is enormously enhanced, and the hysteria that the childlike game of religious pretending has long repressed reappear. Words of anger, condemnation and excommunication, that religious people have used so often against those who seek reformation, will be heard again in language that will be as vehement and violent as it has been in previous times of transition. "You have destroyed everything we hold sacred," they will say. "You have gutted the Christian faith. You cannot possibly be a Christian any longer." At best those of us who seek to call the Church to a new awareness are called 'heretics' or 'infidels'. At worst we are dismissed as atheists. Because I live so totally and self-consciously inside the Christian tradition, I suspect I have heard these words more frequently than most of you who are present at this gathering. It is the particular cross that the Church's ordained servants are called on to bear. Professors and academics can finally be marginalized and ignored by the Church. The ordained and especially those who have been chosen for positions of institutional leadership will face the anger of threatened believers that is simply beyond most people's imagination. It is, however, an unavoidable vocation for me because there is no other way that I can bring together my dual commitments to be a Christian, a disciple of my Lord Jesus Christ, and to live as a full citizen of the twenty-first century.

I hope I have enabled you to feel the full weight of this dilemma. Christianity lives today at a crossroads. The playwright, Edna St. Vincent Millay, once observed that "God is dead and modern men and women gather nightly around the divine grave to weep." The old understandings are increasingly bankrupt. Christianity must change or Christianity will die. Yet the changes required will be so total that there is no guarantee that what emerges from the dust of destruction will be Christian at all. But there is no choice. No religious system can live outside the mindset of its own time in history.

So let me turn now to sketch a vision of what twenty-first-century Christianity might look like.

The first question that must be raised is a simple one: Is God real? By that I mean to ask is the word 'God' merely a symbol created by human beings to give a sense of objective reality to a subjective dimension of human life? Does the word 'God' have any reality outside the mind of its human creator? Can the word 'God' be the word human beings use to describe a dimension of life that is real and that on the edges of our consciousness we are able to enter? These are not easy issues to unlock.

There is no doubt that the word 'God' is a human symbol. There is no doubt that this symbol was created by human beings. There is no doubt that the word 'God' speaks to a dimension of human existence. The question becomes whether or not there is a God reality which can be known and to which the word 'God' points. The non-realist position represented ably by Don Cupitt would say no. But, someone like the novelist Flannery O'Connor would affirm a realist position and would say yes. There seems to be so little room between the two mutually exclusive concepts of realism and non-realism that most people consider it fruitless to search in this place, but it is exactly in this in between place that I believe the twenty-first-century Christian must to be able to speak about God.

When I seek the God beyond theism, I seek to name a human experience of wonder, awe and transcendence. Yes, each of these are human words but they open the human spirit to an aspect of life, which I do not think human beings can create, but in which, I believe, they can participate. It is not an aspect of life different from or over against our humanity; it is not, as one of my critics once suggested, the last vestige of my dying Platonism. It is rather a dimension of our humanity that calls us beyond our normal limits. It is found in the human ability to embrace our finitude so totally that we are led beyond all its boundaries into infinity. It is the willingness to live within the barriers of existence so deeply that we transcend those barriers again and again as we journey toward what might be called an unbounded humanity. It is the ability to live so completely that we discover a transcendence that is not compromised even by the human inability to understand who it is that we ultimately are. It is, to use an Eastern image, to see a particular life as part of the great sea of life, that surging force that appeared perhaps a billion years after this planet earth came into being, animating and vitalizing all living things and finally expressing itself in everything from a single cell of living matter to the more complex entities called plants and animals, including Homo sapiens. The human gift is not so much to be different from other living things as it is to be consciously aware of the fact that we are alive. To be conscious of life is also to be able to commune with life as a dimension of our natural state, but one that enables us finally to escape our biological boundaries. Is that simply something we discover in ourselves or is that a reality calling us to be more than we have yet embraced? Is that something bidding us to see our lives as part of life itself, in communion with the source of life, called to be creatures who can recognize and indeed worship that life force in which we so obviously share but which we did not create?

When some of our less traditional Hebrew forebears, those I now call the minority voices in the biblical story, tried to find symbols that could help them articulate this aspect of their human experience they chose non-personal words to symbolize this experience of God. One of those words was *ruach,* which meant 'wind' and another was *nephesh* which meant 'breath'. *Ruach* and *nephesh* were always related. The wind that animated the forest was to the Jews symbolic of the breath of God. The breath of God was thus the vitalizing force within every living thing. Our breath was itself the sign that we participated in something more than who we are.

Wind and breath were mysterious, elusive, and not capable of being contained in any structure. Our Hebrew forebears knew not from whence the wind came, nor where it went. They could experience the wind on their faces or observe its effects in the rustle of the trees but they could not see the wind, capture it or define it. Their breath or *nephesh* shared in this wind. It was part of who they were, but was always more than what they were. It was another dimension of their humanity which they, as self-conscious creatures, could name but which they could not contain, control or exhaust. It was an experience of transcendence. That is still part of what I mean when I say the word 'God'. God is the source of life to me, not a meddler in life for me. God is part of who I am, but more than what I am.

It is through the lens of this non-theistic understanding of God that I look anew at the life of Jesus. When I do I see Jesus as one portrayed as so deeply and fully alive, that in his particular life the ultimate source of life seems to become visible.

This life force, present in the universe, is quite physical and real. It is seen in the rain that falls out of the sky to nurture all things. It is experienced in the ground water that enables the roots of plants to be nourished and to live. It is operative in the power of the sun that through photosynthesis turns the faces of the flowers and the branches of the trees heavenward to soak up its life giving rays. This life force is, however, also more than just a physical reality. It is in the nurture that so many creatures give their offspring. It is present as the tongue of the cat that licks the kitten or in the beak of the bird that brings nourishment to its nesting young. This life force cannot be named or recognized because the creatures in whom it dwells are not conscious of what they are and what they do. Yet they are agents through whom this unnamed power flows.

Among those of us who have evolved into being self-conscious creatures, we experience this life force as something that flows into us from outside. We are the ones who attach the name 'love' to it. It is a power that enables us to grow, to expand and to give love consciously in return. Since this nurturing love is an aspect of life that we cannot create, which we can only receive from another, it is met as a reality that is both transcendent and unbounded. Yet once we have received this life force called love, we humans have a choice. We can either give it away so that it continues to expand, or we can bottle it up until it dies. So love while always immanent within each of us is not our own. We cannot possess it. Love does not store. Love cannot be kept or saved. The very nature of love is discovered only when it is given away. This seems to me to be in touch with what the Jewish writer meant when he wrote in the fourth chapter of the first Epistle of John, "God is love and whoever abides in love abides in God." If God is love, then is not love also God? The love that interrupts our isolation, binds us together, expands our ability both to live and to love, is that not how God is experienced outside the theistic definitions of a supernatural invasive being? Love does not judge. Love cannot be measured. Love knows no limits. It seems to me that the deepest truth that people experienced in Jesus was the experience of love, the recognition that there was nothing they could do and nothing they could be that placed them outside the scope of the love of God. Is not this the essential message of the gospel, once we allow our spirit to explore the meaning found underneath the blinding power of the popular supernatural words? People could deny Jesus, forsake him, betray him, curse him, persecute him and kill him and yet to each of these actions he responded with the embrace of an infinite love. It made no difference who they were. The barriers that human beings impose on one another faded away. They could be gentiles, or Samaritans, they could be lepers or the righteous and rich young ruler; they could be women taken in adultery or tax collectors; they could be executioners or thieves; they could be cursing mobs screaming for his death or the persecutors of the religious establishment who were so frightened by his freedom. Still the love that set his life apart loved them. Love, like God, is not bounded by any definition, but when love is experienced eyes are opened, lives are expanded, transcendence is known and God is the name we use to symbolize that moment of otherness. Jesus is proclaimed as the life through which this expansive love that is God was met in searing newness. That is why the Church preached Christ and him crucified. Jesus was not the portrait of an invasive rescuing savior in human disguise. Jesus was not the victim of an angry God who sacrificed the Divine Son in order to overcome the wretchedness of a broken humanity. Jesus was, rather, the portrait of a love that gives itself away wastefully, not stopping to count the cost. It was this experience that caused people to say of Jesus "That is who God is, we have met the holy God in the life of this man" or in the ecstatic words of Paul: "God was in Christ." Paul was making no attempt to provide us with the explanation of a theological truth that was destined in time to produce creeds and doctrines like the Incarnation, the Atonement and the Trinity. This rather was Paul's exclamation rising from one whose life had been touched by the transcendent wonder and awe of an in-breaking new dimension of his self-conscious humanity. This is what made Paul aware that at the very depth of his humanity, life could be opened and when it was, his life could become a channel through which the divine, that is the deepest dimension of our humanity, could be known. That is what I believe that Jesus brought to the human enterprise and it was that experience that caused the Church to call him 'Lord' and 'Christ' and to acknowledge that in him was the presence of God.

This is also the reality that has rendered me at times less than comfortable as a fellow of the Jesus Seminar. I am not one who is passionately motivated by the eternal human search to get to the Jesus of history. Please do not misunderstand these words. I honor that task and I am glad that scholars do that work rigorously and carefully for it is important to me to have my Jesus grounded in history. It is not, however, essential to me to know with historic specificity that he said this and not that, that he did this and not that. What is of far more importance to me is to discover what there was about his life that caused people to say of him that when he was born, a star appeared in the sky to proclaim the difference he would make? What was there about him that caused people to assert that gentile magi followed that wandering star until they found the one they too could worship? What was there about this Jesus that caused people to say that at his birth the light of God split the darkness of the midnight sky and that angels sang of him to hillside shepherds? What was there about him that caused people to say the Holy Spirit must have been his father, or that he could still the storm, walk on water, feed the multitude with five loaves, heal the sick, give hearing to the deaf, sight to the blind, loose the tongues of the mute to speak and even allow the cripple to leap with joy. What was there about this life that caused people to say that death itself faded when he confronted it, whether it be the death of Lazarus (John 11) or Jairus' daughter (Mark 5:21ff), or the widow's son at Nain (Luke 7:11–17)? What was there about this Jesus that caused them to say that neither death nor the tomb could contain him? What was there about him that gave people confidence that in him a life power was so abundantly present that even death could not extinguish it? What caused them to suggest that he was the author of a life-giving spirit, symbolized by a mighty rushing wind and tongues of fire, that could be poured out on humanity and could empower people to step outside their tribal identities and begin to speak the language of their hearers, and thus allow a spirit-filled human community to emerge?

The Christian Faith is not about literal virgin births, or the intrusive activities of a supernatural, invasive theistic deity. It is not about miracles and magic, guilt and judgment, or reward and punishment. It is not about creeds and doctrines, institutional maintenance or a sense of religious superiority. It is not about finding, dispensing, or preserving the truth that we have received by some miraculous process called revelation. It is not about theism or atheism, Trinitarianism or Unitarianism. It is not about whether Athanasius was right and Arius wrong or vice versa. It is not about the Council of Nicea or the Chalcedonian formula.

Christianity is about entering the transcendent depth of life, love and being in a human experience with a man named Jesus of Nazareth and calling that experience God. It is about inviting other people not to assent to your creeds but to walk with you into life, which I believe, is also to walk into the mystery of God. It is about carrying out the mission of Jesus by those of us who are his disciples. That mission is not to make people religious, or righteous or orthodox, but rather to call them into the transcendent God experience that expands their life, enhances their ability to love and gives them the courage to be all that they can be. It is about using the name 'God' to understand both the Christ experience and the reality that is met in moments of transcendence. God is neither a theistic being nor a human construction, created to enable us to talk about dimensions of our humanity. 'God' is finally the name we create to make sense out of a power, a presence and a transcendence which is real and which, at the depths and edges of our humanity, we can enter. The word 'God' is not about something more than we are, it is about all that we are. 'God' is about understanding the final dimension of our life; it is about a humanity that has been opened to divinity. It is about stepping into eternity while still walking in time. It is about the experience that Paul Tillich called 'The Eternal Now'. It is about entering humanity so deeply that we taste eternity and experience what we have traditionally called heaven.

I close with words that have become something of a mantra for me because they sum up my constant struggle to hold together my commitment to Christ as my doorway into God and my commitment to live as a citizen of the twenty-first century. I cannot tell you who God is or what God is, I cannot define God in realist or non-realist language. I cannot reduce God to a dimension that my mind can embrace. No human being can do any of those things for these things are not within the scope of the human capacity. All I can do is to tell you how I believe I have experienced God. Even then, I have to face the fact that I might in that experience be delusional. Others have to be the judge of that.

I believe I have experienced God as the source of life. If God is the source of life the only way I can worship God is by living fully and the more fully I live the more I can make God visible.

I believe I have experienced God as the source of love. If God is the source of love then the only way I can worship God is by loving wastefully, never stopping to ask whether this wasteful love is deserved. The more wastefully I love, the more I believe I can make God visible.

I believe I have experienced God in the words of my great teacher, Paul Tillich, as the "Ground of All Being." If God is the ground of all being then the only way I can worship God is to have the courage to be all that I can be. The more fully I can be all that I am the more I believe I can make God visible.

To this formula I add my ultimate conviction. I am a Christian. I walk self-consciously with this Jesus as my guide into the presence of God because when I look at Jesus' life, as that life has been refracted to me through the scriptures and the tradition, I discover one who lived so fully that I believe I can discern in him the Source of Life; one who loves so wastefully that I believe I can discern in him the Source of Love; one who has the courage to be himself under any set of circumstances enabling me to discern in him the very Ground of Being. Since I meet God as the Source of Life, the Source of Love and the Ground of Being, I have no difficulty joining Saint Paul and saying, Yes! Yes! God was in Christ. God is the reality I meet in this life, this love and this being. When I process these experiences I believe I touch eternity.

I want to be a follower of this Jesus. How do I accomplish that? It is not by conversion activity or missionary enterprises, I assure you. I wish the church would get of the conversion business. That business is, I believe, well intentioned but base born. It is, no matter how sophisticated its adherents try to make it, finally nothing but an attempt to impose a religious tradition thought to be superior, on those who are themselves as well as their beliefs judged to be inferior.

I still, however, seek to worship the God I experience in Jesus and to live my life as a disciple of Jesus. This drives me, however, not to creeds, doctrines and dogmas erected to undergird a dying understanding of God, but rather to the task of seeking to build a world, where everyone in that world might have a better opportunity to live, to love and to be, in the infinite variety of our humanity; people of every race and national origin, people who are male and female, left-handed and right-handed, gay, lesbian, bisexual and transgender. The call of the Christ is not a call to conformity. It is not a call to orthodoxy. It is not a call to righteousness. Ultimately, it is not even a call to religion. The call of Christ is first an invitation to be who we are and to open ourselves to that empowerment that is necessary to be all that we can be. It is a call to enter the realm of the divine which is not external to us in some theistic definition, but is rather the ultimate depth of who we are as we transcend finitude and enter infinity, as we escape the barriers of time and enter timelessness and as we embrace our humanity so deeply that we enter the realm of the divine.

This is, I believe, what the Johannine Community understood about the God presence they met in Jesus when they had him say, "I have come that you might have life and have it abundantly."

Facing Up to Hard Questions

Christian Faith for a New Age

Joe Bessler-Northcutt

The moral test of leadership involves helping communities face difficult issues, according to Ron Heiffetz in his book *Leadership Without Easy Answers*. Unfortunately, for several hundred years, many Christian theologians, churches, and denominations have failed that test of leadership. Instead of helping their communities to face the challenges of a scientific understanding of reality, they chose to ignore it; instead of helping their communities to face the difficulties of democratic responsibility, they encouraged subservience to hierarchal or charismatic authorities; instead of nurturing an integrity that follows upon grappling with the intellectual and moral complexities of our time, they have nurtured a narrow spiritualism, based on the too-easy truths of infallible scriptures and infallible teachers.

The result is a culture of what Douglas John Hall has called "religious simplism." Such simplism has achieved impressive polling numbers. According to two separate reports by Nicholas Kristoff in the *New York Times* in 2003, Americans are far more likely to believe in creationism, the devil, and the Virgin Birth than they are to believe in evolution.[1]

Far from representing any genuine sense of cultural or religious growth—which its loud insistence on possessing the Truth suggests—religious simplism represents a form of cultural decline, a retreat that is both religious and secular: religious insofar as religious leaders have failed to insist upon the need for genuine re-interpretation of the faith, secular insofar as politicians cynically exploit simplistic religiosity as an expression of common sense and moral straight-forwardness—a sop to the myth of the "common man."

The issues are not simply between evolution and creationists. Contemporary questions from post-structuralists on the nature of language as well as from post-colonialists questioning the West's and Christianity's constructions of imperial power require similar thoughtfulness from Christian theologians. If words or signifiers do not primarily—much less fully or adequately—point to things, or signifieds, then traditional understandings of representational truth, as well as theological claims of scriptural or doctrinal infallibility, are no longer intellectually viable. Moreover, insofar as the West's pre-modern and modern assumptions of God and Truth functioned imperially and condescendingly to authorize the colonization and economic exploitation of other cultures and peoples, the claims of an almighty, benevolent God—and the requirement of belief in Jesus Christ as the only and universal path to salvation and eternal life—have functioned to authorize the violence of colonial power in both secular and religious forms.

If Christianity is to have a constructive future—one that can be taken seriously on intellectual and moral grounds—it will need to reject theism rooted in its imperial history and theology (i.e., the image of God as a Supreme Being, with a mind and will that governs the world). Recent discussions of a Second Axial Age insist that the notion of God as an imperial, Supreme Being is utterly unintelligible and morally problematic to contemporary persons, a figure of mythology.[2] To be persuasive, Christianity will need to answer at least three hard questions:

- Can Christians articulate an approach to God that is credible to our contemporary understanding of language and reality?
- Can Christians articulate a Christology that rejects the logic of supercessionism and the imperial logic of Christian metaphysics?
- Can Christians articulate an approach to life that respects and learns from both other intellectual disciplines and other religious traditions?

In answering those questions below, I will suggest, first, that while Christians have traditionally understood the word "God" to point to an external and objective reality, we must now recognize that the word "God" is itself a symbol or metaphor within the web of language. That does not mean that the word "God" is simply a linguistic *tool* for expressing our own ideological interests, but it does mean that Christian theologians must be ready to invoke a hermeneutics of suspicion when religious truth-claims function to mask an abuse of power. While attempting, therefore, to maintain an appropriate sense of the genuine transcendence of God, as that mystery within which we live and move and have our being, I will also claim that an important lens for interpreting and constructing the Christian symbol of God is as the mysterious power at work in the ambiguity of human history and human freedom as experienced in public life.[3]

Secondly, I will argue that Jesus' preaching and practice of the Kingdom of God focused not on himself but on the social dynamics of the public realm—"the kingdom of God is among you." A contemporary Christology that avoids the problem of supercessionism will look to the social dynamics of the public sphere, not to Jesus' metaphysical presence, to locate both the Christian interpretation of the incarnate God and the possibilities of human life.

Thirdly, communities shaped around the speech and practices of Jesus exhibit a spirit and ethic of humility not only in the face of new knowledge from its neighboring disciplines in the sciences and humanities, but in the face of new, intimate, and serious encounters with all the world's faith traditions.

Before developing these responses to the three hard questions posed above, I want to highlight a major contribution of the Jesus Seminar to the public theological enterprise.

The Importance of the Jesus Seminar for the Contemporary Situation

One of my favorite cartoons is a Sydney Harris single-frame piece depicting a physics professor standing next to a student at the chalkboard and analyzing the equation proposed by his student. Out of the complex set of numbers on the board, the professor focuses on a statement "Then a miracle occurs" placed in the midst of the equation. Pointing to the statement on the board, he says dryly to his student, "I think you should be more explicit here in step two."

At the considerable risk of explaining a joke, I want to explore a bit further the lessons to be learned from Harris' cartoon. It is funny, first of all, to see *any* words in the middle of a mathematical equation; words are foreign to mathematical equations, and thus their very appearance in the student's answer is itself a point of visual humor in the cartoon. What makes these words yet funnier is that they introduce a second level of impropriety, namely, the claim to supernatural power which, in contrast to the notion of infinity, is itself excluded from mathematical and scientific method. Thus, our student in the cartoon has failed to grasp some very basic assumptions of the discipline. And yet, part of the humor is also its humanity; one feels for the student whose invocation of the divine is a rather transparent acknowledgment of his own limits. Moreover, the professor's words to the student enact that awkward, and hence funny, tension between ironic understatement (the proposed solution is far from adequate) and respect for the student as a person.

There is real pathos in the human tendency to resolve human problems by seeking divine solutions that function as a *Deus ex machina*. And yet, as Harris subtly points out, such invocations tend to short-cut and short-circuit the more difficult, yet genuinely human task of resolving problems with both ingenuity and thoughtfulness.

The scholars of the Jesus Seminar have called Christian theologians to the board to "be a bit more explicit" about our claims to incarnation and deity in the person of Jesus. By closely examining the canonical Scriptures, by exploring texts outside the canon, such as the Gospel of Thomas, and by treating Q as a distinctive and important voice in its own right, the scholars of the Seminar have helped establish an historical, which is not to say foundationally certain, basis for the interpretation of Jesus. Precisely because they pursued a public, historical analysis, they bracketed out of consideration Christian theological assumptions of Jesus' divinity, of his incarnation, of his death as an act of atonement for sin, of his resurrection, and of his return as an eschatological judge of the nations. By refusing to explore the words and acts of Jesus within the traditional limits of Christian theology's imperial, and platonically structured worldview, the scholars of Westar have broken open new and unexpected ways of contextualizing, and therefore, understanding, Jesus' words and acts.

By developing a more historically accurate and debatable picture of Jesus than what is available throughout the theistic, divine-man traditions of Christian theology, the scholars of the Seminar have shown that public discussion of Jesus is not only possible but also theologically fruitful. Through their work, they have provided leadership in helping theologians, and churches, to face up to the problem of Christian theism and its implications for the whole of Christian thought.

Question One: Can Christians articulate an approach to God that is credible to our contemporary understanding of language and reality?

Yes, but it won't be easy. In the classical model of Christian theology, belief in God the Almighty Father structured an imperial and privileged "family," outside of which no one could be saved. Belief in the imperial God involved affirming doctrines that established boundaries of belief and belonging. Failure to share these beliefs (pagans and infidels) or failure to believe them completely or properly (heresy) meant exclusion from the household of God. Over the centuries, and into the modern world, Christianity's imperial logic provided ideological support for Western colonial expansion and its virtual enslavement of peoples around the globe. Inside the church, that same imperial logic functioned to silence or ignore criticisms of church doctrine, leading, over time, to the intellectual and moral decay of the church.

Instead of imagining God as a supernatural *paterfamilias*, ruling over all time and space, through the vehicle of one particular "family" of true faith, it is appropriate to re-imagine God in ways that begin to break down the boundaries separating peoples and faiths. Why? Because the boundaries of old empires, and the social boundaries provided by geography, race, ethnicity, sexuality, and even religion have begun shifting dramatically in recent years. Cultural and geographic boundaries once thought to be unalterable and absolute, have become permeable,[4] and Western assumptions of cultural superiority have given way under the moral criticisms of colonialism, ecological devastation, and nuclear proliferation.

Western Christian theologians, in particular, should acknowledge that while the development of Christian traditions along imperial lines was historically and contextually understandable, the maintenance of such traditions is no longer either intellectually or morally justifiable. Nonetheless, while metaphors of imperial kingship no longer provide either helpful or moral images of God,[5] the domains of history and public life, which such metaphors privileged, remain vital for re-imagining a genuinely public Christian theology.

By the term public theology I mean not only a theology that responds to the changing dynamics of civil society but more importantly a theology attentive to a criterion of contestability—an openness on the part of theologians to revise their received traditions, significantly if necessary, in response to the challenges of neighboring disciplines in the sciences and humanities.

Sallie McFague has been extremely helpful in explaining the problem with traditional imperial metaphors for God. Metaphors, she argues, do not simply describe a reality that is "already there." Instead, metaphors, including metaphors for God, create reality.[6] "Be careful how you interpret the world," she quotes Erich Heller as saying; "it really is like that."[7] McFague calls for experimental theologies, risking new metaphors for God precisely because the God envisioned by the traditional metaphor of kingship is not only irrelevant to, but positively dangerous for, the vastly transformed world of the twenty-first century.

In calling her emphasis on metaphors a "heuristic theology," by which she means one "that experiments and tests, . . . that imagines possibilities that are novel, and that dares to think differently,"

McFague has helped other theologians acknowledge that God language is, and should be, caught up far more in the cultural life—the human crises, dreams, longings and hopes—of a people than traditional theologies have been willing to admit.

In this essay, I respond to McFague's call for multiple metaphors, by reconsidering the relation of God to human history and the dynamics of public life. Like the Deuteronomist, who was struck with the emergence of historical newness and horrified by the tragedies of history, I suggest that the word "God" attempts to name the mysterious power at work in the vastness of human freedom and history. In what follows, I draw upon one of the twentieth-century's most gifted theorists of the public realm, Hannah Arendt, who called that mysterious phenomenon of historical emergence *natality*. It is a term that may provide a helpful metaphorical structure for re-imagining the basic Christian *topos* of God.[8]

In her book *The Human Condition*, Arendt first takes up the issue of natality in a meditation upon the improbability of new beginnings.

> It is in the nature of beginning that something new is started which cannot be expected from whatever may have happened before. This character of startling unexpectedness is inherent in all beginnings and in all origins. Thus, the origin of life from inorganic matter is an infinite improbability of inorganic processes, as is the coming into being of the earth viewed from the standpoint of processes in the universe, or the evolution of human out of animal life. The new always happens against the overwhelming odds of statistical laws and their probability, which for all practical, everyday purposes, amounts to certainty; the new therefore always appears in the guise of a miracle. (178)

Arendt's depiction of the profound improbability of these pre-human beginnings evokes a sense of awe. Yet, her real interest in natality is as a motif that opens up the discussion of history and public life. As Catherine Keller observes: "Natality challenges the western philosophical focus on mortality as the source of both anxiety and action."[9] By shifting away from mortality to birth, from eschatology to natality, Arendt also shifts historical preoccupation with the "decline" of civilizations to a preoccupation with emergence of social and historical change.

> The miracle that saves the world, the realm of human affairs, from its normal, "natural" ruin is ultimately the fact of natality, in which the faculty of action is ontologically rooted. It is, in other words, the birth of new men [*sic*] and the new beginning, the action they

are capable of by virtue of being born. Only the full experience of this capacity can bestow upon human affairs faith and hope, those two essential characteristics of human existence which Greek antiquity ignored altogether . . . It is this faith in and hope for the world that found perhaps its most glorious and most succinct expression in the few words with which the Gospels announced their "glad tidings": "A child has been born unto us." (247)

While Arendt's understanding of natality grasps the startling mystery of newness within a naturalistic frame, her repeated use of religious language—of miracle, of faith and hope, of revelation, of the child "born unto us"—illuminates the contours of an argument she herself did not make; namely, that in the history of the West, "God" is the profound symbol or metaphor for the felt power of natality in human experience. Just as the play of religious language adds a sense of both wonder and renewal to her descriptions of the public realm, so religious faith itself, understood in terms of natality, can appear not as hope for an other-worldly existence, but as hope for justice, for renewal and newness of life within the contours of public life.

Throughout the biblical literature, stories of creation out of chaos, liberation from slavery, social reversals, the pain of ostracism finally undone, or Israel's journey through exile, enact what Arendt calls the "character of startling unexpectedness." From the joy of Miriam, of Hannah, or Mary, to the refrains of despair and joy in the Psalmist, to the Deuteronomist's wrestling with the unsettled and surprising anguish of history, biblical characters both celebrate and long for the creative and purposive power of renewal.

Longing and desire—an eros for wholeness, for love, for acceptance, for freedom and integrity, and fullness of life that they called *shalom*—constituted the most basic frames of biblical God-talk. The language of natality, therefore—as celebrated, as longed for, and even as suffered—lies at the heart of religious experience. In our day as well, whether from the personal bondage of addiction, depression, chronic pain, or meaninglessness, or from the collective experience of economic exploitation, religious bigotry, racism, sexism, or heterosexism, the felt sense of empowerment, revitalization, and renewed purpose comes—insofar as it comes at all—as a miracle, as a gift that re-opens the future. No matter how long one has sacrificed, or worked, or suffered for the arrival of the new, its actual occurrence is felt as a gift, in response to which one is moved not only to humility but to awe and worship.

While Christian traditions have sought to establish their truth claims in the rhetoric of stability, order, and the absolute otherness of

God, Arendt's attention to the "new," which disrupts settled systems of discourse, opens the possibility of re-imagining God as mysteriously involved within the simultaneously vast and intimate domain of human freedom. In a number of passages, Arendt describes how the well being of the public realm is dependent on human words and deeds. We have already seen one of those passages in which she claims that the ontological ground of natality is the birth of new persons. But Arendt is just getting started. More important to the public realm than biological natality is what she names the second birth, the engagement of public life. "With word and deed we insert ourselves into the human world, and this insertion is like a second birth, in which we confirm and take upon ourselves the naked fact of our original physical appearance" (176–77). It is through speech and action that newness emerges in human history. Here the burden and responsibility of human freedom comes to the fore. Arendt describes the human actor not simply as a "doer," but also, and simultaneously, as a "sufferer." The consequences of human action are "boundless," she writes, "because action, though it may proceed from nowhere, so to speak, acts into a medium where every reaction becomes a chain reaction and where every process is the cause of new processes." Arendt continues:

> Since action acts upon beings who are capable of their own actions, reaction, apart from being a response, is always a new action that strikes out on its own and affects others. Thus action and reaction among men [*sic*] never move in a closed circle and can never be reliably confined to two partners . . . ; the smallest act in a the most limited circumstances bears the seed of the same boundlessness, because one deed, and sometimes one word, suffices to change every constellation. (190)

In these and other passages, Arendt enables the reader to grasp both her sense of each person's obligation to risk oneself in public life and her sense of wonder at the vast unpredictability which the global risk of human freedom unleashes. Within this intimate and vast play of both freedom and discourse, I find Arendt's skilled use of religious language and allusion to suggest that what God-talk, or theology, is about is a hermeneutic of the mystery of human freedom in the public realm.

For Christians facing a new world of globalization and cultural hybridity, the instability, uncertainty, and unpredictability of human life and language are the permeable boundaries within and around which contemporary discourse about God must negotiate. To be sure, the classical tradition of Christian theology also invoked a particular hermeneutic of freedom and history, but it was an interpretation governed by the imperial and univocal authority of God, which strictly limited the public realm to approved voices only. As Arendt writes in a very thinly veiled critique of Christianity: "aspiration toward omnipotence always implies—apart from its utopian *hubris*—the destruction of plurality" (202).

If Christians can begin to re-imagine the reality of God apart from the language of power from above and begin to imagine God as emerging in the natality of human history, intimately connected within, but in no way pulling the strings, or controlling the actions of history, then *faith* in God would mean something quite different from "believing" this or that doctrinal formulation. In the experience of faith, we would feel ourselves called and obligated to participate in the public realm in ways that would nurture its present and future well being. Part of that contemporary obligation, which Arendt could not fully anticipate, would consist in welcoming and honoring the participation of all voices in the community, by standing with those who are in need, and by listening to the voices, needs, and insights of strangers. In other words, faith would see itself participating with God in the continuing renewal of public life. Thus, Arendt's focus on human words and deeds can enable a re-visioning of God language far more open to the plurality of public life.

One can now see the importance of historical Jesus studies in a fresh light—namely as a disruptive newness in Christian theology that enables Christians and non-Christians alike to become more deeply aware of Jesus as a fully human historical figure, whose words and acts reflect deep concern for the public life of his religious and social world. In a theology which understands God as the unexpected and even chaotic power of natality in the midst of human history, consideration of the historical Jesus and his public life will be helpful to any construction of what the tradition calls Christology.

Before discussing the historical Jesus and Christology, however, several notes of caution are in order. If Christian theology is to lay claim to the language of natality to imagine the reality of God, it has to face hard questions related to fatality: questions not simply related to questions of natural death, nor even to questions of the death of Christianity,[10] but about the death of others, and others' cultures that Christians have authorized as part of the new reality in Christ. From the Evangelical claim of being "born again," to the Tillichian language of the "New Being," Christian claims of love and renewal have masked Christian claims to superiority and power.[11]

Within the imperial paradigm of Christian theism, the "new creation" of Christian love has been compatible with the dismissal of women from the public life of Christian leadership, the colonization of "pagan" peoples and the destruction of their cultures, and perhaps especially with the hatred of Jews. On this last point: To argue, as Pope John Paul II did, that Christian sins, especially against Jews, were simply individual sins "committed in service to the truth" is to minimize responsibility of the institutional church and its theological claims.[12] However sincerely offered, his overly individualized characterization of these sins obfuscates the role of Christian theology and its truth claims, including that of the Incarnation itself, in authorizing a culture of superiority over both Jewish persons and the Jewish faith.

Question Two: Can Christians articulate a Christology that rejects the logic of supercessionism and the imperial logic of Christian metaphysics?

The boundless, interconnected complexities of human action not only make up the conditions against which natality emerges unexpectedly. Some of those complexities inevitably prove debilitating to public life itself. We know from a selection quoted earlier that Arendt's hopes for the public realm are seasoned with an abiding skepticism. In that selection, she drew upon the Christian language of original sin, saying that the "normal," "natural" state of human affairs is "ruin." Within this state of ruin, Arendt focuses on the everyday tension created by "trespassing" rather than on "crime" or explicitly "willed evil," because, as she writes, "trespassing is an everyday occurrence which is in the very nature of action's constant establishment of new relationships within a web of relations." The inevitability of trespassing, according to Arendt, makes it a more constant threat to the ongoing negotiation of public life. The only adequate response to such trespassing in the experience of public life, she says, is forgiveness. It is only through forgiveness, "through this constant mutual release from what they do," she writes, that human beings "remain free agents." And she adds: "Only by constant willingness to change their minds and start again can they be trusted with so great a power as that to begin something new" (240).

Arendt credits Jesus of Nazareth with "discovering the role of forgiveness in the realm of human affairs." Analyzing the Lord's Prayer, Arendt observes: "Jesus maintains . . . first that it is not true that only God has the power to forgive, and second that this power does not derive from God . . . but on the contrary must be mobilized by men [*sic*] toward each other . . ." "Jesus' formulation is . . . radical. Man [*sic*] in the gospel is not supposed to forgive because God forgives and he [*sic*] must do 'likewise,' but 'if ye from your hearts forgive,' God shall do 'likewise'" (238–39).

That Arendt credits Jesus with a significant contribution to the well being of public life is worth notice, especially in light of recent work on the historical Jesus that extends Arendt's insight. Along with the Jesus Seminar's development of a probable "database" for the sayings of Jesus, scholars including John Dominic Crossan, Marcus Borg, Stephen Patterson, Brandon Scott, and others, outside the Seminar, such as Elizabeth Schüssler Fiorenza, and Richard Horsely, have sought to understand the public realm of Jesus' life—the political, economic, and religious contexts to which the sayings and deeds of Jesus were directed.

The results, by no means unanimous, have been the rediscovery of Jesus as a public figure. In his parables of the kingdom of God, in his aphorisms and practices, such as itinerancy and table fellowship, Jesus pursues an alternative vision of social organization that rejects violence while calling peasants (Jews and Gentiles alike) to stand together as a kingdom of God. Forget the purity logic, Jesus seems to say; forget the barriers of wealth and class, forget the ostracism of women, forget the honor/shame culture instilled by generations—Jesus calls Israel and her neighbors to resist the oppression of the Roman *basileia* by standing together, forgiving one another, reconciling with one another, canceling debts, and eating together.

In a time of suffering, Jesus calls Israel to model a moral integrity that stands against the military might of Roman rule. His parables are practical, but difficult; requiring new ways of seeing across deeply internalized social boundaries, and calling for revolutionary action. In both speech and action he reveals in the midst of the peasant community the social dynamics of the Kingdom of God that can rebuild the public life and space of the community.

Setting aside a Christology that focuses on the uniqueness of Jesus' metaphysical identity, theologians can find in Jesus' poetics of the kingdom, a Christian, theological norm for understanding the authentic power of natality in communal or public life. Jesus' Christological significance is not in himself, as such, but in the public capacity for newness and rebirth that he both pointed to and embodied in parable and practice. Such a Christological shift involves relocating the normative center of Christian life outside the traditional notions of doctrinal orthodoxy and into the public realm where people, and peoples, quite irrespective of their religious affiliation, long for communities that care for all their citizens, hunger and thirst for both food and justice, and celebrate the non-violent renewal and empowerment of their societies.

Question Three: Can Christians articulate an approach to life that respects and learns from both other intellectual disciplines and other religious traditions?

In exploring the importance of forgiveness for the public realm, Arendt argued that the public power of forgiveness could not stem from the private dynamics of interpersonal love.

> Yet what love is in its own, narrowly circumscribed sphere, respect is in the larger domain of human affairs. Respect, not unlike the Aristotelian *philia politike*, is a kind of 'friendship' without intimacy and without closeness; it is a regard for the person from the distance which the space of the world puts between us, and this regard is independent of the qualities which we may admire or of achievements which we may esteem. (243)

I take Arendt's language of respect to invoke the virtue of humility, demonstrated by the public practice of critical reflection open to re-thinking and seriously criticizing the claims of traditions (both secular and religious) in light of new circumstances and in continuing awareness of the fragility of knowledge. Such openness, understood as a public, not private, virtue is required not only of persons but of institutions, and especially, here, of churches.

In today's public realm of bumper-sticker rhetoric, sustaining such openness might itself be miraculous. But the renewal of our communities, both religious and secular, will not happen apart from us, apart from public action and testimony that risks beginning something new. Writes Arendt:

> The melancholy vision of *Ecclesiastes*—"Vanity of vanity; all is vanity. . . . There is no new thing under the sun," . . . does not necessarily arise from specifically religious experience; but it is certainly unavoidable wherever and whenever trust in the world as a place fit for human appearance, for action and speech, is gone. (204)

Ecclesial Tectonics

Non Est Extra

A Position Paper on the Future of the Church

Arthur J. Dewey

T he master said: "To learn something and then to put it into practice at the right time: is this not a joy? To have friends coming from afar: is this not a delight? Not to be upset when one's merits are ignored: is this not the mark of a gentleman?"

—**The Analects 1.1**

Zilu asked: "If the ruler of Wei were to entrust you with the government of the country, what would be your first initiative?" The master said: "It would certainly be to rectify the names."

—**The Analects 13.3**

A Linguistic Foothold

1.1 Any discussion on the future of the church must at the very outset become self-conscious of the language that has been set in play.

1.2 There are two reasons for this need to become self-conscious. First, those who speak of the nature of the church usually presume a privileged position. This masks the power relationships out of which the ecclesial language is spun. The winning or dominating side determines the discourse, sets up the parameters of debate as well as the boundaries of ritual and conduct.

1.3 The second reason is that the usual ecclesial language flees from time and space. It avoids the reality of history. An essentialist language game continues to play out, with brief guest appearances on this planet.

1.4 An ecclesial tectonics functions as a vaccination against these virulent strains in church history. Ecclesial tectonics is a critical understanding of the artisanship that has historically constructed ecclesial communities. At the same time ecclesial tectonics recognizes the global reality in which such construction takes place.

1.5 This paper focuses the future of the church through the lead metaphors found in *tectonics*. This means that an understanding of church is an historical *construction* that occurs within the *shifting formations and deformations* of life on this planet.

Jesus as Peasant Artisan (*tekton*)

2.1 Any reflection on the future of church must begin with the historical Jesus. The relationship between the historical Jesus and the subsequent church has been the traditional subject of ecclesiologies.

2.2 It should also be noted that the question of the historical Jesus has moved beyond the controls of the churches. Since the Enlightenment a new community of critical scholars has entered the discussion over the meaning of Jesus.

2.3 Such a consideration of the historical Jesus must fly beneath the radar of ecclesial defenses. Second- and fourth-century christological developments must be kept at bay for an honest appraisal of the historical Jesus.

2.4 The critical work of the Jesus Seminar has furnished the public discussion with a provocative profile of the historical Jesus. An artisan of words, Jesus of Nazareth through parables, aphorisms and stories challenged his audience to discover the effective presence of God in their midst. Jesus invited his listeners to work out a vision of a present God, who inclusively benefited both good and evil.

2.5 The historical Jesus' use of the phrase "Empire of God" played havoc with his contemporaries' understanding of Empire. The parables of God's Empire shatter the mythic designs of the first-century world. The aphorisms and stories of Jesus challenge those at the bottom of the social pyramid to improvise another way of seeing reality.

2.6 The sayings of Jesus provide his listeners with a new field of imaginative experiment, where the usual power relationships are undermined and taken by surprise. The true force of this experiment comes true when the audience figure out how the Empire of God touches their lives.

2.7 Jesus' use of the phrase "Empire of God" cannot be given an uncritical pass. Unless one sees that the sayings explicitly using that phrase stand over against the Domination system of Rome, then there is no grasping of Jesus' creative juxtaposition.

2.8 Jesus' socially shattering speech was matched by his inclusive table fellowship. Evidently he did not go in for purity litmus tests.

2.9 Jesus was not an apocalyptic visionary. The Seminar has found that Jesus saw the Empire of God as effectively present, not held off for some postponed future.

2.10 There is no evidence that the historical Jesus intended to create a "Church." While he did practice inclusive table fellowship and had an indeterminate number of followers, he did not leave any ecclesial blueprints.

2.11 Jesus died a Jew. Despite the later imaginations of Christian history Jesus was never the first Christian. Such an observation shatters the subsequent history of Jewish-Christian antipathy.

2.12 His death was at the hands of the Romans.

The Exposure of the Domination System

3.1 The Roman Domination System was exposed through the words, deeds, and death of Jesus of Nazareth.

3.2 As noted above, the sayings of Jesus set the imagining of the Empire of God over against the prevalent power system of the first century.

3.3 The death of Jesus further exposes this Roman Domination System. This domination system is the fundamental fact of the death of Jesus. Any other interpretation of the death of Jesus is either post-mortem construction or free-lancing speculation. Yet the domination system has continued to affect the interpretative tradition about the death of Jesus. Instead of exposing the domination system, which made Jesus a victim, the interpretive tradition has maintained ironically a domination pattern, turning the liquidation of Jesus into a vicarious experience and a justification for replicating this shameful domination pattern.

3.4 The traditional confession "Christ died for us" is no longer operative. One can say "Jesus died with us" in the sense that he died among the "disappeareds," those who have been victimized and rendered lost by the prevalent power system. Jesus' death no more can keep us from denying the depths and responsibilities of our humanity.

3.5 The confession "Christ died for us" must be placed in its historical context. Here we see that the death of Jesus had begun to be interpreted as a hero's death that had meaning for others. His death gave possibilities for Jews and gentiles that they could live in trust just as this man did. His death thus disclosed possibilities for humans. With Paul comes a further interpretation about the very understanding of God—a God who surprises by vindicating a man who has taken on the social curse of public execution. This has to be understood as a counter imperial claim.

3.6 We can say that the death of Jesus occasioned new thought. We should not simply repeat the interpretation constructed in the mid-first century. But we can say that we can also allow the death of Jesus to be an occasion for our waking up.

3.7 We must also say—in fairness to the evidence of the first century—that the tradition of the death of Jesus was not a universal concern among the post-mortem communities. Neither the Sayings Gospel nor Thomas is concerned with his death.

Diversity from the Outset

4.1 Contrary to the standard assumption about the unitary origin of Christianity modern biblical scholarship has shown that the early Jesus movement was in fact quite diverse. The Gospels, for example, both canonical and noncanonical, attest to the diversity of understanding Jesus of Nazareth within the tradition

4.2 The notion of a single, unified development comes not from an assessment of first-century evidence but from a critical reading of the ecclesial constructions in succeeding centuries. We do not find signs of uniformity in the first century (e.g., canon or creed). On the other hand, *The Acts of the Apostles* may well be one indication of the second-century's attempts to reread the early years of that Jewish Messianic sect.

The Fourth-Century Watershed

5.1 Eusebius provides a telling example of the embedding of Christology within the political/economic/social concerns of a later ecclesial community.

5.2 Eusebius, the court theologian, constructs a history of the church out of the values of the empire. His history concerns the tracing of the lines of succession from Jesus. This is a continuation of the power games begun with the battles over the succession to Alexander (and then Caesar).

5.3 The origins of the church are not factually based. Rather, they are constructed out of the power premises of the Empire. Antiquity and Divinity were requisite for the power scheme to hold. The implicit structure is hierarchical.

5.4 Not one word or particular deed of the historical Jesus is mentioned. The closest we get is a citation from Josephus; this has been inserted to continue to bolster the external witness for the movement.

5.5 The Divinity of Jesus is crucial for this presentation, for it is the keystone of the imperial arch. Without that there is no authority; the empire will fall asunder. The construction of Eusebius' church history, transforming the peasant artisan into an imperial trooper, rests upon the dreams of the Roman Empire. The Halicarnassus inscription, celebrating the miracle of Actium, anticipates the essential language play for the fourth-century church.

> Since the eternal and deathless nature of the universe has perfected its immense benefits to humanity in granting us as a supreme benefit, for our happiness and welfare, Caesar Augustus, Father of his own Fatherland, divine Rome, Zeus Paternal and Savior of the whole human race, in whom Providence has not only fulfilled but even surpassed the prayers of all people: land and sea are now at peace, cities flourish under the reign of law, in mutual harmony and prosperity; each is at the very acme of fortune and abounding in wealth; all humanity is filled with glad hopes for the future, and with contentment over the present; [it is fitting to honor the god] with public games and with statues, with sacrifices and with hymns.

—Inscription, Halicarnassus (*British Museum Inscriptions, 894*). Circa 2 BCE.

Heretical Tectonics

6.1 Diversity within the developing Jesus community soon becomes shunted off into linguistic ghettoes.

6.2 *Hairesis* originally referred to a philosophical school, whereby a group of people voluntarily joined together to practice a way of life, sometimes in contrast to the prevailing culture. Each person engaged in this school had to make a "choice" [the root meaning of *hairesis*]. This was a significant development not only for the individual but also for the history of culture. Right from the start there is a social reality to the notion of *hairesis*.

6.3 The influence of philosophical schools does not enter directly into the "Christian" tradition until the second century. Even at this point it was not seen as something negative. It was due to the debate over succession and teaching authority that the notion of "heresy" began to take on its negative sense. Indeed, in the third century the question of teaching authority became a major focus of ecclesial debate.

6.4 The notion of "heresy" is always understood in tandem with "authority." What is critical to notice is that the beginning glimmer of personal decision-making by someone who entered a philosophical school is countered and then replaced by the decision of the teacher/office holder. Personal authority is submerged or removed for the benefit of institutional authority.

6.5 In the Middle Ages there grew respect for the individual's coming to faith. Respect for conscience was present. Nevertheless, heresy was seen not as an aspect of an individual's journey in faith but a denial of that fundamental path. Moreover, this denial was inherently social and had to be responded to in an institutional fashion. Hence, heresy hunting, trial, and executions—all done in the name of the good of the faithful and for the good of the heretic's soul.

6.6 The Reformation brought about the beginning of tolerance, at least, over parcels of territory. Clearly there were still charges of heresy and counter-charges. Even those most in need of sympathy waxed eloquently against others they considered heretics. Attempts were made to move the response to heresy from the torture chamber to the debate room. Nevertheless, the religious strife of the seventeenth to eighteenth centuries proved that such attempts were not well grounded or developed.

6.7 What should not be overlooked in all of this history are the cultural assumptions regarding truth. There existed a perduring sense that truth rested in the group (whether philosophical school, ecclesial community, church, reforming church). Little regard was paid to the possibility that truth could exist and be found in the other (group or individual). Of course, the possibility of one's group's being wrong was never in question.

6.8 With the coming of the Enlightenment (and the American and French Revolutions) arrived the rearrangement and re-understanding of authority, the individual and the reality of choice. If Kant was right, then each person was sovereign, following one's conscience. Moreover, the American experiment demonstrated that the given authority structure of society could be changed and transformed as a result of individual choice.

6.9 Both the Reformation and Catholic Churches are heirs of the Age of Reason. Ironically, both proponents of faith and piety have succumbed at times to a rationalistic understanding of tradition and the Bible. Both have, in their own ways, reduced the meaning of tradition and scripture to a univocal, literal interpretation. The use of propositional theology is symptomatic of such a trend.

6.10 Heresy becomes in the modern age a refusal to subscribe to the theological propositions of a religious community. Ironically, those who issue the judgment that so and so is a heretic or that such and such a position is heretical do so without understanding either the context of their own propositions or the sources of faith upon which these propositions are based.

6.11 As noted above, the matter of heresy throughout history has also had a social location. It is crucial, therefore, to understand the particular context, as well as the proximate historical context of any heretical dispute. As this context is unpacked, one can begin to see a nexus or constellation of basic terms: heresy, authority, unity, choice, faith, community, bible, and tradition.

6.12 It is also significant to see that charge of "heresy" is usually imposed upon another individual. No one decides to be a heretic! Rather, the consequences of an individual's choice/s are registered and reflected by others in the community. Such a "reflection" may well be an unwitting reaction. Indeed, the so-called "heretic" may well have touched upon that which the community has neglected in its journey in faith. At the same time, the community may have a neuralgic reaction, sensing that their unexamined assumptions about the life of faith are being put into question. It is not the life of faith that is threatened but the idols of the tribe.

6.13 What should never be overlooked is that good intentions exist on both sides of the heresy dispute. Each side considers itself doing the proper thing. Each may rest well in one's conscience. Both think that this is done for the good of the whole!

6.14 What should not be lost in any investigation of heresy is that the language describing heresy has been historically the victory speech of the winners. The language about heresy masks the power relationship, which has constructed the very language about heresy. The winning side determines the discourse, which sets up the parameters of debate and the boundaries of ritual and conduct. Even modern scholarship has fallen under the spell of such discourse.

6.15 It is incumbent upon the present churches to learn both from the past (from its intimations and its mistakes), from the present (from each side of the dispute), and from the future (where neither side has entered).

6.16 Another way of putting this is asking: what are the sources of revelation—of breakthrough—for us today? Is Wisdom accessible? Where do we preclude the possibility of Reality impinging on us? Are we unable to go where mystery leads? How do we discern wisdom's footsteps? How does this happen in a Global context?

6.17 Further questions to pursue would be: Have we learned anything from our own experience of trust? What does living without any visible means of support do for our debates over heresy? What does a critical reading of our traditions, as well as scripture, do for the conversation?

6.18 The life of trust is truly a journey; thus, our coming to understand goes through stages of growth—from naive through critical to
mature. Many of us respond today towards others with charges of
heresy because we feel that our fundamental experience of the Holy
is being threatened. Indeed, the experience of the Holy is precisely
why certain people find themselves standing over against us! Our
response to another's expression of faith may well be a naive reaction.
Or, even if a critical one, it might lack the imagination to understand
maturely.

6.19 What does it say about us—or our communities of trust—if
we demand a total and complete resolution to the complexity and
murkiness of our unfinished existence together? Are we desirous of
having the final word? Is this not the primal problem—refusing to
detect any depth in our lives?

6.20 What would be the marks, signs, indicators of a community,
which does not have a final solution for everyone within? What sort
of texture would such a community have? Would not forgiveness and
thanksgiving be foremost? What would happen if the Living One (cf.
Gospel of Thomas) were found within?

Looking for Weapons of Mass Construction

7.1 Any reflection upon the future of the church (from a Catholic
perspective) must finally come to terms with the Modernist deba-
cle of the early twentieth century. Church officials succeeded in
destroying the reputations and lives of the relatively few scholars and
writers who tried to introduce the church to the shifting realities of
the Modern world. A fortress mentality, secured by a centralized
authority, kept the demands and challenges of the world at bay until
a fat peasant opened a window on the world.

7.2 The critical issues surrounding the Modernist Controversy
have yet to be fully faced by the present church. The groundbreak-
ing work of von Harnack (*What is Christianity?*) set the terms of the
debate. Harnack brought the question of history to the relation of
Jesus to the church. How did Jesus' preaching of the Kingdom of
God bear upon the later institution? For von Harnack the church
was the husk, not the kernel. The institution of church was not the
essence of Christianity.

7.3 Despite the fact that Loisy in *The Gospel and the Church*
attempted to answer von Harnack, the French scholar nevertheless
concluded, "Jesus foretold the Kingdom and it was the church that
came."

7.4 The Modernist controversy was built upon two opposing
currents. Reflection on the nature of the church required a fun-

damental theology that was developed as an apologetic discipline. Its arguments were structured upon historical demonstrations of the foundation of the church by Jesus. The historical-critical method stood against this endeavor and undermined such proof text attempts.

7.5 The *Syllabus Condemning the Errors of the Modernists* (1907) as well as *Pascendi Dominici Gregis* (Pius X's Encyclical Letter on Modernism) attempted to expose the errors of the Modernists. A critical reading, in fact, discloses the church's consistent refusal to see itself within time and space. In the spirit of Pius IX the documents show a church that has abstracted itself from this world, unsettled by revolutions and movements from below.

7.6 The Catholic demonstrations at historical reconstruction/ apology have taken two routes. Both attempt to provide the facts in an argument post hoc propter hoc.

7.7 One route tries to locate the foundation of the church within the intent of the historical Jesus. This meant ransacking the New Testament for any intimation of ecclesial formation. The so-called parables of growth (e.g., Mark 4) were allegorized to argue for a continued development. The gathering of disciples by Jesus was seen as the foundation of an apostolic college and conferral of power. Of course, Matt 16:17–19 was employed to defend the promise to Peter's primacy.

7.8 The second route uses the post-resurrectional emergence of the church as an indication of the foundational activity of the Spirit and the faith of Peter.

7.9 A third method later was adapted when the first two faltered under withering historical critique. A connection between Jesus and the church was established by a transcendental method. Assuming that Jesus is the "absolute savior," there is a need for this salvific presence to be transmitted. This happens through the church. The church continues to be the public and historical conduit of this presence.

7.10 Both Catholic and Protestant have continued to work on the question of the relationship between the historical Jesus and the church. Both Barthes and Bultmann provided different ways of making the connection. Especially since Vatican II Catholic biblical scholarship has followed the critical paths blazed by Protestant scholarship. Indeed, it can be said that the Catholic Church defends an historical-critical method for scripture.

7.11 A fundamental irony comes home when one observes how the scriptures are now taught at Catholic universities. Almost all, if not all, that was condemned by the *Syllabus of Errors* has become standard intellectual fare.

7.11 The Catholic Church, however, has yet to apply critical historical consciousness to the foundational thinking on the church. In sum, the refusal to enter history remains.

7.12 The church's refusal to see the historical dimensions of its life can be seen in the often-used description of church as "divinely instituted." This is tantamount to special pleading, an avoidance of the fact that this or that structure is an historical development, resulting from the decisions of human beings. Even the organic notion of development (espoused by some Modernists) can be used to avoid limited historical reality.

7.13 If one considers how theologians argued from the sixteenth century even through the twentieth one discovers little concern with the evidence (as fragmentary, etc.) but overly concerned with buttressing up a power position (e.g., the use of the so-called parables of growth to support such arguments). But if one considers the parables are occasions for experiment, where the Empire of God provides the creative space for thinking, imagining, and fellowship, then what? Also if the parables dwell upon the dirty, the unexpected, the other, then?

Colonial Aftershocks

8.1 Recent scholarship (e.g., Jenkins' *The Next Christendom*) points to the seismic shift in church population. It is estimated that by 2050 only 1/5 of the Christian population will be non-Latino whites. The face of "traditional Christianity" will be transformed through significant surges in demographics. While the churches in Europe and America are fussing with ideological matters, Christianity is already flourishing in South America, Africa, and Asia. This new wave of Christian development will be conservative, evangelical and apocalyptic. It will stand in direct competition with Islam.

8.2 While such analyses are sobering, they are also somewhat problematic. Much of the argument is based upon a model for church (the CEO pyramid of power schema) that is top-heavy. This model presumes the colonial infrastructure and indirectly perpetuates it.

8.3 Moreover, the focus turns very much upon a propositional or textual conservatism without noticing that in Africa, Asia, and Latin America there are many, many ways of reading around and about the traditions.

8.4 The church around the world may already be intimating a new way of imagining church. It is a grass roots situation, as well as a situation that is "off to the side" or "in the shadows."

8.5 Listen to the grandmothers. The Pastorals long ago were afraid of them. The reality of compassion and humanity has come down through these unseen hands and hearts. They know intuitively that the traditions are not monolithic but plastic.

8.6 Such analyses are being used by neo-conservatives to bolster their attempt to maintain power. The sad irony is the neo-con argument is another instance of the old colonial position.

8.7 Such analyses bring to light the need to craft new language of church, for that is where the church hovers—in words. Hence the genius of creeds. But now we need new strategies and protocols that are not excluding propositional solutions but ways of establishing breathing room for people on this planet.

Degrees of Complexity

9.1 A more complicated reading of the global shifts in Christian population comes from a long-standing habit within church tradition. When the human has been taken seriously a complex vision has resulted.

9.2 Such complexity of vision was already in place with the multi-level reading of scripture.

9.3 The various architectures through the centuries also indicate the need for a complicated reading of the life of the respective communities. Baroque art was but one facet of Christian life in the post-Tridentine world.

9.4 The imagination, even in medieval times, can be described as a dramatic movement through time, not simply around or above it. Even Dante's *Commedia*, set in eternal stations, exhibited this dramatic human progress through time and space.

9.5 The sacramental tradition can be understood as reinforcing the sense that human life together is more than meets the eye. This is not a magical formula but an appreciation of the use of symbol to gesture at the depth of life together.

9.6 Such complexity, noted even from the beginning in the speech and activity of the historical Jesus, cannot be lost. What must be ended is the perpetuation of the pediatric church. It is time for people to stand on their own two feet and discover the possibilities of life together on this planet.

Non est extra

10.1 Not just the eternal realm has collapsed as its supporting myths fall to earth like aging satellites. The nineteenth-century locomotive of pre-ordained progress also has been derailed. A century of war, genocide, atomic blackmail, and economic rampage has ushered in a democratic refusal to believe unwittingly in the inevitable. We have come to see that the mythic narratives determine the actions of historical players. We have begun to understand that these foundational stories do not lead into the beyond whether in space or in time. Rather, they bring us back to earth, to the human beings responsible for their telling and the social world constructed from them.

10.2 What then is left? The only world there is. The old saw *Nulla salus extra ecclesiam* (no salvation outside of the church) falls from its own weight. Instead, we see that ***non est extra.***

10.3 The stories that we spin do not lead to some other world. There is no other side. Life through a conscious twist (like a Möbius Strip) becomes a sacred continuum. Evolution takes a critical turn through and by us. In the very midst of contingency, finitude and transience our life becomes endless, outsideless, as we give ourselves to life's immanent interconnection.

10.4 While the church has suspended Jesus in the heavens, the dysfunctional control of the church has kept Christians on their knees. But the world did not stand still while the church held its breath. Modernity blew off the ecclesiastical roof and left "bare ruined choirs" under an open sky. Main line churches are on the verge of becoming tourist traps, while the Holy leaks out, diffused throughout our human habitat.

Credo in unam, sanctam, catholicam, apostolicam ecclesiam

11.1 Confucius advised that the first task of governing was to rectify the names. What this paper has tried to do is to sketch out some of the artistic assumptions that have gone into the history of the church. This was done to show that any reflection on the future of the church must be a consideration of the "work in progress." At the same time, such a perspective must take into account the enormous movements at work as these constructions get underway. If anything has been learned from this exercise, it is time "to put it into practice."

11.2 In contrast to the *Syllabus of Errors* this paper is neither a *Syllabus of Dissent* nor a *Grammar of Ascent* (with a nod to Darwin). Instead it is a metaphorical play upon the historical complexities of the history of church. It has attempted to highlight salient features of the history of the church in order to see if the various elements can be rubbed together to ignite the present situation. The church today senses all and more of these historical tremors.

11.3 When these reflections are brought together a rectification of the basic description of church comes to the fore. The church no longer is the only game in town (something that should have been learned from Galileo). Moreover, one church is not alone in matters of tradition. The various churches throughout the world certainly point this out. But also the secular society has much to say about how the traditions are to be understood and explored. Further, critical scholarship presents a crucial angle of understanding.

11.4 The church in a global situation must come to terms with its attempt to dominate. We have noted that the roots of ecclesial imperialism come directly from the very government that liquidated Jesus. Since the time of the Conquistadors the church has buttressed the colonizing efforts of the Western nations. The theology of the church has greatly helped propagate the continual saga of domination.

11.5 How do we speak of church in the encompassing Global community? The following chart begins to spell out some possibilities for critical discussion.

11.6 The traditional descriptors of church ("one, holy, catholic, apostolic") must be rectified within the ongoing Global context. But what happens when "this is it"? When *non est extra?* What happens when members of the church can no longer use the trappings of allegory to avoid the global reality of our life together on this planet?

11.7 The sense of ecclesial unity ("one") can no longer be understood as a monolithic adherence to a propositional confession, nor reduced to a litmus test. The reality of human experience brings us to the recognition that unity is discovered in diversity, brought about by genuine human relations. Dialogue not dictate characterizes such unity in diversity. The hierarchical pyramid of power collapses as a structural principle for church. This sense of inclusive unity agrees right with the vision of the historical Jesus who trusted in a God that benefited good and evil, just and unjust. Paul also intimates this unity in diversity through his understanding of the gifts of the Spirit to the community.

11.8 The "other" becomes the trademark of the "holy" in this rectification of terms. Since there is "no outside," one begins to look for the "holy" in the encounters with the "other." We can discover the "other" right in the midst of our experience. There is no need to go to Mars to do this. The unknown is on our doorstep. Even facets of ourselves become avenues of entrance into the other. Dialogue with members of other religious traditions or none at all

Traditional Term	Rectified Term		
One	Unity in diversity	Relational, intimacy	Unity not defined by propositions, but by experience
Holy	Other	The other is in our midst not outside	Jesus the first-century Jew; The Empire of God in our midst; Paul's body of the Anointed
Catholic	Global, comprehensive, holistic	The experience of wisdom traditions	Not a colonial power nor an imperial power
Apostolic	Historical	Limits	Seismic historical shifts: E.g., Constantine

should be seen under this rubric of otherness. It is not a matter of asserting one's guarded truth but of discovering the truth that emerges from negotiating the dense intersections of history ("To have friends coming from afar: is this not a delight?"). Again, we can start with remembering that Jesus was a first-century Jew. The "other" is at the heart of the Christian tradition. There is no way we can or should baptize Jesus. He was not the first Christian. He remains in the church's memory that bothersome note: a Jew to the very end. But there is more to the memory of the historical Jesus. His speech betrayed a vision of God's Empire that provided an opportunity for others to imagine an alternative way of living and breathing. The Sayings Gospel community continued to trust that Wisdom was available in their lives. The community of Matthew further believed that Wisdom continued to speak in human terms. Paul discovered that the God of Israel joined in solidarity with the forgotten ones. This God did not leave the innocent in the lurch, but joined in the death throes.

11.9 A "catholic" church can discover its sense of "wholeness" in a global environment. This does not mean that the church can indulge in imperial or colonial fantasies or scenarios. The church finds out its global reach, its comprehensive search, and its holistic vision precisely when it confronts the "other." Instead of providing a "totalizing solution, the church can begin to rediscover what it means to listen to the experience of various Wisdom traditions. In so doing, the church will discover what it can contribute to the planet's survival. It will discover that it is involved—not as an eschatological holding company—but as a creative contributor to the continuing history of this planet. Confucius, furthermore, may well have something to say to our situation. Muhammad may be onto something. The Buddha might "push" us to realize our at-one-ment in the fragments of our life together. We can begin to understand what *kata holon* can mean as we detect the life that is our common good and destiny. Artistically we shall look for ways to be transparent, for windows of intersection, to let the "other" in.

11.10 The church becomes "apostolic" when it finally embraces the dramatic density of the historical. No longer will history be used to prove a point, or to establish a claim. Instead, the fragility of human life, the effervescence of time, will allow us to see what is really at stake. We shall begin to re-read our history, our present relationships, and our future prospects in light of the seismic historical shifts that condition our life together on this planet. At the same time, we can begin to see how a creative sense of the "other" in our midst can push us to envision history in constructive, dynamic ways. We may begin to see that we are players in a game that we can help others to keep playing long after we are gone.

> They drew a circle and shut me out,
>
> A heretic, a rebel, a thing to flout.
>
> But love and I had the wit to win,
>
> We drew a circle and took them in.*

---

*This poem by Edwin Markham inspired the congregation of the Unitarian Church of Baton Rouge in 1988 to build, as part of the Sanctuary Chancel, the largest circle window extant in any building in Baton Rouge.

Killing Jesus

Stephen J. Patterson

C hrist crucified rules, and it may be that the true business
of modern Christianity is to crucify him again and again
so that he can never get a word out of his mouth.

—Barbara Ehrenreich, *Nickel and Dimed*, 2001

When Jesus was killed by the authorities in charge of keeping
the Roman *Pax*, his friends and followers were not without cultural
resources for dealing with this tragedy. As they began to reflect on
Jesus' death, they soon came to see it not as a tragedy at all, but as
an inevitable part of his life, an end fitting of the kind of life Jesus
led. They began to develop ways of speaking of the death of Jesus
that would connect it with his life and draw attention to his life as
decisive for their own lives.

One way that these early followers of Jesus could speak of his
death was simply as the death of a victim—a victim of Roman imperial power, a dissident to the great Roman vision of a single empire
encompassing the whole known world, standing alone, without
rival or alternative.[1] They knew that to be a follower of Jesus was to
embrace the foolishness of raising a dissident voice and an alternative vision to the Roman *Pax*. "We proclaim a crucified Messiah,"
says Paul, who is both the "power of God" and the "wisdom of
God" (1 Cor 1:23–24). Power that is weakness; wisdom that is foolishness. These were the realities that determined Paul's new life in
the followership of Jesus. To be a follower of Jesus was to become a
"fool for Christ's sake." It meant embracing weakness, not strength;
shame rather than honor. It meant welcoming vilification, persecu-
tion and slander. It meant becoming "the refuse of the world, the

offscouring of all things" (1 Cor 4:8–13). And as Jesus' dissident life led to his death as a victim of imperial power, so also many of his followers led dissident lives that in turn earned them the fate of victim as well.

But the followers of Jesus soon began to speak of his death not simply as the death of a victim, but as the glorious death of a martyr. The rich and varied Jewish martyrological tradition was perhaps the most fertile and productive interpretive field for early Christians. From it come the idea that Jesus' death was a sacrifice, and the belief that God could, and would raise Jesus from the dead. But the direction in which the martyrdom tradition points is not forward, into the heavenly future life the martyr is said to enjoy, but backward, to the way of life, the values, and the cause for which the martyr was willing to die. The martyr's death is a witness—a witness to the ultimate value of the cause for which he or she died, and a witness to the way of faithfulness to that cause, a way that may well lead to death. The martyr must be willing to pay the ultimate price for the convictions she or he holds. But before one might be willing to die for a cause, one must first be willing the live for it. Thus, the New Testament gospels, all of which make use of the martyrological tradition, present Jesus' life not simply as a prelude to his death, but as the *way of life* one must embrace as one follows Jesus to the cross. This was true of Paul as well—though this is often obscured by the fact that Paul very seldom discusses Jesus' life and only occasionally makes use of his words. But of all the characters that appear in the New Testament, it is Paul who emulates the life of Jesus most thoroughly. If Mark's fictive rich young ruler turns away from Jesus when he learns of the rigors of renunciation Jesus requires, Paul did not. Paul took up the life of Jesus and made it his own. This he says of his own struggles with life as a dissident voice in the Empire:

> . . . we are always carrying in the body the death of Jesus, so that the life of Jesus might be made manifest in our body; for in living we are always given up to death for Jesus' sake, so that the life of Jesus might be made manifest in our mortal flesh. (2 Cor 4:10–11)

For Paul and others who came to understand Jesus' death as a martyrdom, embracing his death was really about embracing his *life*. The martyr's death means nothing apart from the life to which it bears witness.

Finally, the followers of Jesus also spoke of his death as a sacrifice. To speak thus may seem at first glance to take leave of Jesus' life and to draw his death into theological abstraction. A sacrificial lamb is born to die, nothing more. But this was not how the early followers of Jesus made use of the metaphor of sacrifice to interpret his death. The idea that a *person* might become a sacrifice for sin originally came from out of the martyrdom tradition.[2] In the Maccabaean literature, for example, it is because of the martyr's extraordinary faithfulness to God that his or her death might be regarded by God as atonement for the sins of the people. It is the martyr's extraordinary life and faithfulness unto death that finally turns God's anger, and stirs God to come at last to rescue the suffering people of God. Ironically, in the New Testament it is Caiaphas in John's gospel who gives clearest expression to this idea: "do you not understand that it is expedient for you that one man should die for the people, and that the whole nation should not perish" (John 11:50).

But even when the idea of Jesus' death as a sacrifice was not explicitly tied to the martyrological tradition from whence it came, it remained connected to Jesus' life in a very creative way. As Jesus' followers pondered his death as a sacrifice, and considered this within the context of a culture in which sacrifice was the glue that held every stick of the social infrastructure firmly in place,[3] they began to see how Jesus' death could function culticly to free them from that infrastructure, and their culticly-sanctioned places in it. Like the sacrifices that held together family, clan, city, and empire, they found that their common meals—sacrificial meals, as all meals were—could become a place of new identity and new social formation. And as they began to walk away from the sacrificial fires that held the old world together, they discovered once again the freedom to become something new in this new micro-society, "the body of Christ," held together by the sacrifice of Jesus' own body. At these new tables—altars—where slaves and prostitutes sat as equals with merchants, scholars and even the occasional state official, they received a new identity and purpose. But this was exactly what people had experienced in the table fellowship of Jesus himself. Jesus gathered at table the clean and the unclean, those with honor and those with none, prostitutes, sinners, beggars, and thieves. Around those tables all became equals, members of a common family, heirs to a new Empire, the Empire of God. After his death, as the tables of the Jesus movement became the altars around which a new society was formed, this process of personal and communal transformation continued. Thus, what Jesus had meant to people in life was translated into a cultic parlance, and enacted once again through the appropriation of his death as a sacrifice.

And what of Jesus' resurrection? Here, at last, do we not finally take leave of his life? Is not the resurrection a thing of a different class altogether, an event so powerful and transforming that nothing in Jesus' life could carry much significance after that? Not at all. On

the contrary, I have tried to show that apart from Jesus' life the resurrection proclamation would never have been ventured in the first
place.[4] If we were to take the gospel accounts of the resurrection
as historical, they would not be convincing to anyone outside the
inner circle of Jesus' devoted companions—and even some of them
express doubts in these stories. I do not regard them as historical,
but I do imagine that people in the Jesus movement did indeed have
the kind of spiritual experiences Paul and others came to understand
as post-resurrection manifestations of the risen Christ. But why did
they understand them thus? Why did they not see these powerful
spiritual experiences as instances of spirit possession—as the ghost
of Jesus coming back to haunt them, like so many other criminals
and victims of violence and betrayal? Why did they say "God has
raised Jesus from the dead?" They said this because they had faith
in Jesus. Those who said it first, had known him. They believed in
him and in his cause. To them, he was a martyr, not just a victim.
In the ancient Jewish context of Christian origins, resurrection is
part of the martyr's story.[5] Resurrection is vindication. Could God
raise Jesus from the dead? Any ancient would have answered "yes"
to that question. But *would* God raise Jesus from the dead? To this
question, only his followers could answer "yes." And they said "yes"
to it because they believed that Jesus' life had revealed him to be
one of God's righteous ones. They believed that in his words were
God's Word. They believed that in his deeds, Jesus had done the will
of God. Resurrection, too, was a way of proclaiming the significance
of Jesus' life.

I have become convinced that in each of these ways of interpreting Jesus' death, the followers of Jesus were in fact drawing attention
to his *life*. His death mattered to them because his life had mattered
to them. They spoke of his death in ways that affirmed his life, and
reaffirmed their own commitment to the values and vision stamped
into his life by his words and deeds. To the followers and friends
of Jesus, his death was important in its particularity—as the fate
of him who said and did certain things, who stood for something
so important to him that he was willing to give his life for it. That
something was the vision of life he called the Empire of God. They
too believed in this vision of a new empire. And if this vision was
indeed *God's* Empire, then the bearer of this vision was not dead.
No executioner could kill what he was. To kill Jesus, you would have
to kill the vision. This is what the cross could not do.

When Christian believers and theologians approach the question
of Jesus' death today, these are generally not the concerns that lie
close to hand. The things Jesus said that lead to his death are not
at issue. What he lived or died for is of no concern. The event of

Jesus' death has lost its particularity, its connection to the course of real human events that brought it about. In this abstracted status, Jesus' death has become for us a mythic event connected to the universal problem of death and the mysterious and frightening end of human life. As we fret over the moral and ethical failures of our lives and dread the perils and punishments that might lie beyond the grave, we are comforted by the knowledge that Jesus died "to save us from our sins." His resurrection assures us of our own immortality. If Jesus came to fulfill his cosmic destiny and die on the cross so that we might be saved, then anything else he might have done in his life—his own aspirations, his own values and vision, his carefully chosen words and daring prophetic deeds—pales by comparison. Ethics are never so important as salvation. With salvation it is life itself that hangs in the balance, our lives, which we desperately seek to preserve, even in the face of death, whose threat confronts us all. Thus, Jesus' death and resurrection have become the universal saving events in which we find God's graciousness extended even to us, hopeless sinners, who have no intention of giving up the lives we live, oblivious to the vision of human life Jesus espoused and embodied.

The eclipse of Jesus' death and resurrection in their particularity, and their elevation to the status of mythic events in a cosmic struggle, is invited perhaps by the way Paul and other early Christians placed Jesus' death and resurrection at the center of their own traditional apocalyptic hopes. Apocalypticism casts the struggle between good and evil in terms of a great cosmic battle, with the forces of God arrayed against the armies of the Evil One. In Jewish apocalyptic the power and victory of God is marked by the resurrection of all those who have been slain by the forces of evil. In the final struggle their faithfulness and sufferings are vindicated. This is the framework in which Paul interpreted the resurrection of Jesus: he was the first fruits, the first of those countless ones slain in the struggle against evil to come back to life (1 Cor 15:20). The resurrection was for Paul a signal, a cosmic alarm clock sounding the arrival of the final battle, which would begin any day. But Paul and others who interpreted Jesus' death and resurrection in this way did not detach the death and resurrection of Jesus from his life. The cosmic battle they believed they were witnessing was being waged over a specific idea, a real cause. The struggle in which they were engaged was the struggle for the vision of human life their crucified messiah had espoused. For Paul, to experience the resurrection of Jesus was to become possessed by his Spirit, to share "the mind of Christ," and to embrace the life of Christ as his own. And Paul and others formed communities that would be the "body of Christ," embodying the life of love and mutual care that Jesus had died for. What he died for, they would now live for, until God would finally establish the Empire of God as the universal rule of love and justice in the world.

As time passed, however, and that first generation of friends and followers who had known Jesus and actually remembered his life passed from the scene, the connection between the particulars of Jesus' life and the mythic structures of cosmic battle became ever more tenuous and eventually were lost. The struggle became less and less a struggle for a particular set of values connected to Jesus, and more a clash of powers. The power of Christ was pitted against the religion of the Jews, against the pagan gods, and ultimately against the universal foe, death itself. One can see this already in the Apostles Creed, where the life of Jesus has been diminished to a mere comma, a blank space residing quietly between "born of the Virgin Mary" and "suffered under Pontius Pilate." The elements of the Christian creed are the elements of the cosmic drama common to many ancient religious traditions: miraculous birth, death, resurrection, ascension. Jesus became simply another of the many dying-rising savior gods of antiquity, association with whom would assure safety in this world and the next. His table fellowship would for some become a mere dispensary for the "drug of immortality," the *pharmakon athanasias*, as Ignatius would come to speak of the communion bread (Ign.*Eph.* 20).

Eventually Jesus Christ would become the greatest savior god of all. His cross would become a logo, a talisman emblazoned on the shield of Constantine and his soldiers to protect them in battle. Jesus became a partisan, whose name would strike fear in the heart of anyone who by chance had not been born under his sign. In the Middle Ages his cross would become a sign of terror, before which Jews and Muslims would cringe in supplication, begging mercy from marauding hordes of crusaders, or stand in defiance only to be slain. The symbol of weakness Paul embraced became the symbol of merciless power, where it remains today for many Christian believers. One can see this still in its infinitely trivialized American form on any given Sunday—afternoon—where the warriors of sport pause to cross themselves as a solemn prelude to the touchdown victory dance that is sure to follow, taunting those poor unfortunates inexplicably abandoned by Jesus in their moment of greatest need. The cross is for winners, not losers.

Is Jesus dead? Not yet. But what the cross could not do, Christians could. We are killing Jesus. Jesus was a sage, or if your prefer, a prophet. Sages and prophets live by their words and deeds. In this sense, for most of us who assemble in the name of Jesus, he is dead. His words and deeds mean little to us, if anything at all. We do not look to Jesus for a way of life, but for salvation. "He died that we might live." Indeed. It seems we have to kill him in order that we might live whatever lives our power and privilege will allow us to lead. When real life is at stake, most of us will take personal salvation over the Empire of God any day. And so we prefer our Christ crucified, a once living Jesus silenced by a higher calling.

But this was not so for the friends and followers of Jesus. For them, the Empire of God *was* salvation. They saw God's care for them in the communities of mutual care and love founded in Jesus' name. They experienced the acceptance and welcome they received around the tables of the Jesus movement as redemption. Beggars, lepers, prostitutes, and expendables of every sort—the "nothings" of the world, as Paul puts it—embraced Jesus' Empire of God as their one great hope and longing. And others did, too—people like Paul, who gave up lives of considerable status and importance to enter into these communities of the new Empire. Why did they do it? They were responding to the compelling vision of Jesus, who lived on for them, alive in their midst. For them, this was no existential metaphor for commitment. Jesus was really alive, spiritually present with them. Whatever it might mean to speak thus today about Jesus—to say that he is "alive" in our midst—it must above all else mean that he somehow still offers us the vision of a new Empire, into which we are still invited in a very real way. Apart from his words and deeds, the living Jesus would have meant nothing to those who encountered him in the private and public places of antiquity. Neither can Jesus be alive to us apart from his words and deeds. He is alive *to us* only as he was alive to them, as a real invitation into a way of life we can see reflected in his own life. When the life of Jesus no longer matters to those who would claim him as Lord and Savior, then the life that changed the lives of many finally will have come to an end. The killing of Jesus has been a long process. It began long ago in an Empire not so unlike our own, and now we are finishing the job for reasons not unlike those for which the Roman Empire crucified him in the first place. His words are too hard. His ways are too challenging. He does not respect our world and its virtues. And so we are killing Jesus; for our sake, he must die.

Literal Incarnation or Universal Love?

Robert J. Miller

T he purpose of this paper is to stimulate reflection and provoke discussion about the place of the incarnation within Christian theology, both orthodox and non-traditional. To facilitate discussion I have stated key conclusions as numbered theses.

Virgin Birth, Incarnation, and Atonement

A biologist colleague of mine recently asked me what I thought about the virgin birth. I told him that I believed it is true theologically but not literally. After a moment of shock he volunteered that he believed the virgin birth literally. Since he was a biologist, I asked him whose DNA Jesus had and was told that it was a miracle. When I asked my colleague how it would affect his faith if he came to suspect that Jesus had a human father, he said that he would have to stop being Christian because Jesus could not be the Son of God or the Word of God unless he was virgin born.

While this theologically unsophisticated response shows no awareness of a critical understanding of the New Testament, it is completely typical of how Christianity has traditionally construed the significance of the virgin birth, that is, as a support for belief in the incarnation. That is why it is usually futile to argue that the virgin birth can be true theologically without being true literally. Such a distinction makes no sense within the traditional theological framework in which the virgin birth has to be literally true for the incarnation to be literally true.

Thesis 1: The literal virgin birth is important in Christianity primarily because it supports the literal incarnation. (By "literal incarnation" I mean the doctrine that Jesus is the Son of God, fully divine and fully human, one person with two distinct natures, as defined by the councils of Nicea and Chalcedon.)

If Jesus was fully divine, the Christian religion is unique in that it is the only one founded by God in person. *Thesis 2*: The literal incarnation is *the* basis for the belief that Christianity is superior to all other religions.

Though the literal incarnation is the ultimate ground for the claim of the unique superiority of Christianity, incarnation is not the most important belief in the hierarchy of doctrine. In traditional Christian theology it is the doctrine of the atonement which is of supreme importance. Incarnation is important because it is understood as the necessary condition for atonement. Two observations about Christian theological reasoning, one ancient and one modern, will illustrate. First, in the christological controversies surrounding the early ecumenical councils the perspectives that prevailed repeatedly emphasized that if Christ were not truly and fully divine his death could not effect salvation. Second, when traditional Christians today defend the divinity of Christ, they seldom do so in order to claim divine authority for the teaching of the historical Jesus, but rather in order to assure themselves that they are going to heaven. That the certainty of salvation depends on the divinity of Christ is an oft repeated theme in traditional apologetics.

Thesis 3: The doctrines of virgin birth, incarnation, and atonement are traditionally related as follows: We cannot be sure we are saved unless Jesus is fully divine and Jesus cannot be divine unless he was virgin born.

The Incoherence
of a Literal Incarnation

John Hick has demonstrated that the concept of a literal incarnation is not philosophically viable.[1] Many theologians before and after the council of Chalcedon have attempted to explain how one person could have both a fully divine nature (with all the essential attributes of divinity) and at the same time a fully human nature (with all the essential human attributes). However, all those attempts failed to meet the Chalcedonian requirement to affirm both full divinity and full humanity and thus have been rejected as heresies.[2] In other words, every attempt at explaining, as opposed to restating, the orthodox doctrine has resulted in heresy. *Thesis 4*: There exists no orthodox explanation of the literal incarnation.

Most theologians who have wrestled with this doctrine end up pleading that the coexistence of two natures in Christ is a divine mystery beyond human understanding. However, the Chalcedonian formula (two natures in one person) is not a revealed truth. It is a philosophical artifact, carefully crafted over a couple of centuries of christological debate and ecclesiastical negotiation. Since philosophical artifacts are formulated in technical language, they have no natural or common sense meanings; they have only whatever meanings they are defined to have. Any difficulties in understanding the Chalcedonian formula must therefore be attributed to the shortcomings of those who created it. The intention of the formula is to exclude any understanding of Jesus that denied either his full divinity or his full humanity.[3] But this seems to be impossible. If the formula cannot be explained in a religiously acceptable way (i.e., if every attempt to explain it has implications that clash with one of its aims), then the formula is not a mystery, it is a failure (i.e., it cannot accomplish what it was designed to do). It is both a category error and an evasion of theological responsibility to call a non-viable philosophical artifact a mystery. *Thesis 5*: The doctrine that Christ is one person with two distinct natures is incoherent.

The Cost and Benefit of Literal Incarnation

Whether a given belief is philosophically viable does not in itself settle the question of its theological utility. In fact the religious value of a belief has little to do with its philosophical coherence, except for those committed to a strong version of the harmony between faith and reason. For the sake of the argument, then, let us assume that the literal incarnation is a viable belief and go on to ask whether it is religiously helpful. (Humans can easily believe things that are incoherent or otherwise irrational, but very seldom do they believe things they don't want to believe.) The approach taken here is a cost-benefit analysis.

There is no denying that incarnation is an appealing, even beautiful, belief. In the traditional story of salvation history, sin ruined the relationship between God and humankind, but God loves humanity so much that he became a human being and endured suffering and death to make things right between him and us. By freely accepting suffering and death, God gave us the gift of salvation, something we could never gain by ourselves. This story about a loving God is both powerful and beautiful. It is "good news." Indeed, it is almost too good to be true. If you had never heard of Christianity and set out to invent a beautiful way of imagining God, you might well come up with something like this.

As we saw earlier, the incarnation is the foundation of Christianity's claim to uniqueness. In Jesus God came to earth and died for our sins, something which had never happened before and will never happen again. Belief in Jesus and acceptance of his atoning death is therefore the only way to salvation. Every human being therefore should be a Christian. (This insistence makes Christianity unlike any other world religion except Islam.) Not only should everyone be Christian, every person *must* be Christian or else risk damnation. (Not even Islam believes that it is the *only* way to salvation.) This exclusivist perspective makes for an intolerance within Christianity which history shows can have dangerous consequences for both non-Christians and "wrong" Christians. Within this exclusivism, even God is believed to be intolerant, for he will consign you to eternal hell if you do not accept the Christian religion. Here we have the monster god who has driven out of the churches so many of those raised in the traditional Christian worldview. The important point here is that the ugliness of this image of the monster god and the beauty of the image of the God of incarnation are two sides of the same coin. *Thesis 6*: It is the uniqueness of the Christian claim about God's love that nourishes the intolerance of exclusivism.

The Scandal of Limited Access

For several reasons that do not need to be reviewed here, many Christians (maybe most of them) reject exclusivism and the monster god that it entails. The strict exclusivist theology that humans can be saved only by the death of Jesus and only if we beg God to accept Jesus' death as atonement for our sins is now pretty much confined to fundamentalists. It was formally rejected by the Catholic Church at Vatican II and nearly all non-fundamentalist Protestants believe that God has more than one way of saving human beings of good conscience.[4]

Here is the point at which the connection between atonement and incarnation poses a fascinating problem: if exclusivism is rejected, what happens to incarnation? (The Catholic Church, for example, rejects exclusivism but affirms the literal incarnation.) If there are paths to salvation other than through the death of Jesus, what is the benefit of the incarnation? Regardless of how one answers that fascinating question, here I want to consider another problem that flows directly from it, a problem focused on what we can call the scandal of limited access. However one describes the benefit of the incarnation, is there not a contradiction in there having been only one that has affected only a minority of humanity? The contradiction is in terms of God's love. If the incarnation is an act of love, why has there been only one? Why hasn't God come to earth as often as necessary to reach the whole world?[5] (By contrast, Islam teaches that God has sent to every people a prophet from among their own. In Hinduism, Vishnu is believed to have come to earth in human form many times in response to human need for divine assistance. Some Hindus who admire Jesus understand him to be one of Vishnu's incarnations.)

There are several responses to the scandal of limited access. Here we can briefly mention four.[6] (1) Incarnation is not only about atonement, but about God sharing in the human condition. But the scandal of particularity remains because the benefit of knowing about God's sharing our condition is a benefit that only some can experience. (2) The revelation of the incarnation is in principle available to all. This is theoretically true in that the proclamation of God's incarnation in Jesus has not been deliberately hidden or withheld from anyone. Still, the medium of the revelation is limited and therefore so is the actual, as opposed to the theoretical, access to it. (How likely is it that those who are Christians today would have believed in the incarnation if God had become an Eskimo?) (3) The church has the duty to evangelize. Therefore any limitation in humanity's access to faith in the incarnation is due to the church's inadequacy. But if incarnation is an expression of infinite love, why would God outsource the revelation of that love to a limited group, especially since that group has failed to convert the world? Why not plural incarnations? (4) Jesus is the one savior, but a person does not need to know that to be saved. (This is the Catholic position.) This mitigates the scandal but does not remove it, since Christians are privileged to know the truth while others are not.

All these solutions want to have it both ways. But that cannot be done responsibly. One cannot affirm both that there is an important advantage in being Christian *and* that Christians are not favored in a way that is unjust to the majority.[7] *Thesis 7*: Christian theology must make the choice: either a literal incarnation or a God of limitless and universal love.

Incarnation as Metaphor

Can Christianity survive without a literal incarnation? Some forms of Christianity cannot. Those who insist that Christianity can be a true religion only if it is the only true religion cannot relinquish a literal incarnation. Those whose faith is structured to meet the need for certainty cannot. Those who long for a simple faith might think they cannot, but should think again. The concept of a literal incarnation is far from simple. It seems simple enough in hymns, ritual utterances, and popular sermons, that is, when it functions as myth or metaphor [ironic, no?], but when it is pressed beyond that to its actual conceptual content, it is extremely complicated. If it had been a simple matter to state that Christ is true man and true God, the patristic theologians would have been spared a lot of intellectual labor and there would have been no need for several centuries of christological controversies and ecumenical councils. The doctrines of the Trinity (three persons with one nature) and incarnation (two natures in one person) are in fact incomprehensible to nearly everyone who professes them.[8] And despite the sincere intentions of those who developed the classic formulations of those two doctrines, they still seem to fudge on monotheism—just ask a Jew or a Muslim. Compared to the metaphysical complexity of a literal incarnation, a non-traditional Christian faith which accepts incarnation as a metaphor is genuinely simple. Here is one version of such a faith, boiled down to a few affirmations.

There is an ultimate Reality ("God" if you like). This Reality is good, on our side. This Reality is reflected in many ways, but occasionally in human terms, in the lives of the world's great religious figures. Among them we find Jesus to be our principal revelation of that loving Reality. While we can and must learn from other traditions, the tradition emanating from Jesus is decisive for us. We therefore commit ourselves to live by Jesus' wisdom and example.[9]

Such a faith is truly simple in that it is metaphysically uncomplicated. It is more than enough to ground a full life of faith. As a bonus, it is intellectually honest in that it doesn't require us to deny or ignore anything else we know to be true (e.g., critical biblical scholarship or our own experiences of non-Christian traditions). An objection from traditional Christians that a metaphorical understanding of the incarnation amounts to a watering down of Christian truth need not be taken seriously until it is accompanied by an explanation of how a literal understanding of incarnation does not entail a watering down of the infinite and universal love of God.

Tradition and Faith in a New Era

Roy W. Hoover

P articipants in Westar Institute's Spring 2004 Meeting in New York City will be concerned with an array of challenges that must be faced if the Judeo-Christian tradition is to have life-enhancing meaning for its heirs in the twenty-first century. Though all of them are worthy of serious and courageous attention, one seems to me to be primordial: the ability to respond to other challenges will depend in large measure upon the way we respond to it.

This primordial challenge is posed by our involvement in a new era in human history. This era is historically new, but its beginnings are not recent. They go back to Copernicus and Galileo. "As an event that took place not only in astronomy and the sciences but in philosophy and religion and in the collective psyche the Copernican revolution [initiated by Copernicus and subsequently confirmed by Kepler and Galileo] can be seen as *the* epochal shift of the modern age," says intellectual historian Richard Tarnas. "It was a primordial event, world-destroying and world-constituting."[1] What Tarnas here calls "*the* epochal shift of the modern age" others refer to as the beginnings of the second axial age.

One might think that the Christian church would feel deeply obligated to pay close attention to and to reflect seriously upon something as stupendously challenging and significant as a primordial, world-destroying and world-constituting event. In fact, Galileo did his best to persuade the church of his time to embrace the startling new knowledge, but it soon became clear that he had hoped for too much. That church did everything it could to ban the new knowledge as contrary to church doctrine. In their view, church doctrine, tradition, and authority had to be defended at all costs. Those costs have proven to be very high. That early attempt to ban the Copernican revolution as false knowledge and contrary to true

Christian doctrine set in motion a substantial erosion of the credibility and meaning of church doctrine, tradition and authority, if
not their complete collapse. One can commiserate in some respects
with Galileo's ecclesiastical contemporaries: the new knowledge was
indeed disorienting and threatening. Nevertheless, the sad consequences of their attempts to ban the birth of a new understanding
of the world cannot be regarded as the fruits of religious courage,
insight, and wisdom.

What Galileo's church tried to ban the later churches have largely
ignored. In their liturgies, theologies, forms of worship and piety,
the churches have for the most part continued to resort to traditional ideas and practices. Even though almost everyone would agree
with Richard Tarnas's characterization of the Copernican revolution
as "*the* epochal shift of the modern age," the churches have largely
maintained the traditional forms of their faith and religious understanding as if nothing much had happened. This holy narcolepsy
has brought about a crisis of credibility for the churches. Facing and
taking a cure for this evasive somnolence has become an historic
challenge. The very life of the church is at stake. The churches in
Europe are losing nearly a fourth of their remaining constituents
every decade and about half in each generation, reports Cambridge
University professor Don Cupitt. "The main reason for their decline
is a general loss of public confidence in the objective truth of the
major Christian beliefs."[2] The rate of decline is somewhat slower in
the United States, but the primary reason for it is the same. If the
Judeo-Christian tradition is to have a future, especially among an
educated people, this loss of credibility must be openly acknowledged and courageously faced.

An epochal shift in history that destroys one view of the world
and brings another into being calls for a corresponding shift in
religious understanding and commitment. One way to think about
what this means for the heirs of the Judeo-Christian tradition, I
suggest, is to say that it calls for a shift from regarding ourselves as
defenders of the faith to regarding ourselves as apostles of veracity.
Veracity involves more than truth-telling and intellectual honesty,
critically important though they are. Veracity involves what Huston
Smith once characterized as "a sublime objectivity, the capacity
to see things exactly as they are. To conform one's life to the way
things are is to live authentically."[3] Such objectivity is "sublime,"
because it is not directed by defensiveness, righteous causes, political agendas, or self-interest. Such objectivity is an indispensable element of the quest for the humane wisdom that must characterize an
authentic faith in the new era that has come into being after Galileo
and after Darwin.

The principal task of an authentic faith is to expose the meaning of the world as it really is and of human life in that world as we really are. Interpreting sacred texts, recovering historical origins, preserving and reflecting upon traditions and doctrines are useful only insofar as they serve the aims of veracity. If those means are turned into ends, they only get in the way. John A. T. Robinson, author of the celebrated *Honest to God*, made essentially the same point forty years ago when he insisted that the real test of the faith claims of the church is the question of whether or not they are "veridical," i.e., whether or not they correspond to reality.[4]

An epochal shift from commitment to orthodoxy to commitment to veracity is the way to bring the good news of an enlightened faith to our new era. Biblical and theological scholarship have often been viewed as a threat to orthodoxy and as irrelevant to the life of faith. But research and scholarship are not only essential to advances in science and technology; they also contribute importantly to the way we understand society and culture. They have a companion role to play in discerning the moral and life-affirming meanings that are or ought to be served by that science and technology and affirmed and expressed in that society and culture. A commitment to veracity offers the best chance we have of bridging the chasm that has existed for generations between the church and its own scholarship. If both faith and learning were to enlist in the service of veracity, they could be on speaking terms with each other again.

Resistance to the claim that an enlightened faith in our time requires shifting from a commitment to orthodoxy to a commitment to veracity comes not only from fundamentalists and evangelicals, but also from some tradition-bound mainline Protestants as well as from many Roman Catholics and adherents of Eastern Orthodoxy. All of these groups can be seen as committed to what can be characterized as an attempt to live the founding Christian myth from within. One formerly liberal Protestant theologian, for example, has abandoned the pursuit of the modern meaning of Christian faith in favor of a return to early Catholicism. Now a refugee from the radical political utopianism of the 1960s when he "saw the church as a potential instrument for rapid social change," he has been converted from reading scripture selectively, choosing only those parts of it that could be taken to support his "soft Marxist" ideology,[5] to reading scripture canonically, in accordance with "the Vincentian rule: *in the world-wide community of believers every care should be taken to hold fast to what has been believed everywhere, always, and by all*"[6] [at least up to the fifth century when this rule was propounded].

It is symbolic that the hero of what is here touted as the rebirth of orthodoxy is an obscure fifth century monk, Vincent of Lerins, who "retreated to a monastery [on the island of Lerins] off the coast of southern France" where he carefully formulated his rule of orthodox faith. This modern reborn-to-orthodoxy author has found his bearings on a theological island off the coast of the modern world, where ancient tradition is a world unto itself, out of touch with the great world outside its boundaries, and where he can "live within the doctrinal and moral boundaries fixed for millennia."[7] This is a form of traditional faith that has turned in on itself and has no interest in asking whether the faith it affirms is veridical, as J. A. T. Robinson put it—that is, corresponds with reality—but only with whether "the faithful" everywhere have always believed it.[8] It is apparent that for orthodoxy thus reborn "*the* epochal shift of the modern age" need not be considered. It has no bearing on the question of the truth of orthodox Christian faith.

In another attempt to retain the truth and authority of orthodoxy a recent Gifford lecturer, Stanley Hauerwas, responds to the perception that the constitution of the modern world has rendered traditional Christian language unintelligible by asserting that "the truth of Christian convictions requires a recovery of the confident use of Christian speech about God," and that the theologian who, more than any other, offers us "an unfaltering display of [such confident] Christian speech" and whose work "is a resource that we literally cannot live without, if we are to be faithful to the God we worship" is Karl Barth.[9] For Hauerwas, Barth shows us the way to bring the whole of reality within the sacred enclosure of the revealed truth of Christian faith. Barth is the pivotal figure in Hauerwas' Gifford project "because he was engaged in a massive attempt to overturn the epistemological prejudices of modernity. . . . Barth had a single concern: to use every resource at his disposal to show that our existence and the existence of the universe are unintelligible if the God found in Jesus Christ is not God."[10] Barth rejected systematic theology, such as that of Paul Tillich, as a merely human edifice, whereas dogmatic theology is rightly concerned only with the revealed truth witnessed in the Bible. "Directed by the witness of the Old and New Testaments, dogmatic theology is concerned with proving the truth of the message which the Church has always proclaimed and must again proclaim today."[11] Rather than supposing that Christian faith has a responsibility to make itself intelligible to the modern mind, Hauerwas insists, following Barth, that the modern mind must accept the claim of traditional Christian faith that it is the recipient of revealed truth and is therefore in a position to judge the truth of all other human claims to truth. This can be seen as Hauerwas' "I have a dream" speech—the nostalgic dream of the imperium of revealed religion.[12]

"Barth's refusal to submit theological claims to nontheological standards can seem to make Christian theology and Christian practice an entirely self-referential as well as a self-justifying enterprise," Hauerwas observes. "If this is indeed the case, then the story I have told simply confirms what [William] James and [Reinhold] Niebuhr, each in their own way, understood: Christianity makes sense only as a disguised humanism. As anything else, it can appear only as non-sense."[13] This is as close as Hauerwas comes, although only ironically and unwillingly, to recognizing the way things really are.

What Hauerwas shows us is that not even a prodigious theological genius, his famous mentor, can succeed in making the meaning of Christian faith intelligible to moderns, if he ignores the theological significance of so epochal a turn in human understanding as the Copernican revolution. Theology today cannot hope to explicate the Bible by overlooking the fact that the outlook of the biblical authors was conditioned by a now incredible worldview, reflects the limits of the state of knowledge of their time, and by assuming that there was no effect on the truth alleged to have been revealed in scripture when Copernicus and Galileo demonstrated the necessity of seeing the world in a way no biblical author had ever imagined. This failure to pay heed to the theological implications of "*the* epochal shift of the modern age" is what has rendered traditional Christian theology unintelligible in our time, not modern epistemological prejudice.

Those who insist upon the unaltered retention of traditional forms of religious understanding and language and who retreat from the challenge posed by the actual world after Galileo want to direct the Christian community into the confines of a sacred grotto, an enclosed, religiously defined world that is brought completely under the control of scripture and tradition; and they want to turn the ordained clergy into antiquities dealers. This is the only course open to those who regard it as necessary for Christians to live within the world of their sacred texts and in submission to the authority of their tradition. The irony is that the Judeo-Christian tradition can be a resource for an enlightened faith in our time only if its heirs live outside of its sacred texts rather than inside them. By outside of them I mean: see them as texts to be read in the light of an historical and global context, not in the blinkered light of a Christian grotto that is isolated from new knowledge and the wisdom that may be derived from that new knowledge. Withdrawing from the actual world into an ethnic or religious grotto in order to preserve the purity and power of a tradition is a tragic miscalculation. A cave is the most unsafe place for a religious tradition to be: at worst it will entomb the tradition; at best it will preserve it only as an archaeological relic. If there is to be a future for the Judeo-Christian tradition, it will be because its heirs have committed themselves to veracity, not because they have preserved yesterday's orthodoxy. Theologian Gordon Kaufman has this right:

> . . . it is of fundamental importance—if we are truly to help bring about a more humane and just order in human affairs, and are to give proper attention to the ecosystem within which human life falls—for us men and women to think through carefully, in the light of modern knowledge, the questions of who or what we humans are, what sort of world this is in which we find ourselves, which God must be served. Our concepts of God and of Christ must be reconceived with attention to our modern understanding of ourselves and of the universe, and to our new consciousness of the destructiveness we humans have worked in the world as well as on our fellow humans. . . . We dare not continue to use our received religious symbols without carefully analyzing and assessing not only what they supposedly *"mean"* but also their actual effects on ongoing human life and the world at large.[14]

In the introduction to his book, *The Religious Situation*, written when he was Professor of Philosophy at the University of Frankfort, Paul Tillich suggested that "to live spiritually is to live in the presence of meaning"[15]—a remark that resonates beyond the use he made of it in the course of that discussion. Here it can serve to point to the fact that a faith that has lost its credibility has lost its meaning, and that to continue to recite traditional expressions of faith that have lost their meaning is to deprive people of a spiritual life. What our present religious situation calls for first of all is not a set of updated creedal affirmations, but something prior: an unconditional commitment to veracity, to what John A. T. Robinson referred to as "what is veridical"—to what, to the best of our knowledge, corresponds to reality. That is the most pertinent answer, for those who are inclined to ask, to the question, "What would Jesus do?" His parables and aphorisms are expressions of his own vision of reality and of what that reality implied for him and his contemporaries and called upon them to do about the way they think and the way they live. Basing our faith and life on what is veridical is, in that sense, to do what Jesus would do, even if that leads us to understand ourselves and our world in ways that never occurred to him. An unconditional commitment to veracity is the narrow gate that will admit us to terrain where we will be able to identify the meaning that can nourish our spirits in a new axial age.

The Church Organist and the Jazz Pianist

Richard Holloway

I understand this session is being picketed by the New York Guild of Church Organists. They've been sliding up to me all week, like people selling drugs, and saying, "We're a bit unsure of what this is going to be about, but you'd better be careful." So let me hasten to point out that some of my best friends are church organists and I'm not about to traduce them tonight. The meaning of the title of my talk will be made plain in time—I hope.

Let me start with a recent of bit of British social history. We had a medical scandal in Britain a few years ago. It was discovered that the Paediatric Cardiac Section of a hospital in Bristol had an unacceptably high death rate after surgery, and a young anaesthetist blew the whistle on the team. The government set up an inquiry into the matter and during one of the hearings a learned witness let slip, almost inconsequentially, that the Royal Children's Hospital in Liverpool had one of the biggest collections of children's hearts in the country. There was a pause while the significance of that admission sank in. Gradually it dawned on the inquiry that doctors in Britain had been harvesting the organs of dead children for an indeterminate period without anyone's consent. So they set up a new inquiry to investigate the scandal of the stolen organs.

During the inquiry it was revealed that for over fifty years doctors, without anyone's consent or permission, had been harvesting organs from dead children. It was revealed that 100,000 hearts, lungs, brains, and other organs had been so harvested. The most grisly element in the landscape that was exposed was the head of an eleven-year-old boy. The country was astonished by the revelations. During an interview the mother of one of the children whose organs had been harvested said, more in sorrow than in anger, "If only they'd asked." The medical establishment appeared to be bewildered by the country's reaction, because anything they'd done was for the benefit and welfare of the people of Britain. They had harvested these organs the better to understand and minister to our medical needs.

When those words were uttered, "If only they had asked," I realized that the people of Britain had reached what Karen Armstrong would have called an axial moment in their relationship with power and authority. In this case it was the authority of the medical establishment, but it could as easily have been any other major institution in our national life. We were no longer prepared to be meekly obedient to their authority because we knew they had our own best interests in their hearts. Now, in all matters that concerned us, we expected to be asked. In other words, consent had become a fundamental ethical principle that overrode the traditional habit of obedience to superior authority. Consent, not commandment, had become the new norm. The emergence of the new principle had been a gradual process, but its presence erupted into view at that critical moment during that inquiry.

In this presentation I don't want to use axial language to describe that change and what it tells us about human culture today; I want, following something Marcus Borg said earlier, to use the word "paradigm." It was a paradigm shift that was revealed during the Inquiry into the Stolen Organs in Britain. I want to say something about the history and background to paradigm thinking, one of the most important philosophical developments of the twentieth century. So let me spend a bit of time talking about paradigm theory before jumping into the main theme I want to explore with you tonight.

Thomas Kuhn was a young physicist at Harvard in the 1960s when he was invited by the President of Harvard to teach a course on the history of science to humanities students. In his research he made what, to him, was a surprising discovery. He had previously thought that science was a linear, incremental, cumulative process that gradually ate its way into the facts of the universe, like one of those mining machines that chew into a seam of coal. He'd assumed that science was a straightforward process that just mopped up facts about the universe. So he was surprised to discover that it was much more dramatic and interruptive than that, much more violent and revolutionary. He developed paradigm theory to describe it. He said that the scientific community developed a constellation of approaches and understandings, which he called a paradigm. A scientific paradigm was both theory and practice, an explanation and a form of action, which worked till it stopped working, till it no longer did the business. To quote Einstein: "When a paradigm can't solve a problem within the paradigm in which it was created, that's when you get a paradigm shift." The classic paradigm shift, which has been referred to several times in this conference already, was the shift in astronomy from the Aristotelian to the Copernican paradigm. When it became obvious that the new facts that were being discovered by scientists through the telescope could not be accommodated within the operating paradigm, a struggle ensued in which Aristotle was replaced by Copernicus. Kuhn called this dramatic process a paradigm revolution, and he said it was how science operated. We've been through many paradigm revolutions since Copernicus put the Sun at the centre of our solar system.

Paradigm theory has been adopted by philosophers, culture critics and even by theologians, to explain the dynamism of their own disciplines. Kuhn's slim book, *The Structure of Scientific Revolutions*, turned out to be one of the most influential philosophical texts of the twentieth century. A good example of its use outside science was Hans Küng's application of paradigm theory to the study of religion in his books on Judaism and Christianity. Küng says there have been five Christian paradigms and he believes we are on the cusp of a sixth. Paradigm theory has had a profound effect on the way we think about everything today, and it is central to our understanding of change and development within human culture.

But there's a highly significant difference between a scientific paradigm and a social, cultural or religious paradigm, which brings me to the first point I want to make. It is obvious from what Kuhn wrote that when a scientific paradigm's day is done, it dies. If you are being educated as a scientist today you don't start with Aristotle's paradigm and work up to the scientific approach that prevails today; you start right in with the current paradigm. Unlike scientific paradigms, social, religious and cultural paradigms seem to hang around for ever. Though they may only have a shadowy existence, they never really die, are never really abandoned when a new paradigm appears. Rather, they get stacked up like trays in a self-service cafeteria.

This morning Lloyd Geering reminded us why it is that we never bury social, cultural, ethical or religious paradigms. As well as addressing the obvious human fact of cultural discontinuity, he also spoke of the deep human need for continuity. That's because, as T. S. Eliot reminded us, humankind can't bear too much reality. We prize stability almost as much as we dislike incessant change. Change is disorienting and induces enormous anxiety. That's why many speakers at this conference have reminded us of the infectious plague of fundamentalism that is sweeping the world today. Fundamentalism is an understandable response to the anxiety and fear that is provoked by accelerating change.

Those of us who cope well with change ought at least to try to understand why other parts of the human community find it difficult. They are likely to be the kind of people who prize continuity and stability highly. That's why, during this period of accelerating change in the world, the old religious paradigms continue to hold their corners.

This conference has itself been an interesting illustration of that fact. We may occupy a fairly narrow slot on the continuum of Christian paradigms today, but there are significant differences between us. Marcus Borg whispered to me yesterday, "You realize, of course, that I am the conservative at this conference." We've listened to the philosophical differences, eloquently expressed, between Don Cupitt and Jack Spong. Those good friends occupy different slots on the theological spectrum of Christianity. That's why we need a particular kind of imaginative generosity if we are to comprehend the vast array of theological options that are available to people today.

Nevertheless, change is a permanent and often a morally necessary fact of human history. I was moved when Karen Armstrong asked James Carroll how they might turn round the mighty armada of paradigms that is the Roman Catholic Church. How does good change come about in social and religious institutions? What causes a paradigm to shift in religion? I want to try to answer that question tonight.

One of the things we need to understand about any cultural paradigm is that it is, among other things, a power system. And power always creates victims. There is no power system without victimization. Simone Weil said, "To assume power over is to soil." If you have ever been in a position of power, you will know how easy it is to abuse people below you, however subtly and unconsciously.

The best guide to political and cultural revolution is still the last and greatest of the Hebrew prophets, Karl Marx. Marx was a lousy predictor, but he was a brilliant diagnostician of the pathology of power. He understood how power arrangements shift and change. He observed that people in power never relinquish it voluntarily. Revolution comes, he said, not by the weakening of the strong, but by the strengthening of the weak. Power systems, including religions, are changed by the revolt of their victims, the people who pay the price of a particular power structure. Victims inevitably rise against a system that is oppressing them, and challenge it. And the most obvious response they encounter when they try to overturn a social paradigm is that the people in charge of it always oppose the challenge. If they have the means the people in power will use violence, but they also know how to mobilize ideas in their defence as well, they know how to field what Marx called ideology. When women challenged the power of an all-male priesthood in the Anglican communion, for instance, the men in charge of the going dominant paradigm didn't say honestly, "Push off, sisters, we don't want to share power with you." No, what the brothers said was, "Sisters, we'd love to have you in the sanctuary, but it's God whose against it, it's the Bible that won't permit it."

Marx would have loved that classic ideological response to a power challenge. It offered a respectable theoretical justification for what was essentially a power grab. And that's what happens all the time. So one of the questions we must put in our reading of cultural history is, "Who are the victims of this set-up?" The follow-on question is, "How is this particular version of victimization justified?" That's when you'll hit the theory behind the power system, whether it's theological, political or economic. So the first thing to look out for in a paradigm shift is the revolt of the victims, with its concomitant theoretical justification of the status quo from the system's priesthood.

The next bit of the process is equally fascinating, and Nietzsche is the best guide to it. He pointed out that the victims who are revolting against a particular power system make alliances with the heretics within the system itself, people who belong to the reigning social paradigm but are unfaithful to it. The most conspicuous virtue of the conservative mind is fidelity. Conservatives are the kind of people who stick to their commitments. They are loyal to their communities, their churches, their spouses. But what if the thing they're sticking to is dying and needs an infusion of new life from somewhere? Nietzsche said that the people who enable change to take place in any tradition are the immoral, the unfaithful, the people who betray the going paradigm, either because they are morally weak, or because they are intellectually restless. Let me read you, from *Human, All Too Human,* one of the most seminal quotes in social and cultural history.

> History teaches that the best-preserved tribe among a people is the one in which most men have a living communal sense as a consequence of sharing their customary and indisputable principles—in other words, in consequence of a common faith.[1]

That is the standard justification of the conservative principle in education, the passing on of the tradition to the next generation. We can reflect on the significance of the institutions that have done this down the ages. They provide us with an excellent justification of the importance of a stable social and ethical paradigm. They help us to hold steadily to received values. They build a rampart against the chaos that is always threatening to overwhelm fragile institutions. This is the conservative imperative in education, and it is essential to the maintenance of human stability. But Nietzsche then goes on to offer one of his most disturbing insights.

> The danger to these strong communities founded on homogeneous individuals who have character is growing stupidity, which is gradually increased by heredity, and which, in any case, follows all stability like a shadow. It is the individuals who have fewer ties and are much more uncertain and morally weaker upon whom spiritual progress depends in such communities; they are the men who make new and manifold experiments . . . they loosen up and from time to time inflict a wound on the stable element of a community. Precisely in this wounded and weakened spot the whole structure is inoculated, as it were, with something new; but its over-all strength must be sufficient to accept this new element into its blood and assimilate it. Those who degenerate are of the highest importance wherever progress is to take place; every great progress must be preceded by a partial weakening. The strongest natures *hold fast* to the type; the weaker ones help *to develop it further*.[1]

So here is an interesting paradox. Social and moral evolution is generated by a combination of the revolting and the unfaithful. Those who rebel against an oppressive paradigm ally themselves with the heretics within the system itself, who are not afraid to betray it , and thereby effect change. Social and moral evolution is generated by this extraordinary combination. The most powerful recent example of this in cultural history was the emancipation of women, the perfect example of a cultural paradigm shift. Women stood up and said, "We've had enough of this and are determined to change it." Significantly, they made allies with the men within the power system who were no longer committed to its maintenance, and change was achieved. Not everywhere, of course, and not yet enough, but enough to effect the most significant cultural revolution in our lifetime.

Let me stay with this theme of power for a little longer before looking at the new ethical paradigm that is emerging in our time. Related to the creative disloyalty that becomes an agent of change in history is the emergence of pity, a development that Nietzsche did not wholly welcome, though his thinking on the subject has not been entirely understood. What he seemed to be opposed to was weak pity, cowardly pity. But what about strong pity, angry pity? One of the most astonishing things to emerge in human history is the angry pity of the heretic who challenges the way the operating power system tramples upon the weak. You could describe the universe as itself an expression of that kind of naked power, charging through space and time, creating victims, obliterating species, smashing the poor and the weak in both the human and animal kingdoms. Richard Dawkins, the great Darwinian biologist, says that the universe is neither good nor evil, just pitilessly indifferent. Yet from within this apparently meaningless process of indifferent power there have been generated creatures who are angered by that same pitiless indifference. People appear like the Hebrew prophets in the first axial age who stand up and denounce the oppression of the weak by the powerful. The more I think about this the more astonishing it seems. That a pitiless universe, fifteen billion years into its history, produces both victims of power and people who are angered by their misery is a mystery almost as large as the universe itself. But let me enter a word of caution here. Power, like energy, never disappears, it simply assumes new forms. Even when it absorbs its victims into the system, it does not fundamentally change. That's why Alasdair MacIntyre said that "all power co-opts, and absolute power co-opts absolutely." One of the things that saddened me when women entered the Episcopate in the Anglican church was the way they immediately slapped on the mitre, itself a power symbol. For women to take on the full panoply of the ecclesiastical power that had victimized them for centuries was a disappointment, but hardly a surprise.

Now let me move on. One of the most encouraging aspects of our era is that a new evolutionary social paradigm is emerging to join the armada of paradigms that floats on the ocean of human history. The new paradigm seems to have four emergent characteristics. The first is a radical suspicion of power and authority. Until recently, the basis of most ethical systems was obedience to superior authority. Moralities were essentially commandment systems. Moses didn't come down from the mountain with four consultation documents, he came down with ten commandments. But something has changed in the way we think about these things. When we started on Wednesday Roy said, "One of the most significant facts of the cultural era that we're living through is that the house of authority is disintegrating." Authority itself is now viewed with enormous suspicion. Whereas respect for authority was the basis of the previous ethical paradigm, suspicion of authority seems to be the basis of the emerging ethical paradigm. This strikes me as a return to the prophetic subversion we find in both the Hebrew and Christian scriptures. In Mark's Gospel, chapter 10, Jesus described the political reality of his time in this way: "Ye know that they which are accounted to rule over the Gentiles exercise lordship over them;

and their great ones exercise authority upon them. But it shall not be so among you." Maybe we are beginning to see the actualization of that radical subversion of power and a return to the spirit of the Hebrew prophets. That is why American Christians should be asking themselves these questions: "If power always creates victims, and if the United States of America is the most powerful nation in the world, how should we be interrogating its exercise of power? Who are the victims of American power?" The Christian community in this country, in whatever form it expresses itself, should be able to unite in its interrogation of American power, because that is always the Jesus question, the prophetic question. Who? Whom? Who is oppressing whom through this system?

The second element in the emerging ethical paradigm is the principle of consent. We expect to be asked, not told, in every area that concerns our own welfare. Apart from the application of this principle to medical ethics, the other obvious place where it is essential is in human sexuality. According to the new paradigm, we no longer believe that sexual activity is a commodity whose distribution has to be licensed or sanctioned by external authority. It is autonomously ours, it belongs to us, which is why we refuse to be exploited sexually by other people. Personal consent is the principle whereby we validate or invalidate any sexual encounter. This is why there is such public outrage over the sexual abuse of children. It is why we are scandalised when people in power use their status to extort sexual privileges from the weak. These are obvious and incontestable applications of the principle of consent in the field of personal ethics, what is perhaps less obvious is the application of the same principle to the ethics of war.

The latest Iraq war, and the new doctrine of pre-emption which underlines it, is causing a major re-think in this area of moral debate. The traditional Just War doctrine had five elements: (1) the cause had to be just; (2) the war had to be declared by legitimate authority; (3) there had to be strong probability of success; (4) there had to be proportionality in the means used; (5) and there had to be non-combatant immunity. Most modern conflict invariably abrogates the last two elements in this catalogue, but we seem to be in the process of adding a sixth element that will make it increasingly difficult for democratic governments to wage war in our name. Because it is our children who die and our taxes that are consumed in the wars our leaders start, it will become increasingly difficult for politicians to gain our informed consent to their murky adventures. Given the now notorious failures in the intelligence community before the Iraq war, it will be increasingly important for government to be transparent in gaining the public's consent to any future adventures.

The third element in the emerging ethical paradigm is that pleasure is considered to be a good that need not always be delayed. In other words, it's OK to have fun. The old authority paradigm operated a theory of delayed gratification for the sake of the soul's preparation for eternal life. Pleasure was essentially an eschatological concept: the more you denied it in this life the greater would be the gratification in the life to come. Well, many of us are no longer sure that we're going to be around after death to cash in the brownie points we earned down in this vale of tears, so we prefer to take our pleasure now. Where pleasure is concerned, most of us are realized eschatologists, and Hannah Arendt is probably the best guide to the new hedonism. She invited us to think of ourselves as Natals, people who are in the midst of life, rather than as Mortals, people who are going to end up dead. Live while it is yet day, for the night cometh when no one will live. Pleasure is good and we should be suspicious of people who have little or no capacity for it. We will usually find that they are not lovers but haters of humankind. That said, I don't have to remind anyone that pleasure, like misery, can be addictive, so we need to practise it with skill and artistry. But it also follows that we should be wary of those authority figures who think they know better than we do ourselves which pleasures we should be allowed. America's historic penchant for trying to prohibit the pleasures that fleeting life affords its people is not encouraging, the current War on Drugs being only the latest example of its notorious proneness to bouts of damaging Puritanism.

The final characteristic of the new paradigm is that it not only tolerates, it actively celebrates ethical plurality as itself an important way of correcting the abuses of power. Voltaire told us that if there were two religions in a state they'd be at each other's throats, but if there were thirty-six they'd live in peace. Fundamental to the new ethical paradigm is an appreciation of the fact that good people can disagree with one another. Even more fundamental is the recognition that the more groups there are who disagree with each other the less likely it will be that one of them will gain ascendancy over all the others. John Bennett once described the achievement of this kind of balance in society as "the equilibrium of mutual dissatisfaction." There is never going to be a unified theory of ethics on which all of us can agree about everything, and it would be dangerous if we did. We must, of course, achieve a broad consensus in fundamental areas, the negative version of the Golden Rule being as good a guide as any: "Don't do to others what you do not want them to do to you." But the glorious variety of human beings, and the communities and traditions they create, guarantees a saving plurality in our values.

That is why magnanimity is a fundamental characteristic for anyone wanting to negotiate with grace the ethical complexity of contemporary society. Unfortunately, this kind of magnanimity is difficult if not impossible for passionate adherents of intentional moral communities to achieve. If you believe that God has delivered a fixed and absolute moral script to your community, which you are commanded to play from at all times and in all places the way an unskilled parish organist ploughs wearily through the hymn book, then it is going to be difficult for you to live comfortably in the new multi-track society. I use the metaphor of the church organist to describe people who can only play from a fixed script as they respond to the challenges that history throws at them. If you belong to such a group, living in a plural moral community is going to be tough because it will permit activities forbidden by your score, such as abortion or stem cell research or therapeutic cloning or same-sex relationships.

Even so, the pain is not all on one side here. Governments in liberal democracies usually allow religious communities opt-outs from legislative instruments that would lead to prosecutions in purely secular bodies. In Europe religious communities are exempt from many of the requirements of human rights legislation that prohibits employment discrimination on the grounds of gender or sexuality. Religious communities are good at taking full advantage of liberal toleration for their own discriminatory approach to secular freedoms, but they rarely return the compliment. On both sides of the Atlantic they continue to campaign against the extension of the very principle of toleration that protects them against prosecution for their own abrogation of contemporary human values. The saying of Jesus about the speck of dust and the plank of wood springs to mind here. But we should not be surprised at the abiding hypocrisy and serpentine skilfulness of religious communities who denounce the liberal culture of toleration even as they take full advantage of it to pursue their own discriminatory purposes. It hath ever been thus.

In conclusion, let me make a few final points, the first of them a caution. I am not saying that all this change, all this shifting of paradigms, is improvement or progress. It isn't necessarily so. It is a fact that societies do change, and there is always loss as well as gain. However, we must learn to defend the moral gains that we actually do make, the moral equivalents of the fact that we now know that the Earth goes round the Sun and not the other way. For me, the most important moral gain of the last two or three hundred years is our radical mistrust of power and the permanent imperative of emancipation. If you belong to the Christian paradigm in any of its variants, you are committed, by definition, to an emancipatory ethic that is called to the liberation of slaves, of women, of gays, of the poor, of the planet. It is part of the deal. It comes with our commitment to the subversive ethic of Jesus and the axial prophets.

Next, know your own paradigm or your own paradigm mix. And remember, it's even OK to be conservative. I was glad when one or two questioners this week stressed the fact that conservatives also had rights, and that it was all right to be orthodox. An element of the kind of calculus we need to do when we're doing ethics is that we have to acknowledge the importance of stability as well as the fact of incessant change. We need people who know how to hand on the tradition, as well as people who know how to subvert and challenge it.

Finally, we must learn how to do ethical jazz, the art of adaptive improvisation. This is where my metaphor completes itself. The one thing that you never get in human history is absolute stability. If you insist on plonking your way through the same old script year in and year out, then you will not only be increasingly uncomfortable with the dynamism of actual human history, you will also miss a good time, because change is coming at you and engaging with it can be exhilarating. Learn to improvise. Oh sure, you must know the tradition as well. Good musicians know how to read the script, but they are also good at abandoning it and improvising. They have the courage to give themselves to the music and let it play itself through them. Real life is more like a rolling jazz session in a night club than an organ recital in the local church, and it's also a lot more fun.

I want to end with a postscript that sums up some of the things I've been trying to say tonight.

> ONE night I had a wondrous dream,
> One set of footprints there was seen,
> The footprints of my precious Lord,
> But mine were not along the shore.

> But then some stranger prints appeared,
> And I asked the Lord, "What have we here?
> Those prints are large and round and neat,
> But Lord, they are too big for feet."

> "My child," He said in sombre tones,
> "For miles I carried you alone.
> Challenged you to walk in faith,
> But you refused and made me wait."

"You disobeyed, you would not grow,
The walk of faith, you would not know,
So I got tired, I got fed up,
And there I dropped you on your butt."

"Because in life, there comes a time,
When one must fight, and one must climb,
When one must rise and take a stand,
Or leave their butt prints in the sand."

(With acknowledgements to the Rev. Mark Stibbe)

Part II

Wisdom for the Global Age

VERITAS

The Truth of the Matter about Religion

Daryl D. Schmidt

Preface

A s I was preparing this essay, I received an email, forwarded from Westar Institute, inviting me to participate in a Veritas Forum to be held at UCLA. A quick internet search revealed a phenomenon I had missed when it emerged in the 1990s. It traces its roots to a first Veritas Forum at Harvard in 1992, featuring writers who later appeared in the book *Finding God at Harvard*.[1] The subtitle on the book reads: "Spiritual Journeys of Thinking Christians." The title, *Finding God at Harvard*, could easily elicit the one-liner: "You always find something the last place you look." The title might appear to be a response to the bestseller from the early 1990s, *The Search for God at Harvard*, where *The New York Times* religion editor, Ari Goldman, describes his year-long sabbatical (1985–86) studying religion at Harvard Divinity School. The project that became *Finding God at Harvard*, however, was actually in process at the time Goldman's book was published in 1991.

The outcome of Goldman's "search for God at Harvard" was captured by one reviewer in Goldman's statement: "If you know only one religion, you know none at all." The reviewer summarizes Goldman's description of Harvard's premise as: "the view that no religion is intrinsically superior and that therefore every person has to find a religious truth of his or her own."[2] In other words, Goldman made the unremarkable discovery that the study of religion at Harvard takes for granted the basic mainstream assumptions typically associated with the "liberal arts" foundation of most major private universities. Another description of this approach would be: an open-ended quest for "veritas." Rather than be preoccupied with whether that is "truth," "Truth," or "the Truth," let's simply think of it as "the truth of the matter—about whatever matters." In this case, the truth of the matter about religion.

107

The Veritas Forum describes its approach as "an interactive and inter-disciplinary conference to explore the hardest questions of the university, society, and the human heart in relation to the truth claims of Jesus Christ in a quest for truth and real life" (www. veritas.org). In its promotional materials, Veritas Forum claims to base its name on Harvard's motto, *Veritas*, which had been more fully: *Veritas Christo et ecclesiae* (Truth for Christ and the Church), reflecting Harvard's original commitment to a theologically centered education. Veritas Forum cites a statement from the "earliest known account of Harvard College" (1642) that the end of every student's "life and studies is to know God and Jesus Christ which is eternal life, John 17:13, and therefore to lay Christ at the bottom, as the only foundation of all sound knowledge and learning." Veritas Forum thus implies that the *Veritas* of Harvard's motto really means "the truth claims of Jesus Christ" (a phrase found throughout the Forum's materials, and exemplified by the Nicene Creed).

As a "professor of religion" at a university committed to the liberal arts, I find many unexamined claims in the frequent use of "true" and "truth" in this material. It seems to be yet another revival of a neo-neo-orthodox response to the legacy of liberalism. I suggest we are engaged here in a much more generic "veritas forum," one that lies at the very heart of the liberal arts. We must affirm the heritage of "liberal" in "liberal arts," as a commitment to examine the truth of the matter about all matters, especially those matters that we take as given in our self-understanding. The quest for *veritas* at the heart of a university must mean that all areas of knowledge are subject to critical evaluation, certainly including all matters related to religion.

Another context for this essay is found in recent news stories about religion in America. Many of us have seen the popular opinion polls that indicate a significant majority of Americans continue to say they believe in God.[3] However, recent polls also indicate other interesting results. The 2001 American Religious Identification Survey (ARIS) conducted by the Graduate Center, City University of New York, made news when it announced that the third largest religious category after Protestant (52%) and Catholic (24.5%) is now "none" (14%). By denomination the numbers are Catholic, Baptist (16.3%), then "none."[4] Compared with its predecessor 1990 National Survey of Religious Identification (NSRI), the number of "nones" more than doubled, representing over 29 million, with the percent of increase from 8% to 14% (the portion of those identifying themselves as "atheist" or "agnostic" is less than 1% combined). Various news stories appeared in 2003 commenting on the ARIS results. In Salt Lake City the headline (deseretnews.com) read: "'Nones' now

2nd in religion poll," where "none" was the second largest religious category after Latter-Day Saints (Mormons). The Freedom from Religion Foundation (ffrf.org) used the headline "America growing more secular," which noted that, given a choice between identifying their outlook as "religious" or "secular," 16% responded "secular" or "somewhat secular," with 5% not responding. Overall the category "Christian" declined 10% (to 76.5%) and within that 11% were generic "Protestant" or "Christian," with no further affiliation indicated. In a 2002 survey conducted for PBS's "Religion and Ethics Newsweekly" and *U.S. News and World Report,* one emphasis was on religious tolerance. The results are reported in the *U.S. News and World Report* special issue (2003) on "Mysteries of Faith." In this survey over 80% identified themselves as "Christian," but 32% said neither Catholic nor Protestant, and only 19% responded positively to: "The religion you practice is the only true religion," while 77% affirmed: "All religions have elements of truth."[5]

These results reveal, in part, the need for more sophisticated polling, but they also suggest that belief in God has become a generic cultural affirmation of the positive value of religion. We are thus witnessing a noticeable increase in those who continue to affirm religion, yet feel no need to identify with any particular form of religion.

At the other end of the spectrum, we might note one other news story, which the mainstream press overlooked. Theologians Clark Pinnock of McMaster Divinity College in Canada, and John Sanders of Huntington College in Indiana, survived an attempt to expel them from membership in the Evangelical Theological Society (ETS) for promoting the model of "open theism."[6] While many of us were preparing to leave for the annual meeting of the American Academy of Religion and Society of Biblical Literature in Atlanta on Nov. 19, 2003, the ETS was already meeting there in a special business session to vote on the charges that "open theism" is incompatible with the Society's sole doctrinal requirement of biblical inerrancy. The next day, long-time member and past president Norman Geisler resigned his membership in protest against the Society having lost "its doctrinal integrity" by failing to expel such members.[7] Its strict Calvinism will not allow any leeway on God's absolute omniscience. To make explicit the "incompatibility of the view commonly referred to as 'Open Theism' with biblical inerrancy," its executive committee, including Geisler, passed a resolution in 2000: "We believe the Bible clearly teaches that God has complete, accurate and infallible knowledge of all events past, present and future, including all future decisions and actions of free moral agents." The sin of "open theism" is that it takes seriously the biblical passages in which God "repents" and "changes his mind" or alters a "prophecy."[8] "Open theism" interprets such texts as indicating God's desire to relate to humans. In Pinnock's words:

> God sovereignly grants human beings significant freedom, because he wants relationships of love with them. In such relationships, at least in the human realm, either party may welcome or refuse them. We may choose to cooperate with God or work against his will for our lives. God has chosen to enter into dynamic give-and-take relationships with us, which allow God to affect us and also let us affect God. As co-labourers with God, we are invited to bring the future into being together along with him. The openness model of God is a variation of what is often called "free-will theism," and I think it makes better sense both of the Bible and of our walk with God.[9]

I cite this as an encouraging indication that in mainline evangelical circles issues of theism are now the cutting (divisive) edge of the theological conversation. A similar kind of controversy was set off last summer when HarperCollins released *If Grace Is True: Why God Will Save Every Person*.[10]

What does the "truth of religion" mean in this cultural setting? Our "veritas forum" on the future of the Judeo-Christian tradition must consider the larger question of religion itself.

What's "True" about Religion?

Marcus Borg situates his most recent book, *The Heart of Christianity*, within the contemporary shift away from the traditional paradigm of absolutist claims, summarized as: "Christianity as the only true religion." In its place Borg sees an emerging paradigm, which acknowledges "Christianity's encounter with the modern and postmodern world, including science, historical scholarship, religious pluralism, and cultural diversity."[11] I openly affirm Borg's overall approach and many of the particulars he argues in the book. He forthrightly contrasts the authoritative claims made in the earlier paradigm with features of the emerging paradigm, including the Bible as a human response to God and biblical interpretation as historical and metaphorical. He also affirms diversity and pluralism at all levels, including religious pluralism, which treats Christianity as but "one of the world's great enduring religions, the response to the experience of God in our particular cultural stream."[12] Rather than identify the many valuable corollaries that Borg derives from this emerging paradigm, I seek instead to push his paradigm a step further. A more radical edge in the new paradigm would also reconsider the nature and role of the experience of God in his definition of religion.

In his chapter on faith, Borg argues for a kind of foundationalism, asserting that: "three affirmations are foundational":

Being Christian means affirming the reality of God.

Christian faith means affirming the utter centrality of Jesus.

Christian faith means affirming the centrality of the Bible.

I call attention to the decreasing order of the claims being made. Although the three categories of God, Jesus, and the Bible form a foundational trinity of centrality, there is also a pecking order of centrality. It begins with the reality of God, of which Jesus is "the decisive disclosure," both of which in turn are disclosed in the Bible.[13]

It is the unexamined realism of the traditional paradigm that I would like to explore briefly. Borg's commitment to theistic realism is stated quite explicitly: "Without a robust affirmation of the reality of God, Christianity makes no sense." He uses the category "the More" from William James as a more generic term for the sacred, and then faults the modern "nonreligious worldview" as not allowing room for "the More." Modernity affirms "a secular or naturalistic or material worldview" that "has no foundational place for God."[14] He then makes his case for the panentheistic view of God.[15]

"I cannot demonstrate or prove the reality of God," Borg acknowledges. He does, however, "cite the kinds of data to which I would appeal." For Borg, "the collective witness and wisdom of the world's religions" makes it "reasonable to take seriously the possibility that their affirmation was grounded in what they did know, not in what they didn't know." (All the world's religions can't be wrong.) He also cites "the provocative affirmations of postmodern science, especially postmodern physics," which "stretches, indeed shatters, the modern worldview, which affirms only the space-time world of matter and energy." (Science allows room for religion.) While these two categories are suggestive for Borg, they are secondary to the central category:

The data of religious experience is highly suggestive, especially in its more dramatic forms of mystical, shamanic, and visionary experiences. People throughout history and across cultures have had experiences that seem overwhelmingly to them to be experiences of the sacred. There also are "quieter" forms of religious experience in the dailiness of our lives. The experiential base of religion is very strong, and for me is ultimately its most persuasive base.[16]

The reality of religious experience becomes the primary reason for insisting on "the reality of God." In his concluding chapter, Borg asks: "Are all religions thus the same?" He notes certain central similarities, of which the first is: "They all affirm 'the More,' 'the real,' 'the sacred'; and they all affirm that the sacred can be known . . . in the sense of being experienced." Despite the pluralism of expression in the world's religions, "the internal core, the heart of religion, is the experience of the sacred, 'the real,' 'the More'."[17]

Borg does acknowledge different ways of seeing religions since the Enlightenment. His caricatures serve well his heuristic purposes. He contrasts the extremes of the absolutist understanding of religion and the reductionist understanding of religion. The absolutist view claims that "the truth of one's own religion is grounded in God's infallible revelation." The contrasting view "sees all religions as human constructions, as human projections." This "dominant secular understanding of religion" reduces it to "the psychological and social factors that generate religions," including "the need or desire for" basic human features, such as "explanations," "protection from vulnerability and death," "reinforcement of the social order," and "meaning." Borg reduces all this (reductionism) to: "the final truth about religion is 'we made it all up,'" which amounts to: "the religions are all built on a mistake, for there is no God, no sacred, no 'More'."[18]

In the best of the Anglican tradition, Borg offers us a *via media*, a middle way that avoids these mistakes and builds on the best insights of both Catholic and Protestant traditions. The middle way itself is also very Anglican: "it sees religions as sacraments of the sacred." This view is also a kind of classic synthesis, incorporating the best of both extreme views. It accepts Gordon Kaufman's view that religions are "imaginative human constructions," but it affirms that these constructions are *in response to experiences of the sacred*, rather than "built on a mistake." Religions are thus *cultural-linguistic traditions* (in the words of George Lindbeck), reflecting the particularities of their own cultural contexts.[19]

My own sympathies are very much in the direction Borg is suggesting here, on two different counts. First, in my own personal odyssey, I too found my way to the Anglican *via media* as a meaningful expression of religion, although, unlike Borg's Lutheran upbringing, I came to it as a Mennonite, from a distinctively un-Lutheran perspective. In fact, one of my Mennonite mentors made the argument that Anabaptism was radically "neither Catholic nor Protestant," which I learned later was a popular claim among some Episcopalians.[20] Second, Borg's "third view of religion" contains the crucial elements that I want to explore further as the basis for a more radical alternative.

A Neo-liberal Paradigm

My theologian colleague, C. David Grant, has begun exploring a "reclamation of the legacy of liberalism."[21] Grant's proposal provides the basis for suggesting a "neo-lib" alternative to Borg's "emerging paradigm." While Borg's paradigm is a welcomed postmodern alternative to the legacy of neo-orthodoxy, "neo-lib" is meant to suggest a more direct challenge to the conservative claims made by the "neo-cons" of religion. My sketch here can only be suggestive.

Grant seeks to reclaim several important features of classical Protestant liberalism, as expressed especially by Schleiermacher. A vital feature of liberal Protestant theology was its focus on human experience and its insistence that all religious claims, including those of Christian faith, are expressions of fundamental human feelings. In this view, religion gives expression to a common, fundamental human experience, so that all religious experience is rooted in a common consciousness, "the consciousness of being absolutely dependent." Theology then sees religious language as giving expression to God as the source of this feeling. Neo-orthodoxy, as epitomized by Karl Barth, focused on the "objectiveness of God's otherness," as distinct from the feeling of absolute dependence. A direct corollary then is that God's otherness can be objectively demonstrated, e.g., in G. E. Wright's *God Who Acts*, required seminary reading for my generation.

Grant calls our attention to a second vital feature of classical Protestant liberalism, which neo-orthodoxy lost sight of, and that is the understanding that theology is continuous with other disciplines and areas of knowledge, so that theology fully accepts what is learned about the natural world. Grant then notes classical liberalism's deduction that religion itself must be "rooted in a common human experience," so that the "varieties of religious experience" are all rooted in the same common raw religious consciousness. Borg calls our attention to the (reductionistic) tendency in the legacy of the Enlightenment to create a theological chicken-and-egg dilemma out of this: Which came first, "the sacred" or our experience of "the sacred?" Does "the More" exist independently of our encounter with it?

Grant proposes what I am calling a "neo-lib" response. All religious experience shares in the common human consciousness of the need for meaning—whether that is experienced as the need to "make" meaning or to "find" meaning. The fuller, interdisciplinary explanation for "common human experience" is rooted in common human creative capacity to find order, value, structure, wholeness—in a word: meaning. It is "meaning-making" that is indigenous to being human. It is indeed utterly reductionistic to dismiss this as something "we just made up," and certainly to conclude that religions are all mistaken.[22]

The neo-lib corollary would be: human experience can invalidate claims made about human experience. The two-way-street nature of experience applies as well, or even especially to religious experience. Here a caution is in order: appeal to the category "religious" experience brings with it the critique of self-interest. Robert Sharf notes the modern appeal of the category of experience, because it meets the scientific need for empirical data to study. In turn, for the scholar of religion to insist on a distinct category of "religious" experience then implies an exemption from established scientific methodology, while at the same time affirming some validity to all religious traditions. Sharf notes the inherent self-interest of the category even for the secular scholar of religion. "By appealing to non-tradition-specific notions such as the 'sacred' or the 'holy'—notions that blur the distinction between a universal human experience and the posited object of said experience—the scholar could legitimize the comparative study of religion even while acknowledging the specifically Western origins of the category itself."[23]

In Grant's proposal, the neo-lib understanding emerges from the human evolutionary process itself. Humans transcend their biology, not in any supernatural way, but through our historicity. Grant appeals to Clifford Geertz's understanding of culture as the environmental pattern of meanings that influences human evolution. In such an understanding of culture, language emerges as a trait favored for its capacity to embody meaning in symbols.[24] Grant uses Gordon Kaufman's view of humans as "biohistorical beings," with two dynamic evolutionary components. One component is religion—the practices, artifacts, and beliefs that symbolize meaning, through which we say that "life makes sense," and we achieve feelings of wholeness. The other component inherent in our biohistorical being is the drive for meaning, which culminates in religion. The universality we observe about religion indicates a common human *need for meaning*, not a common *experience of meaning*.[25]

If I may spin Borg's language in this theological neo-lib manner, "the More" is our fundamental human sense that "there's More to life than our biology." For this kind of neo-lib, "the More" is Meaning; meaning-making is what defines human beings. But the neo-lib also refrains from locating meaning-making primarily in reason or rationality, which is more about positing certainty than about making meaning. The neo-lib refrains from making claims that cannot be sustained through interdisciplinary discourse. (Another place to repeat Robert Funk's mantra: no special pleading allowed.)

In his preface, Grant gives this summary of how he argues from "remodeled" liberalism to making a claim for Christianity:

> Human Beings need meaning to flourish. Religions provide meaning worlds that can meet the human need. Christianity is such a religion. Christianity, when focused through the concept of the grace of God, can be a viable way of finding meaning in our world today.

I can only unpack a few of the implications suggested here, and add a few corollaries of my own.

If the need for meaning is basic in human beings, religion is then a primary meaning world (worldview) responding to this need. The particular culture in which we first develop the capacity for making meaning provides the categories we use to express meaning (accounting for the varieties of our religious experiences). Two related corollaries provide support for this area of Grant's proposal. Expressing meaning requires both consciousness and language. In the field of cognitive science there are compatible proposals to account for both language acquisition and human consciousness as evolving through neurobiological processes.[26] Noam Chomsky launched the debate over language acquisition by proposing an innate human capacity for language structure that is actualized only in a particular linguistic environment. While basic forms of communication may be learned behavior, the infinitely creative capacity of human language is more than behavior. Chomsky suggests rather that the brain is predisposed for linguistic structures.[27] Current cognitive neuroscience studies provide an alternative to Chomsky's (Cartesian) rationalist approach and argue for a unified theory of development that fits language within Grant's "biohistorical" evolutionary process. The emergence of creative language capacity can be accounted for by neurobiological processes that belong to the same complex of features that Grant suggests produced the need for meaning.

The other corollary that belongs here is the emerging understanding of human consciousness. John Searle has made a strong case for explaining consciousness as a "biological phenomenon," which avoids both classic mind-body dualism and reductionistic materialism. "Conscious states are caused by lower level neurobiological processes in the brain that are themselves higher level features of the brain."[28] In Searle's approach we could talk about ontological experiences analogous to the kind of religious experiences already described. This kind of consciousness would provide a compatible context for talking about the need for meaning, which in turn is realized through human capacity for symbolization, again made possible through the processes of consciousness and language. These components fit together into a matrix of ideas that are accounted for by David Grant's focus on human biohistorical evolution.[29]

Grant's nutshell summary indicates the kind of case he would make for Christianity. Like Borg, Grant builds his case here on the analysis of the language of faith derived from Wilfred Cantwell Smith. Also like Borg, he appeals to the root sense of *credo* as "I give my heart to," and to the cognate sense of "believe/belove." The resulting quality has the characteristics of "faithfulness, allegiance, loyalty, commitment, and trust."[30] Here, however, Borg appeals to the pre-modern sense of believe/belove God, in which "God" is still the object of believing and faith retains its component of assenting to foundational affirmations. Grant rather focuses on the human characteristic of believing as making commitment. He defines the nature of human being as *Homo Fidens* (we are "faithing" people). The primary affirmation of the neo-lib is that all humans need meaning, something to "believe in," to "commit to," to "give one's heart to." We make sense of life by the way we interpret our experiences, and in turn our interpretation is based on our commitments. We tend to call all this "worldview," but it is more than a "view" of things. In life we act on what we trust, on our faith, our commitments. Being "religious" then means committing oneself to living in a particular context of meaning. In this sense, all faith is inherently confessional, in that meaning ("the More") is not a demonstrable feature of reality, but a commitment to interpret reality in a meaningful way. For the neo-lib, this is the reality of "the More." There's "More" to life than factual matters, for those who make sense of life.[31] And we make sense of life by committing ourselves to a certain way of interpreting our experiences of life.

Christianity, David Grant suggests, is one such option for making sense of life. It is about commitment to living in God's grace.[32] To make sense of life involves committing oneself to a "meaning world," which in our cultural context is often a religious world. What about the Christian meaning world commends itself? From the tradition of its myths and rituals, Grant commends the centrality of grace as a meaning world in which to live. The appealing features of grace include: life is treated as a gift, and thus is accepted as good.

Viewing life as a gift further conveys the message, "You are accepted," which in turn liberates us from needing to justify our own existence. The result is a sense of being at home in the universe; we live in a world where we can find meaning. This meaning world comes to us through the language of some particular communal tradition, which embodies it as grace. It this sense there is a sense of dependence that comes with the experience of accepting the gift of grace. Accepting a gift begins as a passive response, trusting the source of the gift. The further response is of loyalty to the source of the gift. Receiving a gift elicits a response of gratitude for the gift, and the in-kind response is to share the gift of grace with others. This meaning world makes sense by committing to it; it is not deduced empirically from raw experience or philosophical reasoning.[33]

To acknowledge that one does not arrive at this position empirically, Grant raises the questions of justice and evil. The gift of grace includes freedom, with genuine choices to act in either gracious or ungracious ways. To believe in God is to commit to seeing good in the world, especially in the face of human evil. Identifying grace as central to Christian understanding is itself a choice that recognizes God's justice is not absolute, or grace would not be truly a gift.

I would suggest that a fitting corollary here from the perspective of grace would be the biblical emphasis on God's impartiality as a manifestation of God's justice, rather than focus on the perceived "fairness" of the distribution of grace in a world in which "life isn't fair."[34] In the meaning world assumed by the apostle Paul, God's impartiality is one of two vital principles, the other being parity: "we'll all be held accountable" in the same way (regardless of religious preference!). These two principles, in fact, constitute God's very integrity/justice.[35]

A further exploration of biblical themes would indicate that the biblical narratives exemplify not just the perspective of God's grace, but more importantly that God's grace is indeed a matter of perspective. We can revisit Borg's use of the story of Joseph and his brothers to illustrate this matter. Borg notes the importance of "retrospective providential interpretation" in the telling of the story of Joseph's reunion with his brothers in Egypt. He focuses on the theme of God's providence in Joseph's speech in Gen 45:5–8: "God sent me before you to preserve life. . . . It was not you who sent me here, but God." I would like to push the interpretation one step further, by looking at the final exchange between Joseph and his brothers. Joseph's initial speech to his brothers, promoting "retrospective providence," is not the last word in this story. After their father has died, the brothers expect that Joseph "will pay us back for all the evil" they did. Joseph's brothers relay their father's request to "forgive . . . their sin because of the evil" they did, implying that justice cannot be avoided. Joseph first reassures them: "Have no fear. Can I take the place of God?" (Gen 50:19). Justice is not to be rendered in the moment. Joseph then insists that his proffered providential interpretation of events does not, in fact, rewrite history: "You meant to do evil to me, but God meant it for good" (v. 20). By introducing the categories of good and evil, the events are now seen from the perspective of the big picture created in Genesis 1–3.

The story of origins establishes the interpretive lens through which subsequent experiences are to be evaluated. The default mode of the universe is declared to be good, even "very good" (Gen 1:31). The created order is neither ambiguous nor duplicitous; its purpose/intent is unified around what is good. The reality of human experience, of course, is often quite different. The story of origins declares that the matter of knowing good and evil belongs to a perspective larger than the human view (Gen 2:9). When humans choose to partake of such knowing, they become "like God, knowing good and evil" (Gen 3:5), which Joseph resists doing. I suggest the issue indicated here is more than accepting the hindsight of "divine providence," although this is an emphasized biblical theme, e.g., "All things work for good for those who love God" (Rom 8:28). However, this in no way nullifies Paul's principle of parity: "God renders to each according to their deeds" (Rom 2:6; Prov 24:12; Ps 62:12).

Justice and grace are not in competition, but are rather two perspectives on the same experience. In the face of experiencing human acts of evil, it is nonetheless meaningful to live with the conviction that humans should feel at home in the world. The longing for justice does not make it a reality. "Retrospective providence" is in the eye of the beholder. It is possible to adopt a perspective that finds a silver lining in every experience, or accept it with the resignation: "That's life." But something else is at stake here. I return to David Grant's suggestion that to adopt the meaning world of grace means "committing oneself to look on the world in this way and live out one's own life in grateful response to it." The only verification must be pragmatic: "Does the overarching context of grace enable humans to flourish in their relations with each other?"[36]

Grant answers with a confident Yes, and the affirmation that "finally the truth of grace is in the believing and committing oneself to follow in the footsteps of the one whom we Christians claim to be the very bringer of truth and grace."[37] But why choose grace as one's "meaning world?" Grant suggests that our experience of the world reveals grace to us, but "revelation will emerge differently for different people in their different cultural complexes." In the end we can only confirm that the truth of the matter is: "the truth is in the believing."[38] We might capture this as, "put your trust in trust," or "trusting is believing."

Grant's proposals are appealing to me at least in part because they seem so compatible with the work of the Westar seminars. Robert Funk identifies three primary aspects of Jesus' vision: (1) The domain of God: "everywhere present but not demonstrable"; (2) Trust: "the door to the alternative reality that is God's domain; (3) Celebration: "the endorsement of trust." In summary:

> Since God's domain is hidden, it is a fiction to be embraced on trust. To trust means to act as though something were true when the evidence is ambiguous or marginal. Human beings can embrace a fiction only if it is undergirded by faith. . . . Celebration is the by-product of trust . . . , the endorsement of trust. Celebration nourishes trust. Celebration is the heart of liturgy in God's domain.[39]

In short: a "trust ethic" is at the heart of Jesus' discourse. It is after all Jesus' truth that: "your trust has cured you" (Mark 5:34; 10:52); "don't be afraid, just have trust" (5:36); "have trust in God" (12:22).

It is also a crucial element in Paul's discourse. He promoted "a total trust like that of Jesus, God's anointed" (Rom 3:22; Gal 2:16), the kind of trust Abraham first demonstrated (Gen 15:6; Rom 4:3; Gal 3:6). Paul's warrant for this focus is itself from scripture: "The one acceptable to God, based on total trust, will have life" (Hab 2:4; Rom 1:17; Gal 3:11). The heart of Paul's theology is thus: God counts total trust as virtue; total trust brings life.[40] And we experience this all as grace (divine favor), as a gift, because it's free: just trust (Rom 4:16). "That's why it's all based on total trust, so the promise [of life] can be a matter of divine favor—something guaranteed to . . . those who share Abraham's trust" (Rom 4:16). After all, "everyone is regarded as virtuous, free of charge, by God's generous gift, through the deliverance provided by God's anointed, Jesus—through Jesus' total trust" (Rom 3:24–25).

We have now revisited Marcus Borg's three fundamental affirmations, God, Jesus, and the Bible, from the "neo-lib" perspective derived from David Grant's suggestions. Rather than summarize the results, I attempt to capture these in the form of some "neo-lib" affirmations and mottoes.

Neo-lib affirmations:

1. Humans share a common experience of the need for meaning.

2. Human biohistorical evolution accounts for the human need for meaning.

3. Religion is the cultural context in which humans construct meaning.

4. "God" symbolizes one cultural component of meaning.

5. The "More" of religious experience is meaning.

6. "Being religious" (having faith) is committing oneself to living in a context of meaning.

7. Christian faith is living in grace.

Neo-lib mottoes:

Humans need meaning; it's the way we evolved.

Religion makes meaning; "God" means "there's More to life."

Faith is a commitment to meaning; promise yourself a meaningful life.

Faith works.

Meaning matters.

Grace happens.

Ballot Propositions [recommendation]:
Representing religious "realism": [Black]

Being Christian means affirming the reality of God.

The reality of religious experience confirms the reality of God.

Religion is the human response to the experience of God.

God is a factual object of religious experience.

Representing religious "non-realism": [Red]

Religious experience is rooted in the common human experience of the need for meaning.

The need for meaning evolved within human biohistory.

Religion is a linguistic-cultural meaning world constructed by human imagination.

Being Christian affirms a meaning world shared with Jesus.

God is the sum of our values.

Appendix: The Trinity in Comparative Mythology

Another corollary that would add insight to suggestions made here can be derived from the comparative mythology theories of Georges Dumézil. In the study of a wide range of cultures that share a common Indo-European (I-E) linguistic base, Dumézil noted a tripartite structure in both their mythologies and their social organization. Scott Littleton's summary will suffice for our purposes here:

> On the basis of his comparative analysis of the varied social and mythological forms presented by the ancient I-E-speaking world, Dumézil has concluded (1) that the parent or Proto-I-E society, before it broke up, was characterized by a tripartite ideology; (2) that elements of the ideology were carried by the inheritors of that society across the length and breadth of what was to become the historic I-E domain; and (3) that these elements can be discovered in most, but by no means all, of the early I-E mythical and epical literature. . . . Moreover, this ideology, whether expressed in myth, epic, or social organization, is asserted to be uniquely I-E, having no parallels among the ancient civilizations of the Near East, the Nile Valley, China, or any other region of the Old World prior to the I-E migrations in the second millennium BC.

> Dumézil claims that this characteristic and uniquely I-E tendency to view phenomena as divided into three hierarchically ranked strata became a deeply ingrained habit of thought; it became, in short, an ideology.[41]

This "ideology," as Dumézil calls it, was manifest in both the mythic structures and social structures of I-E cultures. The three prototypical roles are priest, warrior, and farmer, corresponding to "three fundamental classificatory principles—sovereignty, force, and nourishment—each of which is, in the mathematical sense, a function of the others."[42] More generically, these can seen as order, action, and sustenance.[43] An obvious implication here is that the cultures that shaped Christian trinitarian theology were indigenously tripartite. In other words, a kind of trinitarianism is in the DNA of Indo-European linguistic cultures. We might even call this the proto-"Secular Trinity."[44]

As a corollary to what we have considered in this essay, it seems reasonable that Grant's proposal might well be expanded to identify the "need for meaning" as one of three basic needs that humans expressed in Indo-European cultures. One's "meaning world" then provides the structure within which to "make sense" of life's contingencies.

Beginning All Over Again

Don Cupitt

O
n May 8th, 1942, as the United States entered the Second World War, Vice-President Henry Wallace declared in a much-quoted speech that

> The century on which we are entering—the century which will come out of this war—can be and must be the century of the common man.[1]

Sixty years later, there is general agreement amongst us about who, in the century of the common man, has become the common man of the century. He is Homer Simpson. By now Matt Groening and his team are said to have issued over 360 episodes of *The Simpsons*—an astounding figure—and Homer's world has been described in great detail. He is the modern Everyman, especially of the advanced countries, especially of the Liberal Protestant English-speaking world, and most especially of Middle America.

It is often said that Americans are not good at irony, but the pleasure *The Simpsons* gives us is precisely the pleasure of irony. By deft scriptwriting all points of view and all aspects of the Simpsons' world are mercilessly mocked, but it is done with such unfailing good humour and lightness of touch that we end up, like his gifted daughter Lisa, by loving Homer just as he is and with all his manifest absurdities. In fact the films themselves carry an important religious message, for they first help us to transcend small-town ordinariness, see its limits and laugh at it, and then secondly they *also* help us to return into ordinariness and accept it because in the end it is all there is. Which makes Matt Groening the Jane Austin of our late modern age, for they both faced the same question: How is a thinking person to cope with the banality and narrowness of ordinary life?

Answer: By using her intelligence to see it as it is, to see through it, rise above it, and laugh at it—and learn to do all this with such generosity of spirit that she is enabled to return into ordinariness and accept it, because it is outsideless, and because it is all we'll ever know. There is no More-Real world beyond: there is no place elsewhere that will compensate us for the banality of Springfield. Springfield is all there is, and the Joyful Wisdom is to say a goodhumoured and wholehearted Yes to it, just as it is.

From what I have said you will gather that I agree with all those who say that *The Simpsons* is a considerable work of art, a divine comedy whose message is substantially correct. But it doesn't follow that everything *within* the world of Springfield is perfect. Far from it: and in particular I must draw your attention to the state of religion in that town. Many religions and para-religious movements are mentioned, but only two are permanent social facts and live options[2] for most of the characters. There is the Evangelical protestantism of Ned Flanders and his family, which even Homer can see is goofy and immature and on which we need not spend more time here, and there is the "mainline" or liberal protestantism of the middle-of-the-road church that the Simpsons themselves attend. It may be Episcopalian, it may be Methodist, it may be Presbyterian. No matter: the most interesting figure at the church is the minister, who is known (again ironically) as "Reverend Lovejoy." He is a melancholy and rather tragic character who clearly knows in his heart that the religion to which he has given his life has become an intellectual and spiritual disaster. When he was in training thirty years ago, his teachers assured him, and he believed, that "a critical orthodoxy" was possible. Christianity and modernity were compatible. But the attrition of the years has worn his faith down, and he well knows how hollow the old answers sound today. Unfortunately, they are all he's got, and he has to go on parroting them.

The scriptwriters are cruel about Lovejoy's dilemma here. For example, when he is confronted by people's bewilderment in the face of tragedy, he knows he has to affirm the objective reality both of God's power and of God's love, so the best consolation he can offer is the uplifting thought that "God loves his victims."

Still more devastating is the portrayal of the Simpson family at church. Look at their faces: Homer and Bart are bored rigid. They are there only because Marge makes them come. Marge herself radiates her characteristic vague benignity: she approves of church and thinks it's where the family ought to be on a Sunday, but the truth is that she has no more idea of what's going on there than Maggie has. Only Lisa looks really alert: she's busily working out what it all means. Everything interests Lisa. There will always be one or two Lisas around, but the extent to which they can help normal people is strictly limited.

Many observers of the American religious scene think it a remarkable fact that Americans remain seemingly so much more religious than the people of any other advanced country. Where else in the world do the Homer Simpsons still attend church? Where else can we imagine them one day returning to churchgoing? Nowhere: but is this a good reason for being optimistic and talking about American exceptionalism? *The Simpsons* suggests not, for it portrays a world in which the old religion is no longer understood, is no longer imaginatively inspiring, and no longer makes any appreciable and important difference to people's lives. People do know that religion matters, and matters a lot; but their own religion is already in terminal decline. They are still turning up dutifully, but it makes no sense and is doing them no good. They're bored. It is true that Ned Flanders' religion still makes a perceptible difference to his life; but who wants to be like Ned Flanders? Summing up his own version of the Christian life, Ned says: "You name it, I haven't done it"—which says it all.

Why has this catastrophe happened? The shortest and simplest answer is that the old premodern and tradition-directed type of human being was trained by culture to see everything and to build his world in terms of a great block of grand normative ideas—absolutes, myths, religious doctrines and images. That is how religion used to work. Almost nothing was seen as it was: everything was seen and estimated in its relation to the Ideal order. Not surprisingly, everything was seen, not as itself, but in terms of how far it fell short of the divine perfection. Everyone was a sinner, and everything fell short. They had almost no knowledge in those days, but they did have an absolute standard against which they measured everything, and so they could claim to know the difference between right and wrong. But we post-Enlightenment modern people are very different. We have huge amounts of empirical knowledge, but no absolute truth. We have set aside all the old normative ideas, and instead have covered the world all over with our own minutely-detailed empirical descriptions and theories. This new way of building our world has turned out to be hugely powerful, and the results are in many ways very beautiful—but it has left the older ways of thinking, religious, moral and philosophical, *stranded* and unable to function properly. It has also given us a very different world.

A simple example of the changeover is given by the current controversies about gay bishops and the like. Until the Enlightenment most people could characterize others and fix some knowledge about them only by passing moral judgment upon them. There was no scientific psychology: there was only moral judgment, which enabled you to classify another person as a miser, or a glutton, or a coward, or whatever. People resembled Snow White's seven dwarves, each of whom has only one identifying characteristic. So people were seen as embodying universal qualities—virtues or vices. Everybody was an emblem of the vice or the virtue that she typified. But then about the time of the Romantic movement modern psychology began. We began gradually to develop many new ways of describing other people and explaining how they develop, and how they tick—and all this new vocabulary soon made the old simple-minded moralism redundant. For the first time in the history of Western thought it became possible to see homosexuality as involving more than just a class of actions that were known in advance to be morally wrong: people could now learn to look at homosexuality empirically and see it as a certain constitution of the whole personality, and a way that some people happen to have developed. There's room here for debate about how it happens that different people come to develop different sexualities or sexual orientations, but there's no room for the old reflex moral condemnation. It is uninformative: it doesn't really *tell* us anything. Consider for example, the way we are sometimes pressed to agree that someone or other is evil. We feel reluctant and embarrassed. Sorry, no: that word darkens counsel. Its use creates a feeling of satisfaction, but sheds no light.

In many of the advanced countries the two ways of thinking are nevertheless still struggling against each other. Many ordinary people cling to the old moralism and the old black-and-white view of the world, while in the universities and in "the caring professions" others try to persuade them that it's better to work in the modern way, by building up agreed descriptions, explanatory theories, and ways of understanding and coping. The conflict is fierce, and one popular (not to say, *populist*) way of managing it is to keep the new ways of thinking securely locked up in the universities, where they can't get out and cause any more harm in what is called the real world. In Britain, people tend to see it like this: we are terrified of the new ways of thinking. Above all, we are terrified that if they are applied to religion and morality they will destroy everything we hold dear. So we insist that the universities must not actively spread new ideas, but must instead *act as prisons* for new ideas. At the same time, we hide from ourselves the truth of what we are doing by ridiculing university people as idle dreamers who live in ivory towers! By this ingenious double manoeuvre, the British try to insulate themselves from new ideas and keep their traditional religious vocabulary intact.

To return to Homer Simpson and his family, sitting in a row in their church, I think we now understand better what the cartoons are saying. Like many other people the world over, Springfield folk continue to cling obdurately to their ancestral faith, even though it now does not work and makes no sense at all, having in fact died two or three generations ago. But the present rather strained, awkward period cannot continue for much longer, and it's obvious enough that people like Homer and Bart will not still be sitting in their places a few years from now. In English Roman Catholicism I remember the way the last Irish Homer Simpsons used to sit further and further back during Sunday Mass. Then for a time they could be seen *standing* at the back, hanging about awkwardly, until in the end they disappeared altogether. And the basic philosophical event that underlies this withdrawal is that we have collectively changed over from one way of world-building to another. We used to see everything and to build our world in terms of great normative moral and religious ideas. They were all we had to build our world with, and they seemed to be enough. In the Muslim heartlands there are still a few people who see their world in the same way. Everything is seen and judged in relation to God and his revealed Law. It was a rather cartoonish vision by today's standards, but it seemed good enough then. Today, however, in the West we have changed over to a new *empirical* way of describing and theorizing the world, which gives us much more complicated ideas about human nature. Since the 1950s, mass higher education, mass travel and communications, and ubiquitous high technology have gradually come to involve almost everybody in the new world-view. We need it for our jobs: Homer himself works in a nuclear power plant. And so our old religious and moral traditions have faded away, and nothing can resuscitate them.

That is why a tiny handful of us are not liberal, but radical, theologians. We say that the new culture is so different from anything that existed in the past that religion has to be completely reinvented. Unfortunately, the new style of religious thinking that we are trying to introduce is so queer and so new that most people have great difficulty in recognising it as religion at all.

Here is an example. Trying once again to produce a short clear summary of my own outlook, I recently wrote down my personal creed. You'll think it very odd until I explain it. It is in five articles, four being about true religion and one about faith:

A CREED

1. True religion is your own voice, if you can but find it.

2. True religion is in every sense to *own* one's own life.

3. True religion is the pure solar affirmation of life, "in full acknowledgement of its utter gratuitousness, its contingency, its transience and even its nothingness."

4. True religion is productive, value-realising action in the public world.

5. Faith is not a matter of holding on to anything. Faith is simply a letting-go. It floats free.

The first point to be made about this Creed is that it makes no claims about any supernatural or metaphysical entities supposedly existing out there. Of course it doesn't: everything in the world of human life is transient and contingent, and is always subject to changing human interpretations. We know nothing but the passing show of human life. That's all there is. We have to give up any idea of something purely objective and unchanging that underlies the world. It follows that a religious creed should no longer take the form of a declaration of allegiance to something out there, and I have to confess that I have entirely abandoned the old realistic-dogmatic way of thinking. There's nothing out there: there isn't anything but the disorderly flux of experience and the struggle of human language to build and maintain a tolerably-stable and habitable world out of it. So religion today must follow ethics, and become autonomous— which in effect means seeing religion as a creative human activity, a way of adapting ourselves to life. Religion will become protestant-ism-squared: it will be about our personal *style*—about the way we commit ourselves to the life-world in general, and to our own lives in particular. Religion, I say, is to be about the way you commit yourself to your own living and your life-task. Religion is about deciding what *you* are going to make of your own life.

Article 1, therefore, says that true religion is your own voice. I am sorry to have to risk causing offence, but I now reject all ready-made religious beliefs outright. Instead, I admit that I am pure heretic: I hold that true religion is now very close to art. Like a young artist, the religious person must struggle to find her own voice. She's trying to find the religious idiom through which she can best live her own life and become herself, and at ease with herself. We must therefore frame *our own* religious outlook and shape *our own* religious life, and you will perhaps find—as I have found—that when we are *in extremis* and getting close to death, then the only religious beliefs that can help us at all are ones that we have made for ourselves. That's pure and beautiful heresy: the only truth for you is a truth that you have made up for yourself because it suits you, and have tested out in your own life until it has become a part of you. Thus I believe. Religion is a path to selfhood, and it comes out a bit different for each of us.

Article 2 is about owning one's own life, which means both acknowledging it, and assuming full responsibility for planning and running it. You *are* your own life. Your personal identity is not a secret thing hidden inside you: it is your lived life and the roles you play. Thus your commitment to life and to the task of becoming yourself has to be read as the task of fully appropriating one's own life and assuming full personal responsibility for it. Here I reject the traditional idea that there is great virtue in obedience to religious law and to the direction of religious superiors. Instead I join all those young people who would rather die than put up with an arranged marriage, or any career or life-path chosen for them by someone else. In traditional Christianity the demand for radical personal religious freedom has always been condemned as deeply sinful, but I think we must now insist upon it. One must choose one's own life, *both* making it one's own *and* seeking fully to express oneself in it. One must *come out* in one's own life.

Article 3 of my Creed says that true religion is the pure solar affirmation of life. We don't look for any incorruptible eternal world. We don't look for absolutes. We say an all-out Yes to our present life just as it is, gratuitous, contingent, transient. ('Solar' means all-out and holding nothing back, like the sun.) Of course our life is fleeting and objectively meaningless; but we can and we must *give* it meaning by the passion with which we commit ourselves to it. We'll pass, but something of that passion will live on and be remembered. It alone gives worth to life and to all the things of life.

Talk of solar living brings us close to the biological use of the word life. Struggling for solarity brings us closer to other living things, and may fill us with an overflowing love for them. So at least it is with me.

Which brings me to Article 4: True religion is productive value-realising action in the public world. In the new age we have to do for ourselves what God used to do for us. In *Genesis* God's language creates light and orders the world. Today it is *our* language that runs all over the chaos of experience and makes all things intelligible—that is, bright and beautiful. *We* make the world. Similarly, as in *Genesis* God looks at what he has made and sees that it is good, so we collectively can look at what we have built up and see that it is good.

A favourite example of mine is a good modern illustrated bird book. The labour of thousands of ornithologists over the past two centuries has been sifted and accumulated to build up this beautiful and very highly-accurate inventory of the birds of our country or region. Before the Enlightenment they had nothing even approaching this. Not everything in the modern world is wrong and ugly. On the contrary, by a huge collective endeavour we have already made our world and our life much more worked up, elaborated and precious than ever they were in the past. And everyone, by the way they commit themselves to their own little corner of the world or of our life, can and should contribute something to the work. I call this "the ethics of value creation" or of "world-building." We should seek to build a world that looks as if it is divinely, or disinterestedly, loved.

Finally, Article 5 is about faith. For centuries faith has been fighting a slow, losing rearguard action, and it has got into the habit of seeing itself as clinging to what remains of various old certainties. Orthodox faith has become like a very old person who is fearful, unable to change and clutching at whatever is old and familiar. It demands external support—guardrails, bedrock, foundations. However, no such fixed eternal support is available, nor is it what we actually need. What faith needs is simply the confidence to forget personal anxiety and float free, enjoying life in the face of life's contingency. In the living of our lives, as in our science, anything is indeed possible, but we don't need to take all possibilities equally seriously all the time. We have to pick up the habit of selecting those few hypotheses about what may happen that are worth taking seriously or worth checking out, and then we should give them due consideration. The rest we should airily dismiss, and just get on with our lives. The truly solar person understands that personal life is not really thinkable *at all* except against a background of contingency. Contingency as such is not an enemy; it is a condition of our life, and in particular of our freedom. We should not allow it to frighten us. We should affirm it, dancing out over it and so turning hap into happiness. That is 'solarity'—the art of turning mere hap into eternal happiness by faith. And such faith is entirely rational. It conquers anxiety and helps us to rejoice in life, as the New Testament says, "While we have time." I feel a sense of eschatological urgency. Life is short: I haven't long, so I must rejoice while I can.

So much for my Creed. Elsewhere I have pointed out that this very simple outline can be set against several different backgrounds, and fleshed-out in many different vocabularies:

1. I have argued that it has already become the ordinary person's new religion—an autonomous *religion of life* that is demonstrably built into the idioms of today's ordinary language.[3]

2. In our post-metaphysical and naturalistic age, my Creed might be defended as *Philosophy's Own Religion*.[4] It appears as such in postmodern French philosophy.

3. Alternatively, it can be presented as a new, post-ecclesiastical or Kingdom form of Christianity, that simply takes a step or two further the tradition of Kierkegaard, Bultmann and Christian Existentialism.[5] Thoroughly internalized, commitment to God becomes commitment to existence, which in turn becomes commitment just to our life now, the final goal of religion being just this return into simple immediacy.

4. My Creed can also be interpreted as a lay person's version of Japanese Buddhism, perhaps especially in the Soto Zen tradition of Dogen.[6]

Thus the expressivist, self-outing, self-giving and immediate religion of life that I am describing can be seen as the common outlook upon which several different ancient traditions, each with its own distinctive vocabulary, are converging today in our globalized, postmodern times. Today we are giving up forever the idea that there is a privileged vocabulary that belongs exclusively to a particular community, which on that account controls the road to salvation. No! Nobody has an exclusive franchise. There is no privileged vocabulary. Eternal happiness is available to all. It is easy to find, and ordinary language proves that the common people find it on their own *easily*, without any special help from any priesthood or academy. I sometimes call this "Linux theology." Truth is just sitting there, in public, and available for anyone who wants to use it. If you want to tweak it or add a little to it, you can do so. Why not? Truth is free: you don't have to bow down to anyone, nor pay anyone for it. Truth is common property.

We may also call what I am proposing "democratic theology," a phrase which draws attention to a striking shift in thought. In the nineteenth and early twentieth centuries there was a belief that Great Men made everything. The makers of dictionaries showed how words should be used by quoting canonical writers. Great Men were the masters of language. They also made history, and religious geniuses created religions. But in the most recent dictionaries we see that nowadays it is not Great Men but the common speech of ordinary people that has come to be seen as the principal site of linguistic innovation. Literary gems from Great Writers have become much less prominent, and instead the new dictionaries give long lists of the kind of stock phrases from ordinary language that professional writers usually look down upon. These phrases show that *ordinariness is also creative.*

We are in the midst of a big process of democratization. We are beginning to see the production of all meaning and of truths of every kind as something that comes about, not by Great Men laying down the law, but simply through the everyday conversation of humanity. I am extending this idea to religion and morality, saying that we must give up the idea that in these areas we should look up to any special and exalted mouthpiece of truth. No! On the contrary, we should give up all ideas of revelation and all ideas of traditional authority, and instead look for truth in the midst of common life and in the voices of ordinary people. We don't have to search for truth: it is already here amongst us. I first put forward these ideas nearly five years ago now, and so far there has been little understanding and no serious discussion of them, but I persist in saying that truth in philosophy, religion and morality is public and easy to find. It is for everybody, and the method of enquiry that involves listening to the changing use of ordinary language delivers it to us much more easily and quickly than applying to any of the traditional authorities. I now see the new religion as one that doesn't need to be strenuously propagated. It crops up and propagates itself spontaneously, among the people and all the time.

To understand this process of religious democratization is to understand why in ordinary language in the past generation or two the stock of organized religion has fallen steadily, and the stock of spirituality has risen correspondingly. Organised religion taught us to think of itself as uniquely possessing a large deposit of unchanging and compulsory copyrighted truth, which its own authorities certify to us. That's an idea we are fast abandoning. Spirituality teaches us to think instead of religion and morality as human and changing. Everyone is a lifelong pilgrim, everyone is trying to work out the religious style or idiom that's right for her. We all of us develop and project out our own personal religion, and there's no harm in that. People who are committed to one of the great traditions of organized religion, and people involved with academic theology, usually scorn the new spirituality, saying that it is hopelessly irrational, amateurish and self-indulgent. Well, maybe —though I wouldn't describe the professional apologists of organized religion as being themselves paragons of rationality, either. And in any case, whether you like spirituality or not, it is the future, and my Creed can be seen as trying to give this new kind of personally-evolved religion or principled heresy a rationale.

I have made a very bold claim. I have suggested that we in the modern West are finally abandoning the old dogmatic vision of the world, and are moving over to a new outlook which I have elsewhere called "Empty radical humanism."[7] To put it with brutal brevity, there is no permanent objective reality: there is only the endless human debate through which we struggle, out of the chaos of experience, to build a habitable scene for our common life. Religion in this new era has to take a new form: it is the task of finding and adopting a personal philosophy of life and lifestyle through which we can live, become ourselves, love life, and enhance the value of our own corner of the common human world. We need to find each of us a personal way of committing ourselves, with all the religious intensity we can muster, to life in general and to our own life in particular. So far as we can succeed in this aim, we can help to make the whole life-world more valuable and make it a bit easier for future humans also to rejoice in life and to live well. Your spirituality, then, is your personal lifestyle and life-project, and your contribution within the greater project of humanity as a whole.

That seems straightforward, and even rational. It is rational for all of us to seek for ourselves the outlook and to cultivate the habits that will help us to make the best of the human situation, and be happy. So far so good. But how is my defence of the modern vogue for spirituality to be reconciled with what we actually find in the bookshops? Every big general stockholding bookshop nowadays has sections that are variously labelled "Body, Mind and Spirit" or "Phenomena," or "Spirituality." And what do we find on the shelves there?—An avalanche of terminally self-indulgent tosh. Popular spirituality bears the same sort of relation to mainstream public scientific knowledge as fringe medicine bears to orthodox science-based medicine. Pop spirituality is fringe or alternative—and we should steer well clear of it. It is a jumble of fuzzy language, anecdotal evidence, wish-fulfilment, and the sort of ideas that in ordinary language people introduce after the phrase, "I like to think that. . . ."

What went wrong? I accept—and insist—that there is indeed a large-scale religious shift currently taking place. It is taking us away from the great disciplinary religious institutions with their readymade creeds, and towards a new conception of religion that demands a high degree of personal autonomy. People need to work out their own religious *style*—their own way of life and path to self-hood, their own way of loving life and cherishing their bit of the world, and somehow their own way of saying Yes to life just as it is. But this quest for a valid personal religion certainly does not have to take the form of a compensatory fantasy. On the contrary, it can only really satisfy us if it is firmly based on a cool recognition of the facts of the human condition: we are alone, everything passes away, we'll die, and there is no magic formula or specially-provided way out of all this. **All this** is outsideless, and there is no supernatural escape-route or consolation. But by faith and love and commitment to life it is possible to turn the pure hap of life into eternal happiness. I call the trick 'solar living', and *that* is true religion. There is no other way.

From all this you will understand why I don't just admit, but insist, that religion today has to become beliefless. There is nothing out there to believe in or to hope for. Religion therefore has to become an immediate and deeply-felt way of relating yourself to life in general and your own life in particular. Live it out, hard, and I promise that you'll find it works.

This explains why it is that although I strongly sympathize with the general movement from organized religion to spirituality, I regard it as essential that we make ourselves very unpopular by being severely critical of soppy fringe spirituality and telling people that they should have nothing to do with it. Under the old régime the religious life used to begin with something called the Purgative Way, which was designed to purge the mind of illusions. Modern spirituality still needs something like that, and knows it, for of course every human being knows and has always known the basic facts of the human condition: everything passes, everything is chancy, we'll die, and because everything is outsidelessly this way there is not and there can't be any kind of magical escape or consolation. Everyone knows all these things, and everyone therefore knows that fringe religion is nonsense and that the old kind of organized religion with its readymade Creed was only a temporary stopgap. Now it has broken down, and we all of us know in our hearts that it is time to move on to the fully grown-up kind of religion that awaits us next. It starts from and it clings to a cool and unflinching recognition of the truth of the human condition, and nevertheless, it *still* wants to say an all-out Yes to life—right up to one's last breath.

What, however, is its relation to the Judaeo-Christian tradition, whose highly-problematic future is the main theme of our present gathering? It must be obvious that I personally think that the ecclesiastical Christianity that we have received from the past is now in precipitous and final decline. Its theology, which was chiefly systematized by St. Augustine of Hippo in his book *The City of God*, involved a hugely large-scale and long-termist cosmological myth of Creation, Fall and Redemption, and a highly-illiberal and precritical politics of truth. Today, the great medieval doctrine system—even in the refurbished version that has reached us *via* Calvin and Karl Barth—is way beyond any possibility of rehabilitation; and as for the politics of truth that represses religious creativity and tries to bully us all into passive conformity, it is morally unendurable. Sooner or later, we must either break it or break with it, before it breaks us.

I am not suggesting though that we should or even *can* break with Christianity altogether. It is too much a part of us, our world and our values. Personally, I still admire the original Jesus, and see Christianity as the religion that is always coming down, from God to man, from the world above into this present world, and from mystical rapture into everyday life. In Christianity, God himself is a secular humanist, for he becomes man in the world, and everything comes back in the end to the world of human life and human relationships. Christianity still is and always was trying to develop in the way I've been describing: religion, it said from the first, is made for man, and not man for religion (Mark 2:27f.). Accordingly, I have still not entirely given up hope that there may yet be another Reformation of Christianity, which will need to press on with and radicalize the great tradition of Luther, Kierkegaard, Bultmann and Christian Existentialism. Along these lines, as I have tried to show, those themes in Christianity which are most precious may yet have a future. But, as I have insisted, it is vital that we give up the old politics of truth—and especially the community politics. We *must* abandon the idea that *we* are the chosen people, *we* use the right vocabulary, and *we* alone have privileged access to eternal salvation. If the human race is to have a future we must give up all forms of nationalism and ethnocentrism—and most especially the religious forms of these ideas. So my future reformation will require Christianity to give up its own identity and its own privileged status. And that is the last, the most difficult, and the most necessary sacrifice.

On Behalf of
John Robinson

Don Cupitt

A fter forty years, to revisit the great controversy that in
the mid-1960s surrounded the name of John Robinson
is to re-enter a lost world. The Church of England today is only half
the size it was then, and of what remains over half has been taken over
by the Evangelicals, who as is well known prefer to live on another
planet. But in those heady days of forty years ago Christianity was
still of public importance in Europe, and Christian ethics had high
prestige. People were conscious of the task of rebuilding European
culture after the War, and they mostly saw Christian values as making an important contribution to the work of reconstruction. They
do not think like that today.

Because things have now changed so much, John Robinson is
in many ways a dated figure. He was almost completely untouched
by the feminism and environmentalism that have so greatly influenced us. In philosophy, he knew nothing of the new stirrings in
Paris, nor even of British empiricism and analytical philosophy. He
had been born in 1919 in the cathedral close at Canterbury to an
elderly father who was culturally a High Victorian churchman. This
meant that John's background lay in the now-forgotten tradition
of Personal Idealism, and his Ph.D. dissertation was about Martin
Buber, a Jewish personalist who sought to reconstruct religious
thought after the violent impact of Friedrich Nietzsche.

Robinson's philosophical vocabulary is so unfamiliar nowadays
that most people are hardly aware that his Ph.D. topic was in the
philosophy of religion. He is more usually seen simply as a New
Testament scholar who, like Rudolf Bultmann, dabbled unwisely
in doctrinal revision. But in fact Robinson's religious teaching was
shaped by his personalist philosophy. The Personal Idealists whom
he followed—people like the great churchman William Temple—

tended to see the universe as multi-levelled. The main levels were—in ascending order—those of Matter, Life, Mind and Spirit. The physical sciences explored and theorised reality at the material level; the biological sciences studied the world of life, and the historical sciences studied the world of human thought and action. The highest level of reality, that of Spirit, was the world of love, spiritual values and personal relationships. People influenced by these ideas tended to think of ultimate reality as a society of persons, and if they believed in God they were often drawn to the almost-uniquely-English "social" doctrine of the Trinity.

The attractions of this scheme of thought to the English clergy are obvious. Theology was still the Queen of the Sciences and religion presided benevolently over everything else, just as a Victorian clergyman-headmaster presided over the entire syllabus taught in his school. And for this liberal-academic-Christian world view, just as for the artists and writers of Bloomsbury, human personal relationships and values were the key to the nature of reality at its highest level. Of the philosopher McTaggart, people said jokingly that he saw Heaven in the likeness of the Senior Common Room at Trinity College. And so he did. More seriously, this type of thinking had first been launched by the German philosopher Ludwig Feuerbach a century earlier. For Feuerbach—who was, arguably, the first important heterosexual philosopher—the meaning of all religion could be found in the depths of the relation between I and Thou, an idea that passed through Lotze into Personal Idealism, and through Martin Buber to John Robinson. One late exponent of it was the Quaker philosopher John Macmurray, who was a notable mentor not only of John Robinson, but also of Tony Blair today.

Against this background, John Robinson was acutely aware that nineteenth-century thought had climaxed in Nietzsche and the Death of God, and that the modern world had become in many ways profoundly atheistic. But his study of Martin Buber and his background in Personal Idealism persuaded him that the way forward for Christianity was through a theology of the personal and personal relationships. If *in that area* the Christian teaching was demonstrably superior, then Christianity had won the highest ground, and its long-term triumph was assured.

In Robinson's day the emergent new Western culture was, and looked, liberal scientific-humanist, just as the culture of the Soviet bloc was *planned* scientific-humanist. This new science-based culture was serviced by an army of new professions whose work was broadly pastoral and enabling. Their task was to help the individual to fit into the new order and to flourish. They included therapists, social workers, counsellors and advisors of many kinds. John Robinson's personalist theology showed these people how they could find religious depth and Christian meaning in their daily relations with their own clients. God was the depth of the personal, and Christ was the man for others. No wonder that amongst these younger professionals there was for years intense enthusiasm for Robinson's ideas. He had given religious meaning to their daily work. He had shown that the fully-developed modern world, now being built, could still be a Christian world.

As it turned out, however, Robinson was completely misunderstood, especially by the Church. The Evangelicals demanded action against him because he was being widely accused of atheism, and the then Archbishop of Canterbury Michael Ramsey duly complied by publicly criticizing this most Anglican of Anglicans. John Robinson's career was abruptly terminated at the age of 44: he never got any further preferment in the Church, nor any university teaching post. Through the good offices of a friend, the New Testament scholar Dennis Nineham, he was appointed Dean of Trinity College, Cambridge, and he had to be content with that. As for the Evangelicals, they realised that they could now call the tune in the Church, for by making sufficient noise they could bring the bishops to heel. Michael Ramsey had begun a process by which traditional liberal Anglicans have since been progressively eased out of the Church in order to allow the Evangelicals to consolidate their takeover. But I leave it to the Bishops to explain why control of the Church has been handed over to people who don't even believe in episcopacy.

What about the charge of atheism? It is certainly true that many philosophers who read Robinson concluded that he had reduced God to the status of a mere metaphor, and was therefore an atheist. Robinson's God, said the Christian philosopher G. C. Stead, is a mythical embodiment of love. Robinson's God is just a way of talking about the depth of personal relationships, which is atheism, said the moral philosopher Alasdair MacIntyre. Robinson's God has gone the same way as the gods of pagan antiquity, who by Renaissance times had become no more than just personifications, said Renford Bamborough. These writers assumed that Christian language must be read in a 'realist' or metaphysical sense: for them, someone who believes in God has got to think that God exists objectively, out there, independent of us and in a distinct and timeless spiritual world. But I have said that Robinson was much influenced by Idealism, for which *nothing* exists quite objectively and independent of the mind. *All* existence was, for the idealists, mind-dependent. This means that Robinson could have been a non-realist about God, without being an atheist. And perhaps the same was true of Paul Tillich, who studied Nietzsche and gave up the realist idea of God in his youth. He used language very like Robinson's, but was not called an atheist.

Somehow, Tillich (like Albert Schweitzer) got away with it, and one is left wondering how the philosophers know that the essence of Christianity is not a religious doctrine, but a philosophical doctrine about how all religious statements are to be interpreted? And how do bishops have authority to determine questions of *philosophy*, as well as questions of theology?

The whole controversy becomes rather complicated at this point. Robinson was well aware of the slipperiness of the word atheism, and certainly knew Feuerbach's famous comment on its historical relativity: What today is religion, tomorrow will be atheism; and what today is atheism, tomorrow will be religion. What is more, there are many philosophers such as Spinoza and Hegel who are atheists for some, and theists for others. Atheism just is a rather bendy word. When challenged, Robinson himself always denied the charge of atheism, and of course he always wanted to go on talking about God, worshipping God and praying to God.

At the same time, we should also note that when my own take on all these ideas came out in 1980, Robinson was very quick to take the initiative in approaching me, and gave me much support. He invited me to preach at Trinity College, took part in discussions with me, and even engaged me in public debate in Great St. Mary's, the University Church. On all these occasions (1980 to early 1983) he never dissociated himself from nor expressly disagreed with my ideas. On the contrary, he made it clear that he was handing down to me the mantle of Elijah.

Somewhat later, a certain difference became apparent. In his later writings Robinson seemed to be back-pedalling, and when he died he left his papers to Lambeth Palace Library, as if he very much wanted to end up still a part of the Establishment that had treated him so badly. His widow Ruth thought he had been wrong to back-pedal: he should have pressed on, she said. Hearing about this, I took Ruth's advice, and have not followed John's example. One shouldn't appear to be asking for rehabilitation, because the Church is not a forgiving organization and never grants it in such cases. No *real* heretic has ever been rehabilitated. Since I do not expect that there will ever be a Last Accounting, at which the final truth on this and all other matters will be unrolled, I must be content to say my piece in full, let events turn out as they will, and leave it at that.

A full dissection of all the nuances in the question of Robinson's atheism would take a whole book. I have been able only briefly to recall a few "old, unhappy, far-off things/And battles long ago," and should perhaps end by recalling that on several occasions John Robinson himself declared that he was probably erring by not being radical enough. He was right, of course. In his day the reform and renewal of the churches still seemed possible: today, we cannot be quite so optimistic. But just for so long as the churches can still occasionally produce people like John Robinson, they have not yet quite died, and perhaps still deserve some attention and support from people like us. It is an honour and a pleasure on this great occasion and in this greatest of cities to be able to salute the memory of John Arthur Thomas Robinson, Bishop, 1919–1983.

Anti-Realism and Religious Belief

John C. Kelly

I n their books both Elaine Pagels and Marcus Borg have
emphasized the importance of faith and practice, as
opposed to doctrine, in a Christian life. This emphasis is surely
faithful to the image of Jesus in the Gospels, and it also reminds us
of the very important logical point that the meaning of a religious
doctrine or belief is only made determinate within the context of an
established practice. For religious beliefs that are not embedded in
practice are simply notional.

But, the emphasis on faith, understood as trust, and practice
should not lead us to overlook the extent to which Christianity
has always been a highly self-reflective religious tradition in which
particular practices are informed by, and understood in terms of,
religious concepts that transcend those practices. Wayne Meeks, for
example, has shown how, in the earliest years of the movement long
before the establishment of a body of doctrine, rituals, such as baptism and the Eucharist, and social practices, such as hospitality, and
care for the needy, were understood by Christians as the expression
and embodiment of their religious beliefs. Thus, a ritual like baptism
was surrounded by a cluster of beliefs about the overall structure
and meaning of a person's life before and after baptism.[1] As Meeks
puts it, "it is not simply a case of certain beliefs being added to practice; the beliefs interpret the practices, while the practices reinforce
the beliefs."[2]

Meeks' account suggests that while it is certainly a mistake to
think of early Christianity as simply a belief system, it is equally
mistaken to view it as a body of shared practices which were only
later given a theological interpretation. Rather, there seems to have
been an ongoing dialectic between belief and practice within the
Christian tradition from virtually the outset; and, if we are to judge
by the example of Paul, this dialectic included attempts to reach a

reflective understanding of the web of belief and practice. In other words, Christian practice within a generation of the death of Jesus embedded concepts that were theory laden, and the notion of a pre-theoretical form of Christianity, whether in liberal or conservative garb, seems to be a myth.

Given the self-reflective character of the Christian tradition it is hardly surprising that there has been a long and intimate, but frequently ambivalent, relationship between Christian thought and philosophy. On the one hand, Christian thinkers have often attempted to use the conceptual resources of philosophy to system-atize and defend their beliefs. While this approach has had some distinct advantages, it has also meant that Christian thought has sometimes been held hostage to the fortunes of the various philo-sophical systems with which it had identified itself. For example, in the seventeenth century the rejection of Aristotelian cosmology by the practitioners of the new science was seen by the Vatican as a threat to Christian faith. On the other hand, there have always been Christian thinkers who have seen philosophy as hostile to Christian belief and practice. But, in many cases these thinkers have used the resources of philosophic thought against itself, as when arguments taken from Academic Skepticism were used in late classical antiquity to defend Christian faith.

The twentieth century was not a good time for systematic phi-losophy in the grand manner of Kant and Hegel. Thinkers like Wittgenstein and Heidegger subjected the very concept of provid-ing metaphysical foundations for thought and practice to searching criticism and, in the opinion of many, decisively undermined it. Furthermore, a number of other thinkers also raised doubts about whether the conception of rationality presupposed by traditional systematic philosophers was applicable to actual practice in either science or everyday life. Interestingly, the rejection of traditional ideas of metaphysics and rationality opened up new conceptual pos-sibilities for Christian theology.[3]

An interesting contemporary illustration of the interaction between theology and philosophy, and the opportunities and pitfalls therein, can be found in the work of Don Cupitt. Cupitt is not an apologist for orthodox Christianity. He has moved from being a self-professed Christian non-realist to holding that it is now time to abandon Christian vocabulary in favor of what he refers to as a religion of "Everyday Speech."[4] In his many works he has offered a number of penetrating objections to Christian orthodoxy on the level of both theory and practice, and in this respect is a true heir of thinkers like Hume and Kant. But, unlike traditional liberals, he has not appealed to Enlightenment idealizations of science and rationality to support his criticisms. Both Cupitt's earlier Christian non-realism and his present religion of life are to a very considerable extent the products of his having applied certain twentieth-century philosophical ideas to theology. In particular, his philosophical theology has been decisively shaped by two prominent motifs found in both Anglo-American and continental thought.

First, he has adopted the view that all thought, experience, and conscious awareness of any sort is mediated by language.[5] This idea has its intellectual roots in Kant's doctrine that experience and thought are constituted and regulated by a fixed body of a priori concepts. In the twentieth-century this doctrine was naturalized and historicized, in somewhat different ways, by thinkers like Wittgenstein and Heidegger who, while rejecting Kant's belief in the existence of universal and a priori necessary concepts, retained his insight that there is no such thing as pre-linguistic experience or pure intellectual intuition. The result is the now familiar idea that human beings understand and interact with the human and the natural world through a contingent and historically conditioned vocabulary.

Cupitt's acceptance of the idea that all thought and experience is mediated by language has important implications for his understanding of religious experience. Religious experience has often been thought of as a self-authenticating perception, or awareness, of the holy or the divine. A classic example in the history of Christian thought is Paul's appeal in Galatians 1:12 to the personal revelation he received from Jesus Christ as a justification for his (Paul's) understanding of the gospel. Paul's position here is strictly analogous to that of the classical empiricists who claimed that ordinary sense perception provides us with incorrigible data that can be used to confirm or disconfirm claims about the world. That is, both positions regard experience as providing us with an uninterpreted given that can function as a foundation for truth claims—e.g., "I know this is red because I see it," "I know my Redeemer lives because I have seen Him." What both of these positions fail to appreciate is that the ability to recognize something as an instance of a concept requires that one have already mastered the concept in question. And concepts acquire their meaning from within the nexus of a vocabulary. In short, there are no unconceptualized experiences.

As Cupitt has put it,

> Language doesn't copy or convey experience; language determines or forms experience as such. Language "forms" certain events and thereby makes them into conscious experiences. . . . St. John of the Cross did not first have a language-transcending experience and then subsequently try to put it into words. On the

contrary, the very composition of the poem was *itself* the mystical experience.[6]

This does not necessarily imply that religious experiences are nothing more than the projection of fantasies onto the world, but it does mean that vocabulary, or mind, and world are systematically interconnected "all the way down." Consequently, we cannot simply appeal to the fact that believers within a specific religious tradition regularly report experiences couched in terms of the vocabulary of that tradition as proof of the tradition's validity.

The second major motif in Cupitt's thinking is his rejection of what he refers to as realism. The term 'realism' is understood in a variety of ways in contemporary academic philosophy, and Cupitt seems to have two, not always clearly distinguished, ideas in mind when he speaks of realism. On the one hand, there is the view, associated with Plato, that there are eternal, unchanging, transcendental norms of truth and value that function as standards of judgment and justification. These universal norms are held to be objective in the sense of being independent of merely human beliefs and desires. Such norms, according to Plato, cannot be found in experience, but must be grasped by the mind, either by rational argument or through intellectual intuition.

Platonic realism played a major role in the history of Christian thought because it seemed both plausible and attractive to meld the idea of an eternal transcendental realm of norms with the images of God found in the Abrahamic tradition. In fact, Nietzsche believed that Platonic realism and Christian theism were simply two sides of the same coin, so that the "death of God" also marked the demise of the idea of a transcendental realm of norms. Cupitt has basically endorsed Nietzsche's diagnosis, and when he criticizes realism what he frequently has in mind is Christian Platonism with its characteristic dualism of an eternal realm that is perfect and unchanging standing over and against a temporal realm that is at best a pale, distorted copy of the eternal.[7]

On the other hand, Cupitt sometimes identifies realism with the idea that the natural world has a fixed, determinate, intelligible character, existing independently of human thought, that can be grasped through the use of the correct vocabulary.[8] These two conceptions of realism have frequently been conflated in western thought because God was seen as the author of the "Book of Nature." However, in recent philosophy the idea that the world has a fixed, determinate character existing independently of human thought has usually been identified with scientific realism, which is the view that the natural sciences reveal the structure of the world as it is in itself. On this view, physical entities and processes function in accordance with natural laws and principles that hold whether we are aware of them or not. This form of realism is typically associated with the idea of scientific progress, whereby succeeding generations of scientists build on the work of their predecessors so as to achieve an ever more accurate and complete understanding of nature. It is important to note that scientific realism, understood in this sense, does not identify reality with any particular scientific theory, but rather, sees the scientific community as converging, over time, on the truth about the nature of reality.

Finally, there is commonsense or pre-reflective realism which is the view that the ordinary objects of experience—plants, animals, other people, dry goods—exist independently of our perception of them, and continue to exist whether they are perceived or not. This is the realism of the "plain man," and it is thoroughly embedded in our ordinary ways of talking about the world. Cupitt's attitude towards commonsense realism is unclear, as his recent embrace of the religion of everyday life might seem to have committed him to the commonsense realism inherent in ordinary language.

Clearly, there is realism and realism, and one should not assume that one size fits all when it comes to arguments for accepting or rejecting some particular form of realism. However, while there are different forms of realism, realists do share the common intuition that there are certain things—such as the physical world, or other people, or God, or mathematical truth, or the moral order—that exist independently of our minds and any particular form of life in which we may happen to participate. Realists need not deny that a significant number of our beliefs and practices are largely, or entirely, social constructions. What they do deny is that this is true of all the norms that regulate our thought and conduct.

If we accept the realist intuition, then getting it right with respect to those things that do exist independently of our minds means being answerable to norms not of our own making. For example, for the scientific realist questions about the causes and effects of global warming are to be resolved by appealing to facts about our climate that exist independently of our awareness of them, and that cannot be altered by how we describe them. Similarly, a moral realist will insist that certain social practices, such as slavery or infanticide, are wrong regardless of the fact that these practices have been very well entrenched in a number of societies.

Cupitt rejects this fundamental realist intuition in favor of a position he refers to as linguistic idealism or discursive idealism.[9] As these labels suggest this view is related to Kant's transcendental idealism, from which Cupitt takes over two key ideas. On the one hand, he accepts what I would call the skepticism inherent in Kant's idealism. This skepticism is expressed in Kant's claim that we cannot know the nature of things in themselves, but only things as they appear to us. Cupitt presents a linguistic version of this skepticism in his claim that all human knowledge is necessarily perspectival and interpretive.[10] The underlying idea here is that a language is a framework that structures that which it depicts or represents in such a way that we cannot separate the mode of representation from that which is being represented so as to grasp the intrinsic nature of the latter. And since we cannot step outside of language, as it were, so as to directly apprehend the true nature of things, our understanding of the world is always conditioned by some linguistic framework or other.

The other major idea of Kant's that Cupitt adopts and modifies is the notion that the human mind is itself the source of the principles used in organizing experience. However, Cupitt rejects Kant's view that there is only one such set of principles in favor of the idea that there are an indefinite number of ways of characterizing and understanding the world in which we live. On this view, which Richard Rorty claims has its roots in nineteenth-century Romanticism,[11] we make our worlds through our various vocabularies, and, it is important to note, there are on this second view a plurality of worlds, no one of which can claim to be the "real world." World-making, on this Romantic understanding, is a creative activity that expresses our interests and values, and the only limits on this activity are those imposed by our imagination and powers of creativity. Seen from this perspective, scientists like Newton or Einstein, or religious visionaries like Jesus or the Buddha, are just as much poets—or makers—as the novelist or painter.[12] The presumption underlying the Romantic idea of language as world-making is that the world in itself is sufficiently plastic as to accept an apparently indefinite variety of forms—an idea that Cupitt has endorsed.[13]

The skeptical and the Romantic aspects of Cupitt's non-realism appear, on the surface, to complement one another, in that the former undercuts any form of realism, while the latter provides us with a reinterpretation of what is going on when we do deploy our various vocabularies. However, I think that, in fact, Cupitt's skepticism and Romanticism are deeply at odds with one another. If the Romantic view is correct, then the world, as it is in itself, is analogous to Aristotle's unformed matter awaiting the organizing activities of a linguistic community. But, how could we ever know this? By hypothesis, all of our awareness of the world is through the medium of some particular vocabulary within which our world has some sort of determinate structure. Furthermore, our interactions with the world, from within the framework of a given vocabulary, reveal that our capacity to alter it is very limited. Can we change, for example, the adverse consequences of diabetes by altering our vocabulary? Can we even significantly alter social realities, such as institutionalized economic inequality, simply by changing the way we talk about them?

It may be that Cupitt is led to believe that we are free to create any world we may choose[14] by the idea that all of our vocabularies are contingent and historically conditioned. But, the fact that none of our vocabularies are a priori necessary does not imply that we can alter them in any way we may wish; for any alteration in a vocabulary will itself be historically conditioned by the context in which it occurs. For example, the so-called "Copernican Revolution," which did involve a significant shift in our way of talking about the earth, the sun, and the planets, was the result of an attempt to deal with problems inherent in the older Ptolemaic astronomy. However, Copernicus literally could not have gone straight to General Relativity, bypassing Kepler and Newton, because the background knowledge necessary for such a shift would not be available for another three hundred and fifty plus years.

The Romantic idea of creating a world, ex nihilo, through a vocabulary, only makes sense from the perspective of a Kantian transcendental ego constituting the principles of experience and knowledge. But, the skepticism inherent in Cupitt's linguistic or discursive idealism undermines the very possibility of such a perspective. Furthermore, if we cannot assert that a particular vocabulary succeeds in capturing the nature of reality, as it is in itself, because doing so would require a "God's eye view" of the world, then for the same reason we also cannot affirm the truth of anti-realism. For the anti-realist does claim to know something very important about the nature of reality, as it is in itself—namely, that none of our vocabularies succeed in capturing it. And how, on his own principles, could he possibly know such a truth? In other words, Cupitt accepts the Kantian idea that it is possible to determine a priori the limits of human knowledge, but he rejects the possibility of a transcendental perspective from which such a determination could be made. More generally, what I am suggesting is that the skepticism inherent in Cupitt's rejection of realism is similar to ancient Pyrrhonian skepticism in that it degenerates into a dogmatism that undermines itself if one attempts to defend it as a systematic theory about the relationship between language and the world.

At this point I want to turn to the question of the pragmatic implications of adopting Cupitt's non-realist interpretation of religious belief. It might seem that the process of abandoning a realist interpretation of Christian vocabulary has been going on in philosophy and theology since at least the time of Kant and Hegel. And in a way it has, as evidenced by those thinkers who over the past two centuries have rejected literalism in favor of the notions of myth, metaphor, and symbol in explicating Christian scripture and belief. Typically, theologians in the nineteenth and twentieth centuries rejected a literal reading of, say, the Biblical stories of miracles, because they believed such a reading is in conflict with the account of nature provided by modern science. That is, they were scientific realists, of one stripe or another, and believed that given our knowledge of physics and chemistry people cannot do such things as walk on water or turn water into wine. However, those modern theologians who have evoked the concepts of myth or metaphor or symbol in interpreting the Gospels, or Christian doctrine, have tended to understand these concepts in realist terms. That is, religious myths, metaphors, and symbols were understood as pointing to something real beyond themselves which cannot be described in literal terms. This view was explicitly defended by Paul Tillich a generation ago,[15] and it is still to be found among contemporary thinkers whom he influenced.[16] In other words, while theological liberals tended to reject the reality of certain elements in the tradition they have continued to affirm the reality of other aspects of their faith, particularly the reality of God, however that might be conceived.

Thus, I think it is more accurate to say that historically the disputes between liberal and conservative Christian theologians over the past two centuries have generally taken place within a realist philosophical framework, and the differences between these groups of thinkers have to do with the kind of reality each affirms as fundamental. These differences might be roughly characterized as follows: Liberals have typically accepted the main principles of the modern scientific account of the natural world, and, consequently, have either rejected or reinterpreted those elements of the Christian tradition that appear to conflict with that account, while attempting to preserve what they take to be the fundamental truth of Christianity. Conservatives, on the other hand, have taken one form or another of traditional Christianity as universally and unqualifiedly true and, as a result, have either rejected or reinterpreted those aspects of the scientific understanding of the world that they believe conflict with their faith.

Though Cupitt typically comes down on the "liberal side" of theological issues, his philosophical theology actually bypasses the whole controversy between Christian liberals and conservatives. On the one hand, the skepticism inherent in his anti-realism undercuts any attempt to answer the sort of epistemological and ontological questions—such as those concerning revelation and the divinity of Jesus—that have divided liberals from conservatives. While, on the other hand, the notion that our vocabularies create our worlds implies that theological liberals and conservatives, or fundamentalists, simply have different ways of talking about such things as the resurrection, atonement, revelation, and God, that express different, though related, constructions of the Christian life. From the perspective of Cupitt's linguistic, or discursive, idealism there is no "right" way to engage in such talk, as that very notion presupposes, on his view of the matter, the possibility of a "God's eye view" of reality.[17]

I think it is fair to say that the overwhelming majority of practicing Christians would reject Cupitt's account of their faith, were they to become aware of it. They do not regard this faith as a linguistic construction that has no reference to any reality external to itself. Rather, they view disagreements between Christians and non-Christians about such things as the possibility and extent of divine action in the world as not just a matter of how we choose to talk, but as having to do with "what really happens."

The sharp contrast between the way in which most Christians understand their own beliefs, and Cupitt's non-realist interpretation of those beliefs is analogous to a situation where an anthropologist offers an interpretation of the beliefs and practices of a tribe that the members of that tribe reject. In such situations it is always possible that the members of the tribe are radically self-deceived, and that the anthropologist is benefiting them by helping them shed their illusions and change their ways. This certainly seems to be Cupitt's view of the matter.[18] On the other hand, it may be that Cupitt's own interpretation, and subsequent redescription, of the beliefs and practices of those who identify with the Christian tradition is fundamentally misconceived.

The question of which of these alternatives to accept is sharpened by the fact that a widespread acceptance of Cupitt's views by Christians would, in all likelihood, result in significant changes in both their beliefs and their practices. For example, the vocabulary of prayer and worship is filled with expressions implying the active presence of something other than a product of contingent human activity to which we should be responsive in both word and deed. If large numbers of Christians embraced the idea that this vocabulary is no more right or wrong in terms of capturing an extra-linguistic reality than any other vocabulary, something would have to give. Either they would simply give up using the traditional words, or those words would be radically reinterpreted, or the words would be emptied of meaning and "go dead," all of which is already happening with many liberal Christians. In fact, I would suggest that

Cupitt's own intellectual and spiritual odyssey that has led to his finally abandoning traditional Christian vocabulary altogether is simply the working out, in his life, of the logic of anti-realism.

In other words, I think that the "pull towards realism" is too strong in traditional Christian vocabulary for that vocabulary to survive the sort of reinterpretation of its function required by Cupitt's anti-realism. In this respect, anti-realism has a destabilizing effect on ordinary Christian belief, and, by implication, practice. The situation might appear to be different with respect to a religious vocabulary—i.e., a vocabulary that enables us to talk about the world and life as a whole in such a way as to give meaning to our lives—in which the concepts of a transcendental deity and a realm beyond this world are absent.

In recent years Cupitt has focused on what he thinks is the emergence of a new religion of everyday life that lacks any notion of a divine being and that is thoroughly committed to this world. He finds evidence for this new religion in the very widespread use of a number of idioms containing the word 'life' that he claims are replacing older, more traditional religious idioms as our operative totalizing terms for talking about life and its meaning.[19] In *Life, Life* Cupitt discusses a number of these "life-idioms," and attempts to show that their use implies some fairly substantive claims about life and the world. I want to put the question of the merits of Cupitt's analysis of so-called "life-idioms" to one side, and turn, instead, to the question of how we are to interpret those claims about life that, on his view, are implicit in our use of these idioms. For example, when he says,

> But the way we use metaphors, and other expressions as 'the run of the balls', 'the luck of the draw', and 'the lap of the gods', shows that in the end we know that everything is the product of time and chance: everything just happens (13)

we have to ask whether this assertion is to be interpreted in a realist or a non-realist mode. Cupitt's answer is that it all depends on whether one is an insider or an outsider. As he puts it, "And is it not also obvious that a big religious system looks like a communal dream to outsiders, but feels like plain fact to insiders?" (93). Thus, insiders—those whose lives are guided by a belief such as "Everything just happens,"—will interpret it in a realist sense, in that they will take it as a comment on the ways of the world, whereas outsiders—those whose lives are not so guided—will not. For example, an outsider like a traditional Christian will say "It only appears to you secular humanists that everything just happens; in reality everything that occurs is the will of God." But, Cupitt also goes on to claim

that it is possible to, in effect, be both an insider and an outsider at
the same time and maintain a double perspective on such claims as
"Everything just happens." This possibility is one that he suggests
we accept with irony and humor (93). Presumably it is the final step
in our becoming fully self-conscious of our own role in creating
meaning for our lives.

All of this sounds like a post-modern update on Kant's idea that
the subject is the source of those principles which create the possibility of both empirical knowledge and genuine morality. Thus,
for Kant, what from the perspective of the empirical self is objective
knowledge of the world and the external constraints of duty is, from
the perspective of the transcendental, or noumenal, self, a product
of its own autonomous rationality. But, the possibility of this double
perspective in Kant's philosophy is crucially dependent on establishing and maintaining a rigid dichotomy between the two selves and
their respective realms.

Thus, we need to ask whether Cupitt's suggestion that it is
possible for a person to maintain stable realist and anti-realist perspectives on the same beliefs at the same time makes sense in the
ordinary world in which we live. At first glance the suggestion looks
plausible because there are real-life cases where belief and an awareness of the possibility of doubt about the same subject matter can
co-exist. Let me explain: When we choose a course of action we
do so from within a network of interrelated beliefs. If we are honest with ourselves we will recognize that future experience, or the
criticisms of others, or reflection, may lead us to modify or give up
entirely some of our beliefs. Furthermore, we also recognize that
we cannot tell beforehand which beliefs we will be led to modify
or give up. This recognition is nothing more than an acceptance
of our fallibility as finite human beings. Now it is quite possible to
combine resolute action, which does require some stability of conviction, with an awareness of one's fallibility. For example, doctors
typically make diagnoses and prescribe medications on the basis of
what they recognize is a very incomplete and imperfect understanding of important relevant factors, such as the possible side effects of
the medicines they prescribe.

But, the conscientious doctor who acts for the good of the
patient knowing full well that he could be mistaken in his diagnosis
or prescribed course of treatment is not an anti-realist. In recognizing his fallibility he is not entertaining the thought that his entire
network of belief regarding the practice of medicine is, or might be,
mistaken. Such a thought, if not merely notional, would put him in
a position where he would have no reason on the basis of his medical

beliefs to choose one diagnosis or treatment over another, which is to say that he would cease to be a doctor, except, perhaps, in name only. The point here is that we can doubt a belief within a network of beliefs only when we continue to trust the others. And while such a generalized trust is quite compatible with the recognition that it is sometimes misplaced, it is not compatible with global doubt.

There are situations, however, where global doubt about a network of belief and associated practice can, apparently, be combined with belief and engagement in that practice. For example, imagine an attorney who in practice is thoroughly committed to the norms of her profession, but who, on reflection, has fundamental doubts about those norms. This seems to be a case of a person who is both an insider and an outsider, though not really at the same time. While arguing a case in court she has to be convincing, and the best way to do this is to be convinced—a fact of which she may well be aware—but, after the dust of battle has subsided she may view the norms of the legal profession as a sham and a fraud whose primary function is to serve the interests of the wealthy and powerful. Is such a possibility believable? I think so, up to a point. The problem for our hypothetical lawyer is keeping her private doubts about the legal profession out of her public life, and this will not be easy. As Michael Williams has pointed out, even Rorty is concerned about the impact of private irony on public commitment.[20]

There is a philosophical model for Cupitt's idea of a double perspective on our beliefs, but it is one that does not comport with his own principles. According to Hume, we cannot establish that objects of perception exist independently of the mind and continue to exist when unperceived, or that those objects are linked by the principle of cause and effect. But, he also believed that this skepticism cannot be sustained in practice. Once we leave the study and become engaged in life our skeptical doubts on these subjects vanish. Thus, reflection generates skeptical doubt that cannot be resolved through further reflection, but these doubts have no effect on conduct.

Hume's explanation of this phenomenon involves distinguishing between two sources of belief. On the one hand, our basic, "natural beliefs," such as that water quenches thirst and where there's smoke there's fire are the products of what he calls custom and habit, which is a form of conditioning. These natural beliefs are inculcated in us from our earliest years as a result of our interactions with the world, and they are quite literally unshakable in practice. On the other hand, there are "higher order" beliefs that arise from various sources, including reflection. And reflection leads us to realize that our basic "natural beliefs" not only have no rational justification, but are, in fact, contrary to the dictates of reason. According to Hume, both our "natural beliefs" and our skeptical doubts about the world are stable because neither is able to subvert the other.[21]

Thus, Hume can make sense of the possibility of our having a stable double perspective on some of our beliefs with his view that the beliefs in question are the causal consequences of our interactions with the world. Moreover these "natural beliefs," which we do not choose and which we cannot alter at will, are those that constitute the common public world in which we live. It is the beliefs that arise from other sources, such as religious belief, which Hume sees as the product of imagination, that can be destabilized by doubt. But, this theory of "natural belief" is fundamentally at odds with any form of idealism in which a subject freely constitutes his world. On Hume's view, we are animals within the world, subject to its causal laws, and many of our beliefs are to be explained in those terms.

Let us return to the question that prompted this discussion: it seems to me that we can make no sense of Cupitt's idea of a stable double perspective on our beliefs—where one and the same belief can be interpreted in both realist and non-realist terms by the same person at the same time—unless we have recourse to Kant's idea of a double subject. But, this is surely a desperate strategy. Hence, the only people who can be insiders as far as the religion of everyday life is concerned are those who lack full self-awareness. And what of those people who become aware that the world in which they live is "just another interpretation" which is no more correct or incorrect than any other? As Williams asks, "Why doesn't such skepticism lead to cynicism, to a lack of commitment, to a life of self-involvement?"[22]

It is time to step back from the present discussion and take stock of the situation. Anti-realism is a deflationary theory that undermines any attempt to establish some particular vocabulary as the uniquely correct vocabulary with respect to capturing the nature of reality, as it is in itself. For some anti-realists, like Richard Rorty, the primary target is modern scientism that privileges the vocabularies of the natural sciences, and in particular physics. While Cupitt also rejects the metaphysical claims associated with scientism, I think it is clear his primary target is traditional Christian orthodoxy and those pre-critical metaphysical theories that have been used in the attempt to provide intellectual foundations for that orthodoxy.

One of the apparent advantages of adopting a non-realist interpretation of Christian vocabulary is that it relieves Christian theologians of the onerous task of having to come to grips with those intractable epistemological and ontological issues that have bedeviled Christian thought in the modern era. For from an anti-realist perspective all vocabularies, as vocabularies, are on the same footing—they are the various expressions of an individual's or community's self-understanding. Thus, anti-realism appears to do away with the idea that Christian or other religious vocabularies are intellectually suspect, and have to be justified in a way in which, say, the vocabulary of carpentry does not.

But, these apparent virtues also harbor vices. As I pointed out at the outset, Christian vocabulary is inherently theory laden, and its use commits one to some rather large claims about life and the world that go well beyond the realm of ordinary life and experience. Thus, the concept of Christian non-realism is an oxymoron, and the attempt to realize this concept in practice will inevitably destabilize ordinary Christian belief and practice. Cupitt's idea of a religion of everyday life suffers from similar problems. If it makes sense to develop a vocabulary for talking about life and its meaning as a whole it will necessarily involve those sorts of large claims—e.g., "Life is contingent"—that qualify as metaphysical assertions, if anything does. And the attempt to interpret such assertions in non-realist terms will have much the same effect as it does on Christian vocabulary.

The idea that all of our vocabularies are simply different ways of constituting different worlds also has its problems. Some vocabularies, such as those of witchcraft and racism should be abandoned altogether, whereas others, such as that of traditional Christianity, need, in the opinion of many, to be significantly modified. Anti-realists like Cupitt and Rorty are absolutely correct in their insistence that there is no "God's eye view" from which we can separate the sheep from the goats in our various vocabularies. When we do criticize or modify a vocabulary we necessarily do so from within a vocabulary. Sometimes we criticize a vocabulary from within the same vocabulary, as when Christian civil rights advocates criticized other Christians for attempting to defend segregation by appealing to passages in the *Bible*, or scientists modify theories on the basis of their commitment to other scientific principles. At other times the criticisms are external, as when scholars urge that critical historical studies of Christian origins warrant modifications in traditional Christian vocabulary. Thus, in practice, we are always privileging one vocabulary, or part of a vocabulary, over another. Though, unless one is an ideologue or fanatic, it is not always the same vocabulary that gets privileged.

From the perspective of anti-realism all of this looks more or less arbitrary, which Cupitt, in effect, acknowledges when he says in *Life, Life,*

A consequence of the view of our human condition that I have just described is that it is much less easy than it used to be to draw clear lines between fact and fiction, and between what's real and what is 'merely' a communal dream. (92)

The issue here is not merely a theoretical one, as we have all sorts of people in our world who wish to impose their fanatical and frequently violent "communal dreams" on the rest of us. Now it is, of course, naïve to imagine that religious or political fanatics will be swayed by philosophical arguments over realism and anti-realism. But, we do need both the intellectual resources to combat superstition and bigotry, and a common public forum in which these resources can be deployed in order to try to reach those who are not yet caught up in communal fantasies or who, while being participants, have doubts and reservations. Our problem is that the older Enlightenment values which once provided such resources, and created a public forum for their application, have been justifiably criticized, and in some cases justifiably rejected. But, this only makes our present situation more serious. And my concern with anti-realism is not only that it does not contribute to the task of providing such intellectual resources, but that it further undermines those we already have.

Relational Theology in the Second Axial Age

A Response to Don Cupitt's Religious Theory

Darren J. N. Middleton

Difference is the big question that bedevils us today.

—**Diana Eck**

Introduction

I thrum to Don Cupitt's theory of religion.[1] His outline
of platonism's demise and non-realism's rise as well as
life's prominence and religious short-termism's value describes my
Western liberal Christianity. Yet I must also admit some misgivings.
Certain qualms emerged as I discussed these ideas with my wife, an
historian of American evangelicalism, who helped me sense the gulf
between my world, which is, in many ways, the world of the Western
academic theologian, and that of her subjects, the 46 percent of
Americans who describe themselves as "born-again Christians."[2]
A joint trip to the African subcontinent, which, according to several missiologists, holds the key to Christianity's future, as well as
involvement in the African contingent of the World Council of
Churches (Zimbabwe, 1998) only confirmed this disconnectedness.[3] And this disconnectedness, I think, comes from my sense that
Cupitt captures the ways in which life has changed in the last two
hundred years but also falls prey, like many of us, to the Western
academy's tendency to underestimate the vastly *different* ways others experience these changes. It is precisely these differences that
make any universal assessment problematic. Yet Cupitt's own methodology–searching for, collecting, and upholding applied *stories*
within a relational philosophy–provides a means to build and cross a
bridge of understanding between multiple worlds.[4]

What I suggest here is that Cupitt offers some powerful pro-
nouncements on religion in the new Axial Age. After rehearsing several of his insights, I will sketch my main idea: Christianity's future
lies in those local assemblies who articulate their grasp of the gospel

155

against their own cultural backgrounds, and who embrace their indigenous traditions while remaining open to initiatives beyond their own circles. Unless we Western academics learn to engage difference through the mutual exchange of local stories, we will find ourselves, as the popular series indicates, "left behind" in the First Axial Age.

Cupitt's Theory of Religion

Cupitt says that with respect to contemporary life, pluralism prevails. In his last two books *Emptiness and Brightness* (2001) and *Life, Life* (2003), he announces that humankind is entering its Second Axial Age.[5] According to this Age's world view, there is no ready-made, Real World out there, separate from life's shimmering flux and mutability. For Second Axial Agers, there is only becoming, an emergent evolution signifying happenstance's victory over pre-established Metaphysical Fact.[6] In Cupitt's own words:

> Everything is contingent, everything is transient, everything is "Empty" (in the Buddhist sense: it lacks a stable, permanent essence of its own. It consists merely in its own shifting relations with everything else). Everything is a product of time and chance. We should see the world–that is, we should see all reality–as a fountain, a silent ceaseless outpouring of purely contingent Being, which all the time is getting coded into signs in our seeing of it and then passes away, perhaps to be recycled . . . Everything just happens, everything is just hap, and of course all this is as true also of ourselves, our ideas, our words, our values, our thoughts and fears, as it is of the so-called external world.[7]

Cupitt clearly rejects the platonic and classically Christian vision for the truly Nietzschean and Nagarjunanian one, with its emphasis upon universal contingency, impermanence, and emptiness.[8] Emptiness, however, is not where it ends. Cupitt holds that language takes life's emptiness, encodes it, and makes our world bright and beautiful. As he puts it, we see "everything in terms of words and numbers and thereby make it all into a brightly lit, consciously seen and possessed world of our own."[9] In other words, we create reality, or brightness, through language. The world receives fullness through us. By concentrating intently on the idea that nothing is stable or fixed, we find ourselves dealing with everything in disinterestedness. The phrase, "Empty radical humanism" describes this process of nothing(ness) and everything(ness):

> We are, we live, we represent ourselves to ourselves and to the world in our language—that is, in the flow of language through

us. That's why I am talking about *Empty* radical humanism. I am proposing a theatrical view of the self: a person is not a substance but a role, a *dramatis persona*. We live and perform only in the show we are putting on: and when the show is over, so are we.

Not only the world, but we also—our lives, our thoughts, our faith and our values–are held within and formed by the ceaseless dance to and fro of language. It enfolds everything—including us. That is why humanism (the world fully becomes itself, formed, theorized, "bright," only in *us* and in our description of it, so that we are the only world makers, and our philosophy is rightly anthropocentric), this radical humanism of ours turns Empty. For we find that we must take a thoroughly naturalistic and post-metaphysical view of the self, as of the world. The consolation, as we will see, is that Emptiness is bliss. The more I understand that I am but part of the universal flux of everything, the more I am united with it. I begin to see the possibility of solar ethics and of a new kind of eternal happiness as I burn, burn out and pass away in union with everything else.[10]

In the end, Cupitt challenges us to befriend our own constructed-ness, finding irresistible the empty world we ignite with imagina-tion's fire, even if it will, along with us, burn out and pass away.[11]

Three Qualms

Cupitt's world of emptiness and brightness delights, admonishes, yet also unhinges me. Perhaps he intends this unhinging as part of the process toward brightness. However, three qualms persist.

First, we are hundreds of philosophical years from Heraclitus and Plato. We have journeyed through the Age of Renaissance, the Age of Reason, and we are now in the Second Axial Age. But who forms this Second Axial Age? Is it Western academics and liberal skeptics, devout religious practitioners and participants in popular movements, or postcolonials and non-Western thinkers? According to Cupitt, ordinary people shape the Second Axial Age. They are creating reality. But what reality, or realities, are they creating? And how do these realities reflect Cupitt's outline of Second Axial Age thinking? Looking at the West, we might ask if ordinary people really believe in non-realism, or is it more accurate to say that most women and men, living in a world with all its change, subscribe to philosophical and theological foundationalism?[12] And what does this matter? It is no secret that North American Protestant evangelical-ism, marked by non-denominational Christianity, Pentecostalism, and other, new forms of orthodoxy, holds an enormous appeal at the present time.[13] Certainly, we can claim that this is the *possible* result of realism's collapse. It seems, however, that Cupitt is at least more prescriptive than descriptive when he speaks about the Second Axial Age.[14] What, then, is our responsibility to the everyday experience of religious people? How do we account for beliefs and practices that often fly in the face of our own? How do we write of them without dismissing them?

Second, Cupitt suggests that "so much literary art will be required to maneuver the ordinary person into seeing" the value of what he calls the Second Axial Age's "immediate" and "beliefless religion."[15] In his view, however, this literary art will not revolve around the Christian story-cycle of Fall and Redemption, since such stories are spent forces, utterly obsolete, "and the number of writers who can usefully be kept employed in retelling them is clearly very limited."[16] If we look at popular culture, however, this story-cycle holds wide appeal. While Western academics like Cupitt are abandoning the story-cycle, for many it continues to fill an essential need.[17] How do those of us who experience it as a spent force explain its persistence in the lives of so many?

Third, we are just now beginning to encounter other, non-Western stories in postcolonial nations. Such stories reflect fresh, at least to us, understandings of the everyday lives of women, children, and men struggling for religious identity, cultural renewal, political freedom, and economic development.[18] If we listen to these stories, we find that they illustrate how diverse people in various locales respond to the worldwide cultural revolution Cupitt names the Second Axial Age. We Western academics often consult non-Western sources. Cupitt, for example, is drawn to Buddhist stories. But we often underestimate their cultural specificity, how the stories non-Westerners tell stem from their own unique challenges, quarrels, compromises, and victories.[19] Today, Africa, Asia, and the Pacific are sites of open, plural conversations on their ancient traditions of thought and ways they may be used to engage the West. In one sense, then, Cupitt has never been more right. Rapidly shifting social and cultural changes permeate the world. But people are forging distinctive identities from divergent contexts as they address the challenges that such changes cause.[20] What do we do with stories that might create meaning in a specific environment yet raise serious questions about what contextualization and interreligious encounter means for the church catholic?[21] What do we do with stories that confront and even affront our Western liberal values?

Cupitt is correct. Things are falling apart. Wholesale change is loose upon the world. People are constructing their own realities. But the realities they are constructing are vastly different and many, if not most, do not reflect his understanding of Second Axial Age thinking. If most of us find ourselves in Cupitt's camp, what do we do with thriving evangelicalism, the continuance of Christianity's story-cycle, and non-Western stories that counter-read our own thinking, beliefs, and dare I add, faith?

Relational Theology in the Second Axial Age

While these qualms persist, Cupitt's theory of religion begins to suggest a way to address them. Cupitt might seem at first to concentrate almost wholly on the individual and thereby fall prey to privatism or isolationism. But his emphasis on language and dialogue suggest that it is essential to bind ourselves with other people. *Emptiness and Brightness* closes with these words: "We are seeing Second Axial Period thinking as dominated by the themes of communication and constantly shifting, always emergent consensus. It tends to see meaning as current use, truth as the current state of the argument, and reality as never more than provisionally constructed within an endless open conversation."[22] Like life, religion is relational. That being so, the answer to these three qualms, or more generally the faith's future in the Second Axial Age, is a dialogue characterized by constant movement between differences, the ceaseless to and fro of cultural perspectives, the endless back and forth of ideological nuances, and a conversation that does not fear life's messy verities (with its misunderstandings, setbacks, and disappointments). As Cupitt himself avers, truth depends almost entirely on context. More than ever we need truth that is always in process, avoiding the homogenizing gaze with which we Westerners often view non-Westerners, and that resists settling in any one locale.[23]

The irony is that in an age characterized by global connectedness, and by connectedness I mean here that our thoughts and actions have ramifications far beyond our local context or usual sightlines, disconnectedness seems more prevalent than ever before. It is little wonder that many theologians underscore the dialogical imperative. If we fail to dialogue with, talk to, and engage one another, then we fail to take ideological construction seriously. Moreover, if we fail to take the local, the situational, and the culturally specific seriously, then our only option is to privilege the Western academy or religious liberalism. And such privileging, of course, keeps us stuck in the First Axial Age, under the influence of its most nefarious tendency, namely, the tendency toward using and justifying colonial or imperialist discourse (Western hegemony). This is where Cupitt's work

is so enormously instructive; to maneuver ourselves into the Second
Axial Age, he says, we must conduct endlessly open conversations
in service of more purposeful, integrated, productive, fruitful, and
satisfying lives.[24]

Yet dialogue is an easy answer. The challenge occurs when we
experience realities constructed so differently from our own. Today,
there is no *one* faith to discuss and debate, if ever there was one,
only an explosion of *faiths*–numberless Christianities.[25] How, then,
do groups like the Westar Institute communicate with those outside
its circle? How do Jesus Seminar Fellows and Associates talk to, say,
Vietnamese Catholics, Nigerian Pentecostals, or American Southern
Baptists?

It will not be much help if we, those of us who represent religious
liberalism within the Western academy, seek to speak over other
voices, especially those associated with "Southern Christianities."
After all, postcolonial women, children, and men are entitled to feel
suspicious if at a time when they are beginning to find their voices,
they suddenly find themselves "informed" by Western postmod-
erns—the very individuals who are losing their "privileged" status as
speakers and writers—that language's polysemy rules out notions of
"truth" and "reality." The subaltern must speak. And when it does,
we Western academics would do well to resist rendering the Other
as the negative of what we are and what we do. A similar hermeneutics of generosity must be applied to those Northern Christianities
that we often regard as slipping into the dark ages. The question
concerning what doctrines have become, or should become, fos-
sils in faith's museum is *not* the question that bedevils us today.
Difference—what it looks like, where it appears, what questions it
addresses, who it embodies, and how we respond to it–is.

Let me venture a playful thought-experiment, by way of explaining what I think is at stake here. While Cupitt sees Homer Simpson
as "the modern Everyman, especially of the advanced countries,
especially of the Liberal Protestant English-speaking world, and most
especially of Middle America," I would turn to Hank Hill, star of
the animation series, "King of the Hill," now in its eighth season.[26]
Hank reads life through his Texan lens, including his bafflement at
the Laotian Buddhists, Kahn and Minh Souphanousinphone, who
live next door. Week after week they talk, engage one another, and
yet we sense from their conversation that dialogue, much less understanding, is difficult. In Arlen, their fictional yet very real Texas
town, difference is the question that bedevils Hank, Kahn, and
their loved ones. Two illustrations come to mind. In one episode,
the Kahns throw a part on the eve of the Laotian New Year, called
"Pimai," and three visiting monks identify Bobby, Hank's son, as a

potential lama, or "chosen one." No one is more traumatized than Hank. And when Bobby starts meditating, attending Buddhist Club meetings, and peacefully solving conflicts within the neighborhood, Hank is appalled and tells Bobby, "There will be no enlightenment in this house." He takes Bobby to see Reverend Stroup to get him back in touch with his Methodist roots. But the Reverend feels this is a great opportunity for Bobby to explore his spirituality. The rest of the program is given over to humorous, yet poignant exchanges between the Hills and the Kahns, who, it is clear, must learn to live together in community. Another episode moves these exchanges further. Here Hank's wife, Peggy, finds herself bonding with Kahn's mother. After encountering one another in their backyards, they begin to discuss the problems that mark their own lives–the busyness of Peggy, for example, the loneliness of Kahn's mother, and their sense of place in their families and the community.

How, then, do we incorporate the relational thinking that Cupitt calls for (and that Hank, Peggy, and the Kahn's attempt)? What should we, as Western academics, expect to learn from listening to local stories? For my part, I am "beginning all over again," as Cupitt says we must, by listening to stories from Southern Christians, especially Africans and most recently Ghanaian Rastafarians.

First, I am learning here that various categories and labels appropriate to the West neither hold nor apply to various non-Western Christians. In fact, I am persuaded that the cultural specificities in each case only serve to unfasten our timeworn theological tags. If an Asian Catholic bishop, for example, possesses a lively sense of the supernatural, should we describe him as a "conservative" or a "liberal"? If he then challenges hierarchicalism and endorses indigenization with the curial office, as many in the 1998 Synod of Bishops for Asia did, is he a "liberal" or a "conservative"?[27] Relatedly, how do we characterize African Episcopalians who point to the New Testament to disfavor women's and homosexual's ordinations as well as protest capitalism, the World Bank, the International Monetary Fund, and the World Trade Organization, proposing more just and socialist governments in the face of imprisonment and sometimes torture? What is the meaning, or even helpfulness, of "fundamentalist," "conservative," "liberal," "radical," "pre-enlightenment," and "post-enlightenment" here?[28] Put differently, what is the value of judging others by our own standards? A simple reading of the conferences of the Ecumenical Association of Third World Theologians (EATWOT) confirms that such judgments carry little-to-no value whatsoever. I might add that these publications offer some of the most exciting and challenging theological discourse of this age. Indeed, numerous scholars maintain that we have really learned nothing about non-Western Christianities if we, as Westerners, insist on using our old terms, categories, and criteria for others. As Arun Jones maintains, "it would be helpful to keep in mind that Christians outside the West are highly sensitive to westerner's sense of their own superiority, especially because westerners came preaching a gospel of equality and mutual respect."[29]

Second, I would also insist that we need not completely abandon Western liberal values, creeds, and terminologies. I say this because liberal presuppositions form the basic makeup of my world. They are part of my local story. And whenever I engage others, especially those who model difference to me, I engage them candidly. I do this by spinning my life's yarn, weaving its many strands together, including those strands that signify Western liberalism. But I know it is not helpful to assume, as many in the First Axial Age did, that the way we liberals read stories, evaluate life, and inform ethics should be canon for others. This does not mean that we throw away our readings, philosophies, and moralities. But it does mean that we use them cautiously, particularly when moving outside our context. Western philosophy defined the First Axial Age, in more ways than one, and along the way, this worldview created colonialism and imperialism, patronage systems that assumed theories of right and wrong. Yet now we declare that the Second Axial Age is among us. But there is no Second Axial Age if, once again, Western academic elites are still telling Africans, Asians, Pacific Islanders, lay persons, and all those outside their boundaries, how they should think and act, what stories they should be telling, and what type of churches they should attend. If we take Cupitt's claims about the Second Axial Age seriously, then we must regard it as something brand new. We only mislead ourselves if we claim something novel yet continue to practice business as usual. If we live in a truly different age, then we, as Western academics, must interrogate both Western hegemony and its drive for homogenization, including that of the liberal agenda.

Gianni Vattimo notes that because we live in the midst of a Babel-like postmodern pluralism, hospitality is the best response, at least for now, to this new era together with its many, divergent challenges.[30] Our task is to allow the guest, the Other, to guide our conversations. This strategy entails that hospitality precedes consensus.[31] If everything is emergent, as Cupitt claims, then this means that truth never settles, never becomes stable or fixed, but is constantly on-the-move.[32] Western liberalism only reinscribes First Axial Age hegemony if it desires "settling" in the form of "consensus." In the end, I think dialogue and listening affirm impermanence, the sort of impermanence in which Cupitt delights. Yet if we truly desire to enter and live in the Second Axial Age, with its "endless exchange and change," we must be prepared to go back-and-forth, to-and-fro, between local stories, vernacular faiths, and grassroots theologies, those of our own as well as others. We cannot give up our own stories, faiths, and theologies, but through movement, the movement of dialogue, we all might find ourselves in a different place.

A Path of Faith to
the Global Future

Lloyd Geering

H umankind today stands today at a critical point in its
long and complex history. Too few people realise this.
We are moving into an increasingly global future. Not only are we
becoming dependent on a global economy but the many diverse
cultures of the past are being drawn into a cultural maelstrom. All
this, coupled with the advanced state of our technology, means that
humankind faces a common future or no future at all. These alternatives were well expressed in the Mosaic tradition in words, not
written by Moses but by Jews some six hundred years later, trying
to interpret the God of Moses for the critical times in which they
lived.

I have set before you this day life and death, blessing and curse.
Now choose life, so that you and your children may live.

But whoever would choose death and curse? The words are really
challenging us to become wise enough to know the path that leads
to life?

The cultural paths that led us to the present were not only diverse
but must now adapt themselves to the new global context. Just as
our view of the universe has changed out of all recognition in the
last four hundred years, so also has our understanding of culture,
of religion and of the human condition itself. Far from the human
species being created in its current form at the beginning of time, it
took aeons for humanity and culture to evolve in tandem. By "culture" I mean "that complex whole which, grounded in a common
language, includes the knowledge and beliefs which constitute a
particular worldview, along with a set of customs, morals, skills, and
arts, with which to respond to that world."

From time immemorial our ancestors took their respective cultures for granted. Being immersed in culture from birth they were

unaware of their dependence upon it. They took language for granted, much as we take for granted the air we breathe. People never
thought of language as something humanly created. Language was
assumed to have existed before the beginning of time; indeed, in
the biblical myth of origins, it was the very instrument by which the
world was created. God had only to say, "Let there be light!" and
there was light.

It is only since the time of Charles Darwin that all this has been
turned upside down. We have come to realise that human languages
and cultures have slowly evolved out of the primitive social life of
our pre-human ancestors. They began more than a million years
ago. Whether there ever was a proto-language and a proto-culture
we do not know. What we do know is that, as the human species
spread around the globe, it created thousands of languages, cultures
and subcultures.

What made human culture possible was the human ability to create symbols; it is the symbolization of sounds that formed the basis
of language. Culture is the man-made environment of thought and
meaning by which we interpret our experience of reality. Culture
differentiates us from the other higher animals even more than the
genes which determine our physical form. We become human as we
are shaped by the culture into which we are born. But we in turn
help to shape the culture we pass on to the next generation.

Each culture is an ever evolving and developing continuum of
words, stories, ideas, codes of behaviour and social practices. It flows
through time like an ever-changing stream. Today the many cultural
streams from the past are flowing into one global sea. They not only
have to compete with one another but they are contributing to the
formation of an (as yet incipient) global culture.

The coming global culture will be humanistic because all cultures, being human creations, have a common human base. It will
also be secular. By secular I mean "this-worldly and natural" as
opposed to "other-worldly and supernatural." The modern knowledge explosion has brought about the gradual dissolution of the
worldview, which divided the universe into the dichotomous realms
of natural/supernatural, earthly/heavenly, and material/spiritual.
That worldview has been replaced by one that sees reality as one
vast physical universe of astronomic dimensions of space and time.
This universe operates according to its own internal laws and is self-
evolving. What our forbears took to be signs of supernatural forces
turn out to be the products of primitive interpretation and human
imagination.

Secular does not mean "non-religious." Religion is the depth
dimension of every culture. It is that which provides culture with

motivation and cohesion. It is not **some thing** that can be added to culture or taken away from it. Religion has been usefully defined as "a total mode of the interpreting and living of life." Because the popular use of the word "religion" is too often identified with supernatural beliefs, that distinguished scholar of world religions, W. Cantwell Smith proposed that we should replace the word "religion" with two other terms—the "cumulative tradition" and "faith."

The term faith refers to the internal attitude of trust in relation to life in the world. Christians have no monopoly of it, even though it has been one of their basic words. Faith of some kind is essential to human existence. We humans cannot live well without faith or trust. The absence of faith leads to depression, lack of motivation and despair. When Jesus said to the woman, "Your faith has made you whole," he was not referring to her beliefs but to her trust and attitude to life. I shall return to this later.

Smith's term "cumulative tradition" refers to the objective products of faith within a particular culture—such as stories, Holy Scriptures, temples, and sacred practices. The cumulative tradition marks out the path of faith being trodden in that culture. It is the product of faith, and though it serves to nurture the faith of later generations it is not to be confused with faith. Where this confusion does unfortunately happen, faith is replaced by idolatry. Most cumulative traditions become strewn with fallen idols. In a vibrant culture the inner experience of faith is continually manifesting itself in new creations as it responds to the circumstances of its time. As Smith said, "One's beliefs belong to the century one lives in, but what endures from generation to generation is the inner experience of faith."

Now let us turn to the path of faith that is often referred to today as the Judeo-Christian tradition. It has always been manifesting some change; there have been innumerable examples of both continuity and discontinuity in its four thousand year history. But there have been two major periods of quite radical cultural change. The first was when it came to birth during what is now called the First Axial Period.

The year 500 BCE marks the approximate centre of the First Axial Period. It divided the cultural evolution of humankind much more distinctively than did the Christian division of time into BC and AD. During the First Axial period, and for the first time in known human history, many great cultural traditions came under critical examination. Courageous new steps were taken by thinkers and charismatic teachers. They are known today as the prophets of Israel, the Iranian prophet Zoroaster, the Buddha, Mahavira, the Hindu seers, the Chinese teachers Confucius and Lao Tzu, and the philosophers of ancient Greece.

Out of the First Axial Period emerged the new cultural traditions of Buddhism, Hinduism and Confucianism in the Far East; in the Middle East they were chiefly Zoroastrianism, Judaism, Platonism and Stoicism. Judaism further evolved into the triple-stranded monotheistic tradition of Judaism, Christianity and Islam. All these not only influenced one another but also increasingly replaced or absorbed the cultural traditions that had preceded them—traditions based both on ethnic ties and the veneration of the forces of nature.

The term Second Axial Age refers to the cultural and religious change by which the Western world gave birth to the modern global, secular and humanistic world, which is now spreading round the globe. The Second Axial Age emerged out of the Judeo-Christian tradition, just as the First Axial Age arose out of the ethnic and nature cultures that had preceded it. We can trace it in part to the philosophy of William of Ockham, already labelled the *Via Moderna*. That and other seeds began to germinate in the Renaissance humanists, the Protestant Reformation and the Enlightenment. No one of its pioneering figures, such as Erasmus, Luther, John Locke, ever thought of himself as departing from the Christian tradition.

Yet it became clear, as time went on, that the emerging secular and humanistic world is not Christian in the way pre-modern Christendom was. But neither is it anti-Christian. It is best described as post-Christian, for it still reflects the values and customs of the tradition that gave it birth.

Too few recognise the continuity between the modern secular world and the Christian world out of which it emerged. Fundamentalists, both Christian and Muslim, treat the coming of the humanistic and secular world as the spread of the domain of Satan and hence an enemy to fought. This is because they identify their respective traditions with doctrines formulated to fit the supernaturalistic world-view of the past. Even the main line churches, struggling to retain their identity, too often fall into the same superficial judgment.

Those Christians who treat past creeds as absolute and unchangeable not only replace genuine faith with idolatry and blind superstition but they impede the legitimate evolution of the Judeo-Christian tradition. Instead of being the promoters of faith, as they claim to be, they become the defenders of idolatry and superstition. I define superstition as any belief or practice that has outlived the now obsolete cultural context in which it was appropriate.

Today's secular culture evolved out of Christian culture in much the same way as Christian culture evolved out of Jewish culture. Just as the Christian tradition claimed to be the legitimate fulfilment of Judaism, so the modern, secular and humanistic world is

the legitimate flowering of some basic Christian affirmations, such
as the incarnation. The enfleshment of the divine within the human
condition can be expressed in today's terminology as the humanisa-
tion of God, the secularisation of the divine, and the earthing of
heaven. Indeed, the post-Christian culture of the West should now
be called the Judeo-Christian-secular tradition, in order to specify
the chief phases through which it has passed.

In each of the Axial transitions there has been both continuity
and discontinuity. The old and the new exist in tension alongside of each other for quite some time, giving rise often to bitter
antagonism. Only when viewed from a distance does the continuity
become apparent. That is why, living as close as we do to the Second
Axial Period, we are much more aware of the discontinuity than of
the continuity. On the other hand, we are so used to affirming the
continuity in the Judeo-Christian tradition that we often fail to see
the discontinuity that occurred at the First Axial Period.

Up until then all human cultures explained the phenomena of
nature as acts performed by a plethora of gods and spirits. These gods
were created by the symbol-making capacity of the human imagination. Each god had his or her own proper name and was allotted a
particular function to perform. The word "god" was a generic term
referring to a class of spiritual beings.

In the sixth century BCE the Greek philosopher Xenophanes
subjected the gods to critical examination. He condemned them for
their immorality and poked fun at their anthropomorphic character.
In India Gautama the Buddha took a different approach. He judged
the gods to be irrelevant to the religious quest for human fulfilment;
the gods were marginalized, and eventually faded from Buddhist
terminology.

The Israelite prophets pioneered the Judeo-Christian tradition
by openly attacking the gods of the other nations, warning their
people not "to go after other gods to their own hurt." In the sixth
century BCE they went much further, poking fun at all the gods,
scornfully dismissing them as having no reality; gods were simply
human creations. Here was radical discontinuity with the past. But,
unlike the Buddhists, the Israelites retained the Hebrew word for
"the gods"—*elohim* (plural in form). Here was continuity. But the
word received a new meaning. The word *elohim*, which once denoted
a class of beings, now came to be treated as a personal name. For
the Jews, henceforth, all divine power became concentrated into one
unseeable spiritual force. Thus was born monotheism.

There was further discontinuity. Before the Babylonian Exile the
people of Israel, like all other peoples, had a land of their own, and
the gods had their own dwelling-places, called temples. During and

after the Exile the Jewish people ceased to be united by a dynasty and land possession and they eventually they learned to do without a Temple. They became a community held together only by their faith in their cultural tradition. It was then that Judaism came to birth. Thus, in the process of this birth, a radical religious transition had taken took place, to be summarised this way.

1. The traditional gods were rejected and replaced by one God, conceived as the spiritual Creator of the universe and the controller of history.

2. The temple and its priesthood began to be replaced by the synagogue, Holy Scriptures and lay-leadership.

These same radical reforms carried through into the two derivative forms of monotheism—Christian and Islamic. All three were monotheistic, all three had their respective Holy Scriptures, and the non-priestly institution of the synagogue became the prototype of church and mosque. Unfortunately, as the three separate cumulative traditions subsequently developed their own elaborate complexities, Jew, Christian and Muslim lost sight of what all three had in common, including the radical nature of the religious transition that had taken place in the Axial Period.

Jew, Christian and Muslim all claim to worship one God. But is it the same God? The God of monotheism, being invisible, can be known only by appeal to divine revelation; and here lies the problem. The Jewish God revealed his will in the Torah. The Christian God revealed himself in Jesus Christ. The Muslim God revealed his final will in the Qur'an. It is impossible to reconcile these three forms of revelation. Since two of them must be in error, appeal to divine revelation must be fallible. It was only going to be a matter of time before the concept of divine revelation fell into disrepute. This occurred with the critical rational enquiry that gave rise to the Second Axial Period.

At the First Axial Period the gods were declared to be unreal, being the created products of human imagination. In the Second Axial Period the God of classical monotheism has lost reality as a divine person and has come to be seen as a humanly created symbol, referring to a cluster of supreme values. During the last five hundred years our understanding of origins has been turned upside down. We humans used to see ourselves as the creation of a supernatural deity; now we find it is we who created such symbols as God. We can even write a history of God, as Karen Armstrong has done so brilliantly.

Instead of believing ourselves to have been made in the image of a divine being, we find we are earthly organisms who have evolved on this planet. And, like all other planetary organisms, we live a finite existence between conception and death. Compared with the time span of the earth, and even with the life of any particular species, the life of us individual persons seems infinitesimally short. All this and more is what we mean when we speak of the modern world-view as secular or this-worldly.

In this secular view of the universe, God along with his heavenly dwelling-place have lost their objective reality. The concept of divine revelation has proved to be faulty. There is no need to postulate a supernatural creator to explain natural phenomena. Neither do we now expect divine providence to deliver us from our misfortunes. That is why, as theologian John Macquarrie observed, "among educated people throughout the world, the traditional kind of God-talk has virtually ceased." Here lies the discontinuity. As Dietrich Bonhoeffer observed, "People can no longer be religious in the traditional way." The traditional way was dependent on the dualistic world-view that has now become obsolete.

But a new kind of god-talk is taking the place of the old. Here lies the continuity. Just as the Jews retained their word for god but gave it a new meaning, so at this Second Axial Period, god-talk now plays a different role. This had its roots in the biblical tradition itself when it spoke of "the god of Israel," "the god of Abraham," "my god," and "your god." The "god of Abraham" was unseeable; so if one were to ask, "How can I learn about the god of Abraham?" the appropriate answer would be, "Watch how Abraham lives his life. Try to understand what motivates him at the deepest level. That is all you will ever know of the god of Abraham." So, by god-talk in the secular world, one is referring to the values we live by and the goals we aspire to.

In the modern secular world the supernatural forces and the objective personal God have lost their reality. What survives from the Christian past are its human values and motivating aspirations. Some of these, such as love, compassion, and justice, were long treated as the attributes of God. "God is love," says the New Testament. Jesus exhorted us to live like God—"You must be as completely good as is your Father in heaven." The fact that we can now refer to them as human values, and find some of them highly honoured in other cultural traditions also, does not make them any the less important.

Other values, such as freedom, were long prominent in the Judeo-Christian tradition. The pursuit of human freedom started when Moses led the Israelites out of slavery. It went further when Jesus freed people from religious legalism. That is why Paul exclaimed to his Galatian converts, "You were called to freedom" and the Fourth

Evangelist put into the mouth of Jesus, "You shall know the truth and the truth will make you free."

With the coming of the modern world, however, the pursuit of freedom has flourished as never before, starting with the freedom to think for oneself. It was quickly followed by the freedom to speak and to publish. This led to a whole series of emancipations—the democratic emancipation from absolute monarchy, the emancipation of the slaves, the emancipation of women from male domination, and, currently, the emancipation of homosexuals from homophobia. Sadly, the churches have often been initially opposed to these emancipations, just as they now fail to see the signs of the kingdom of God in the coming of the secular world.

The values most highly prized in the secular world are the continuation and expansion of values in the Judeo-Christian tradition. These values, such as love, justice, and freedom, convince us by their own inherent worth. They do not need the support of divine authority. The authority their worth exerts over us has replaced that of the now departing deity. Those persons who love their fellows because they are convinced of the value of love are more morally mature than those who love because they are commanded by a higher authority.

That is why this new cultural age has been called "Humankind's coming of age." Just as an individual, on attaining adulthood, must leave behind the security of parental control, and take responsibility for his or her own actions, so the human race must now learn how to practice love, justice and peaceful co-existence because it recognises their inherent value and not out of fear of Hell or the reward of Heaven.

But "humankind's coming of age" also means that individuals are freer to choose their way of life or path of faith. This is why we have come to value diversity more than conformity. The conformity of belief and practice so dominant in the past made 'heresy' the most heinous of sins. "Heresy" is derived from a Greek word that means "choice"; it is used in the New Testament to refer to those who have the audacity to choose their own way of life in contrast with that of the majority. As Peter Berger pointed out in his book *The Heretical Imperative*, modernity has brought to human life an extraordinary expansion in the choices to be made. This is not only in the supermarket; much more importantly it is in the area of religious belief and practice. We are now free to choose our personal way of life; we do so from a veritable smorgasbord of options. In the free and open society of today the exercise of personal choice is not merely permitted but has become a necessity. We are all forced to be choosers, that is heretics!

The new freedom to choose our way of life, however, brings no guarantee that we shall make wise choices. Just as many an adolescent goes off the rails on reaching adulthood, this danger becomes greatly magnified when the whole human species comes of age, and becomes free from the cultural restraints of the past. The path of faith, along with the moral life, has become personalised as never before, as we are challenged to make new moral decisions and work out our own solutions to the problems of life. Too often people selfishly engage in anti-social behaviour. Too often people abandon one form of superstition only to adopt another one. Too often people abandon the traditional God only to make idols out of material objects or turn to drugs to escape from mundane boredom.

What is the answer to these unfortunate consequences of the new freedom? Some opt to return to the apparent security of the cultural womb from which we all emerged. That is the attraction of the widespread rise of fundamentalism. In so far as this seems to bring immediate relief and spiritual satisfaction, fundamentalists receive their reward, as Jesus might have said. But the fundamentalist response requires one, in ostrich-like fashion, to shut one's eyes and close one's mind to everything that is in conflict with its beliefs.

But though fundamentalism provides no lasting solution, there is one thing we can learn from this modern religious phenomenon. If we are going to find a satisfactory path of faith into the global future, we need to study our cultural past to understand who we are, how we got to where we are, and how we came to discern the supreme human values which still lay a claim upon us. The study of the past illuminates the present but it does not dictate the future. That is why the Bible remains an invaluable set of documents. We learn much from it but we are not bound by it.

To exemplify this I now take three themes from it, which are basic to the Judeo-Christian tradition, and yet universal to the human condition.

The first is faith. Every cultural tradition is a path of faith. The Bible itself emphasizes this when it starts with the figure of Abraham. In these days of increasing contact between the Christian and Islamic worlds it is salutary to remember that the figure of Abraham is equally important to the faith traditions of Judaism, Christianity and Islam. Jews honour Abraham as the father of their nation. Christians honour Abraham as a model man of faith. Muslims honour Abraham as the first Muslim.

But what made Abraham a model man of faith? It was because he heeded the voice he heard within him and, as the New Testament says, went out not knowing where he was to go. He had no map.

He had no Torah, no Bible, and no Qur'an to guide him. The Midrashic Jewish legends even tell how Abraham smashed his father's idols before setting on his journey. **Faith requires us to surrender attachment to all tangibles. For the journey of faith we must be free of all excess baggage.**

The Judeo-Christian tradition has on many occasions found itself so weighed down by its accumulating tradition that it has had to jettison its excess baggage. The Protestant Reformers abandoned a great deal of what had accumulated in mediaeval Christianity, including the belief in Purgatory. The Second Axial Period requires us to jettison a great deal more than the Protestant Reformers did—heaven and hell, a divine saviour, an objective personal deity, and the whole system of dogma constructed around them. Important as these doctrines may have been in the past as the expression of faith, they have now become a hindrance to faith.

Faith is not dependent on belief in a personal God or in any particular object. In common human experience faith is multi-faceted and operates at a variety of levels. That is why, in various secular contexts, we may be exhorted to put faith in ourselves, in our ideas, in other people, in the natural world. It is over to us to clarify for ourselves just what we put our faith in; for that, whatever it is, has become our god. That remarkable Christian visionary and scientist, Teilhard de Chardin, was so awestruck by what he had learned of the self-evolving universe that he once said,

> If, as the result of some interior revolution, I were to lose in succession my faith in Christ, my faith in a personal God, and my faith in spirit, I feel that I should continue to believe invincibly in the world. The world . . . is the first, the last and the only thing in which I believe. It is by this faith that I live. (99)

In this ecologically sensitive age, that is a good place to begin. The evolution of life on this planet is an awe-inspiring mystery and was the process that Teilhard had come to understand as God. The capacity of life both to diversify and to renew itself is more breathtaking than any of the incidental events that were traditionally called miracles. The creativity manifested by the human species in its evolving cultures more than compensates for the vandalizing and destructive tendencies it also possesses. All these observable facts are sufficient to generate faith even though they provide no guarantees. Dispensing with all of the supposed certainties of the past we have to walk into the future depending on faith alone. Faith is a matter of saying "Yes!" to life and all that it offers.

The second theme is hope. This is as basic to the human condition as is faith. "Hope springs eternal in the human breast," said

Alexander Pope. Where hope dies, faith grows weak, for the two are closely allied.

The experience of hope has played a dominant role in the long history of the Judeo-Christian tradition. Abraham looked forward to a city which has foundations. Moses looked to a land flowing with milk and honey. The Babylonian exiles hoped for the restoration of the Kingdom of David. Christians looked for the coming of the Kingdom of God, the very words becoming permanently captured in the Lord's Prayer—"Thy Kingdom come." In the course of time, however, this hope became transformed into a post-mortem personal destiny in heaven, which even became known theologically as the Christian Hope.

The coming of the secular world has brought us back to earth again where something like the original intention of the "the Kingdom of God" is once more relevant. Our chief hopes for the future are much more this worldly. Individually, of course, we hope for a long and healthy life. Collectively, we hope for social harmony, for economic prosperity, and for international peace. More recently our hope has incorporated the conservation of the earth's ecology.

Hope must not be confused with blind optimism. As I have tried to show in a book, *The World to Come*, the century we have entered is presenting us with so many frightening challenges that it is becoming quite difficult to hold out hope for a better world. Yet, as theologian Jürgen Moltmann has said, "It is just because we cannot know whether humanity is going to survive or not, we have to act today as if the future of the whole of humanity were dependent on us" (176).

My third theme from the Bible is love. There has always been general agreement that this is central to the Judeo-Christian tradition. Jesus named, as the two major commandments, injunctions selected from the Jewish Scriptures—"You shall love the Lord your God with all your heart and mind and strength," and "You shall love your neighbour as yourself."

But Jesus went further than anything in the Jewish tradition. He said, "Love your enemies." This is the most original dictum in all of his teaching. It is sadly ironic that through Christian history the exhortation most central to the teaching of Jesus is just what Christians have found most difficult to respond to. Not only have professing Christians been little better than anybody else in loving their enemies but even the centrality of love itself became obscured. The love for others that we were exhorted to fulfil was projected on to a divine Saviour so that his love for us would provide us with personal salvation. The original message of love, which exhorted us to save others, became distorted into one of exploiting it to secure our own salvation.

It is strange that so few have ever noticed the conflict between Christian dogma and the most authentic sayings of Jesus. In the Sermon on the Mount a sharp contrast is drawn between the wise builder who built his house on bedrock and the foolish builder who built his house on sand. This little parable occurs in one form or another so much in the Jewish Wisdom stream that the Jesus Seminar could not regard it as original to Jesus, yet he may well have used it, for it is copybook wisdom material. We should note that it was not because of divine providence that the one house stood firm while the other perished. It was due to the wisdom of the man who built it. This, like so many of the exhortations of Jesus, manifests the moral philosophy of Pelagius, which Christian orthodoxy judged to be heresy.

The deconstruction of Christian dogma has brought back to light the bare outlines of the original Jesus, the teacher, the man of wisdom, the one who, while sharing the tensions and uncertainties of human existence, also revitalised the path to freedom, the way to live life "more abundantly." No wonder people are said to have heard him gladly. No wonder, after he was crucified, they came to assert, in the symbolic language of their time, that he was so alive himself, and brought so much new life to others, that it seemed that not even death could conquer him.

Paul rightly said that the lasting values in life are faith, hope and love and the greatest of these is love.

I have tried to show that the secular, global world, far from being the enemy of Christianity, is the legitimate continuation of the Judeo-Christian tradition. It still honours its abiding values, while shedding much of its past symbols and creedal formulations. The more we acknowledge this relationship, and give due respect to the matrix out of which the modern world has emerged, the more it will continue to support us on our path into the future.

The traditional worship of God has now become the celebration of life. The wisdom to choose life lies in the exercise of those values which promote life in all of its planetary complexity. Chief among them is the moral imperative to love, coupled with justice, compassion and a host of others. Faith requires us to be free of all excess baggage. Hope requires us to be open to an ever-evolving future. Love requires us to be inclusive of all people and of all cultural traditions.

Part III

Religion, Science, and the Future of Life on Earth

Evolution, Creationism, and the Myths of Nature

Eugenie C. Scott

T he science of evolution is claimed by some to be the foundation for a new, modern, nontheistic religion—an origin story for our times, unshackled to the superstitions of the past, if you will. But is it? Can evolution provide a truly mythic vision? To answer this question first requires some definitions—something especially useful when communicating across disciplines as divergent as science and theology. Different scholarly traditions often use the same words, but in very different ways. The Lutheran theologian Paul Santmire and I have quite different definitions of the term "reconstructionist," for example. As an activist opposing the introduction of creationism into the schools, when I hear "reconstructionist," I first think of R. J. Rushdoony and his school proposing theocracy for the U.S. To Santmire, a "reconstructionist" is someone like Bishop Spong. One should not ordinarily confuse Spong and Rushdoony, so I will ask you to please use my definitions as you read this paper. I will present definitions for "religion," "science," "evolution," and "myth" and then discuss creationism and evolution as potential sources for myths of nature.

Definitions

In my training as a physical anthropologist, I was fortunate that both my undergraduate as well as graduate training institutions took the "4-field" approach, wherein I not only was trained in the natural sciences of human biology and evolution, but also in the social sciences of cultural anthropology, linguistics, and archaeology (though I encourage low expectations regarding my knowledge of linguistics). So as an anthropologist, I use anthropological definitions of terms like "religion," "myth," and "evolution," terms of art in my field which are given different meanings on the street, and also in other scholarly disciplines. So let us begin with the toughest term to define: religion.

Religion

To most members of the American public, "religion" usually means Christianity. Our more sophisticated citizens might extend their definition, or at least the picture in their mind, to the Middle Eastern monotheisms, and some of them might include some of the world religions. But to an anthropologist, the definition of religion has to include not only well-known world religions like Christianity, Islam, Judaism, Buddhism, Hinduism and the rest, but religions practiced by perhaps only a few hundred people. We also include within religion not only modern belief systems, but the traditions that have been important to members of cultures that lived millennia ago. The definition has to stretch from world religions to tribal religions, traditions of many Gods as well as one, and animistic traditions of spirits, ancestors, and even more amorphous forms. The definition has to be flexible enough to extend to traditions which include rules of behavior—and those that do not. Some cultures' moral and ethical systems are not associated with religion, as is the case with the Abrahamic religions, but rather with custom and tradition. A definition of religion has to extend to traditions which include stories of empirical explanations of the world—and those that do not; traditions which include conceptions of an afterlife—and those that do not.

So what qualities do *all* religions have in common that would allow us to define this human universal? Like art, religion is very tough to define, though we know it when we see it. Religion can be defined, I suggest, as those beliefs and behaviors associated with the relationships of humans to a nonmaterial, or transcendent, ultimate reality. This reality is sometimes conceived as a place, such as traditional Christian conceptions of Heaven or Hell, or the Norse Valhalla, or it can be a non-place, such as Nirvana. This transcendent reality is usually conceived of as populated with entities: Gods, spirits, hero figures, ancestors or other agents, and most of the time, these agents have the ability to interact with human beings. Regulating or at least coping with this interaction is the primary concern of religious behaviors, especially rituals.

Now, it seems to me that the existence of this transcendent reality is something that has to be taken as a First Principle: it cannot be "proven," nor can it be "disproved"; it must be taken on faith. The vast majority of human beings accept it, and even with the growing secularization of European societies, many people who say they don't believe in "God," do believe that that there is "something" other than this mortal, material existence. Many people claim certainty that such a reality exists, and as proof, attest to their personal experiences. Most familiar to us is the experience of grace claimed by born-again Christians, but mystical experiences are not uncommon in other cultures as well. The Plains Indian vision quest is an example of this, and is duplicated in many cultures.

However, personal transcendence is not usually persuasive to outsiders who have not had such an experience themselves, and especially not to someone of a different culture. Most of us would doubt that we would see a white buffalo appear if we exposed ourselves on a mountain top for three days without food or water. Therefore, the existence of this transcendent reality cannot be empirically demonstrated and must be taken on faith.

Humanists, followers of a religion that "reject[s] supernaturalism and seek[s] man's fulfillment in the here and now of this world,"[1] and atheists do not accept the existence of this reality, arguing that because such a reality is not demonstrable with empirical evidence, it is unreasonable to accept it. The personal "supernatural" experiences given great meaning by many people are given material explanations by nonbelievers: when a religious person sees a bright light at the end of a tunnel during a near-death experience, interpreting it as representing a glimpse of the Hereafter, a materialist would explain the tunnels and light as typical brain function under conditions of hypoxia. But I would argue that the assumption that there is *no* ultimate reality is equally a matter of faith, as by definition, such a reality cannot be demonstrated by empirical evidence. So we are left with the truth of such a transcendent reality being left to faith—a first principle, which the vast majority of human beings have accepted.

Science

Science is an effort to understand the natural world, limited to natural or material explanations. It is, then, a limited way of knowing. When answering questions scientifically, scientists limit themselves to explanations based on matter, energy, and their interaction (material causes) regardless of their personal religious or philosophical beliefs about the existence or nonexistence of a transcendent reality. The limitation of *scientific* explanations to material cause is called "methodological materialism," and is distinguished from philosophical or ontological materialism, the view of humanists and atheists.

In science, we limit ourselves to material explanations because the essence of science is *testing* explanations against the natural world, and rejecting the explanations that don't work. One of the important components of testing is to hold constant (or "control") some variables so that the effect of others can be ascertained. If there is a transcendent reality beyond the material which includes nonmaterial forces, perhaps omnipotent, how could we possibly hold their effects constant? You can't put God in a test tube—or keep Him out of one, either. It is by definition impossible to hold constant the effects of an omnipotent power; hence science is incapable of evaluating explanations involving omnipotent powers. This is not, as the atheists would claim, because such powers do not exist, but because, logically speaking, any empirical outcome of a test is compatible with the action or nonaction of an omnipotent power.

So scientists restrict themselves to material explanations because they lack tools to test explanations of nonmaterial, supernatural forces. We await the invention of a Theometer; lacking one, we muddle along as best we can with natural explanations.

So that is the context in which I will be using the terms science and religion.

Evolution

Evolution—in the broadest sense—is the extremely well-documented theory that the universe has had a history: that galaxies, stars, our planet, and the living things on it are different today than they were in the past, and that galaxies, stars, planets and all the other components of the Universe cumulatively have changed through time. Biological evolution is a subset of this broader definition, and refers specifically to the inference that living things have common ancestors—that in Darwin's terms, they have "descended with modification" from common ancestors.

There are good reasons for distinguishing between evolution as something that happened and the mechanisms of evolution. First, it is conceptually clearer. Darwin's claim that living things had evolved—that they have common ancestors—was accepted long before his mechanism of natural selection. Today, with natural selection well-accepted as the primary mechanism of evolution, other mechanisms or processes have been suggested in addition to natural selection, thus underscoring the conceptual distinction between common ancestry and mechanisms of evolution.

Second, parsing the components of evolution deflects a longstanding antievolutionist argument that confuses the public about evolution. Antievolutionists contend that if a proposed mechanism of evolutionary change is shown to be ineffective or inadequate as an explanation of some aspect of evolution, then the whole case for common descent itself is weakened. But this makes a conceptual error. I traveled across the country to get from California to New York to give the talk upon which this paper is based. I could have come by train, or by air, or driven a car, or maybe even walked. *How I got to New York* is a separate issue and independent from the fact that I *was* in New York. Similarly, the claim that living things had common ancestors is conceptually different and must be evaluated separately from *how* evolution occurred.

Because natural selection will come up again later, let me quickly describe this important mechanism of evolutionary change. Natural selection—like evolution in general—affects populations, not individuals. Individuals are born, live, and die; they do not evolve. And, although we sometimes joke about someone "losing out to natural selection," natural selection doesn't work on individuals, either: it works on populations of genes. Population thinking, actually, is rather difficult to get used to, but it is essential to understanding evolution.

Populations of organisms consist of genetically different individuals. Some organisms have genetically-based variations that allow them to live longer and reproduce more offspring than organisms that lack these genes, therefore these genes become more numerous through the generations, and the population gradually changes as a result. When you think about it, natural selection is survival of the fit *enough* more than it is survival of the fittest. As a result, living organisms tend to be a mixture of structures that work really well and are beautifully "designed," and klugy stuff that barely works. Jacob used the analogy of a tinker making something out of whatever was handy vs. the engineer who carefully designed the artifact and used precisely the right structural components; natural selection is the tinker of evolution, not the designing engineer.[2]

So we have the Big Idea of evolution (common descent), and the *processes* of evolution, but a third component of evolutionary theory is the *pattern* of evolution. Evolution can be thought of as the branching and splitting of species—a genealogical relationship of species through time. As such, evolution naturally generates nested hierarchies of more and more inclusive groups. Linnaeus, a special creationist, observed the pattern and devised a classification system where species were grouped into Genera, Genera into Families, Families into Orders, Orders into Classes, and so on. Darwin realized that the same pattern of nested groups could be produced by common descent; evolution by its branching, genealogical nature, generates an immense pedigree of species, forming a tree of life. When we consider the *pattern* of evolution, we are trying to reconstruct this banyan tree of trunks and branches and twigs—and great progress recently has been made through the integration of molecular data with information from traditional comparative anatomy, embryology, and paleontology.

So the modern theory of evolution has three parts: the Big Idea of common descent, the processes, and the patterns of evolution. I will return to these three components later, and how they are related to religion.

Myth

This leaves us with the final term to define: myth. Here anthropologists and theologians probably converge in our thinking—our shared understandings of this term largely agree and contrast with the definition most common in the general public. A caveat here, however: I do not use "myth" in the sense of John Dominic Crossan, nor am I using "myth" as does Levi Straus—I have in mind something far simpler for the purposes of this paper. To most people, "myth" means "something false" or untrue. To anthropologists, myths are some of the most important elements of a culture. Myths are symbolic representations of values or cultural motifs that are central to the culture. Myths are often used as enculturation vehicles, and may appear in ritual, and even be repeated several times a year to make sure that people (especially younger members of society) internalize the message.

Some myths are secular, others are religious, but all involve a symbolic representation of some societal or human truth. The story of Persephone and Hades not only symbolizes the passage of seasons, but also is a metaphor of the realities of death and birth. Chinese culture reflects a strong sense of the importance of balancing opposites: yin/yang, light/dark, hot/cold, good/evil, wet/dry, earth/sky, female/male—there are many examples of this duality. A Chinese origin myth reflects this important cultural concern with balance: the creator God Phan Ku separates chaos into a series of dualities including the separation of earth from sky, and other elements of the physical universe.

Given this enculturation role, narrative myth-making tends to be more common in nonliterate societies dependent on oral traditions, but myths also occur in our own, literate society, even if we have other ways of passing on values. The "little engine that could," for example, expresses an important value in American culture: persevering in the face of adversity. The Horatio Alger myth of the poor but plucky youth, who achieves success through hard work, pulling himself up by his bootstraps, is classically American. Both of these secular myths also express American values of individualism—a cultural trait characteristic of Americans, but not that common in cultures world-wide, most of which stress a cultural identity based on kin relationships. Mythic elements arise around historical and popular heroes as well: there are many myths associated with Abraham

Lincoln and George Washington, for example, which reinforce positive values such as truthfulness (the myth of the cherry tree, for example, or "honest Abe").

Myths are not intended to be taken literally: they often have elements of the fantastic about them, such as talking animals or plants. They have conventions of language that set them apart from other kinds of stories—the equivalent of "once upon a time," that let the listener know "Oh, we are in the world of myth now; I'm not supposed to believe there really are fairy Godmothers." Yet myths are meant to be taken seriously, and as *true* in that the values and messages are considered important and to be learned. *The Little Engine that Could* is no more about talking steam engines than the Garden of Eden is about talking snakes—it is the *meaning* of the myth that is most important, not the literal details. This is especially true about the subsection of myths known as origin myths.

Creationism

By "creationism," I intend the broadest definition: that God (or some other superior entity—perhaps many Gods, or ancestors, or other agents of the transcendent reality) created the universe and all that is in it. *How* this creation event took place, of course, varies with the religion, and may well vary within a religion. In the Christian tradition, creationism takes many, many forms, from Special Creationism of six, 24–hour days about 10,000 years ago, to a variety of Old Earth creationisms, to various forms of theistic evolution and deism. I will use specific tenets if I am referring to any particular creationism, such as Young Earth Creationism.

Evolution, Creationism and Myths of Nature

All people try to make sense of the world around them, and that includes speculating about the course of events that brought the world and its inhabitants to their present state. Myths therefore often include *views* of nature. For example, at different times in the Western tradition, nature has been seen as hostile, at other times, romantic, at other times as machine-like. In some Native American views as well as some modern Christian views, nature is seen as in union with humanity—a seamless connection of all living things. *How* nature is viewed influences a culture's view of humankind's *relationship* with nature: whether there is a perceived relationship of domination or hierarchy, separateness, unity, or some other relationship. Although the empirical truth or falsity of a myth is not the most important issue—what matters is the symbolic representation of values—nonetheless, myths must at least be consistent with the view of nature of a people, or they cannot fulfill their function of communicating cultural values. Part of a people's view of nature includes empirical reality. So myths must incorporate the perceptions ("facts") of nature, as well as reflect—even as they help shape—the culture's relationship with nature. Do the various forms of creationism do this? Does evolution do this? Let's look at creationism(s) and evolution in the light of this question.

Young-Earth Creationism

Young-earth Creationism (YEC) is founded on the Genesis creation story of the special creation of unrelated "Kinds" of animals, the historical reality of a flesh and blood Adam and Eve who lived for hundreds of years and begat hundreds of children, their Fall, God's curse, Noah's flood, and so on. Symbolically, the Genesis account is thought by traditional Christians to symbolize the relationship of humankind to God, and to all the rest of the created order. God gives humankind the entire world and its creatures—in fact, the *purpose* of everything God creates is for the use or pleasure of humankind. In return for this, people are expected to worship and obey God in gratitude for being chosen from all of the other created beings for this special position.

Both the story of the expulsion of Adam and Eve from the Garden and of Noah's Flood symbolize the importance of obedience to God. To traditional Christians, the expulsion from the Garden is the foundation upon which Christianity is built: if Adam and Eve had not sinned, then Christ's sacrifice would not have been necessary to redeem their (and by extension, humankind's) sin. Young Earth Creationists view Genesis as the most important book of the Bible. If it is not true, or if it is to be interpreted symbolically, then, in their view, the entire edifice of Christianity falls. The rest of the Bible has to be true, too: as one Fundamentalist minister explained to me on a radio show, "If I don't know that Genesis is true, how do I know that Revelation is true?"

Of course, there are two creations described in Genesis, and they are contradictory in most plain readings. And, of interest to us in considering the role of myths and nature, there are two separate cultural perspectives presented in the two Genesis creation stories: that of the urban/agricultural Israelites, and that of the pastoral/ nomadic Israelites.

According to the theologian Conrad Hyers, these two creation stories of Genesis 1 and Genesis 2 reflect different foci of settled and nomadic populations:

The clue to the differences is to be found within Israel itself where, broadly speaking, there were two main traditions: the pastoral/nomadic and the agricultural/urban. Genesis 1 has drawn upon the imagery and concerns of the farmers and city-dwellers that inhabited river basins prone to flooding, while Genesis 2 has drawn upon the experiences of shepherds, goat-herders, and camel-drivers that lived on the semiarid fringes of the fertile plains, around and between wells and oases. For the pastoral nomads and desert peoples the fundamental threat to life was dryness and barrenness, whereas for those agricultural and urban peoples in or near flood plains the threat was too much water, and the chaotic possibilities of water. It is also revealing that Genesis 2 does not mention a creation of fish, whereas fish in abundance are prominent in Genesis 1 (fish occupy half of day five, with "swarms of living creatures").[3]

Hyers also points out that the two Genesis versions express the different ways pastoralists and agriculturalists interact with nature:

In Genesis 1 human beings are pictured in the lofty terms of roy-alty, taking dominion over the earth and subduing it—imagery and values drawn from the very pinnacle of ancient civilizations, which Israel itself achieved in the time of Solomon. In Genesis 2, however, Adam and Eve are pictured as *servants* of the garden, living in a garden oasis: essentially the gardener and his wife. And while Genesis 1 refers to humans as made in "the image and like-ness of God," in the continuation of the garden story in Genesis 3 the theme of godlikeness is introduced by the *serpent* who tempts Eve with the promise that by eating of the fruit of the Tree of Knowledge, they would be "like God," knowing good and evil. Celebrants of science and technology beware!

Thus, while Genesis 1 is comfortable with the values of civili-zation and the fruits of its many achievements and creations, Genesis 2 offers an humble view of humanity, a reminder of the simple life and values of the shepherd ancestors, before farming, and even before shepherding, in an Edenic state of food gathering and tending. In this manner these two views of human nature are counterbalanced.[4]

Young-earth Creationists are biblical literalists. They do not even recognize that there are two stories in Genesis: because there can be only one narrative, Genesis 2 must be just an elaboration of the same story—contradictions notwithstanding. They do not recog-nize the mythic elements: it's not a representation of the temptations that we must all face, nor a reminder of the difference between God and mankind—it's a talking snake.

The Bible, of course, is a book not only proposing the special creation of living things, but also proposing geocentrism, and arguably proposing a flat earth. But modern cosmology is no longer consistent with these views, which is one reason the majority of Christians are not strict biblical literalists. With the Copernican and later the Darwinian revolutions, the predominant view of nature in western culture changed from a fixed universe to one that changes, from a relatively recently-created universe to one that is ancient, and from the idea of fixed "kinds" of plans and animals, to a nontypological view of the species as being composed of genes that change. YECs thus reject modern physics, astronomy, geology, biology, and anthropology; their view largely is incompatible with the knowledge we have from empirical observation. I contend that YEC would therefore fail as a modern source of myth—at least for anyone who understands and accepts modern science. Of course, not everyone does, making YEC possible.

Intelligent Design Creationism

Intelligent Design Creationism (IDC) is a relatively new form of antievolutionism that grew out of antievolutionist dissatisfaction with YEC. Academics and other educated people rejected YEC because its science was so bad and because biblical literalism was not mainstream theology. Furthermore, as an antievolution strategy, YEC was a legal failure: the 1970s and early 1980s efforts to pass laws requiring equal time for creation science when evolution was taught foundered when courts declared that the teaching of creation science was prohibited by the First Amendment. A new antievolutionist strategy was needed that was not based on biblical literalism, and that could have greater success in the courts.

The content of IDC is a subset of YEC: all the claims of IDC preexisted in YEC, but there are claims made in the name of YEC that IDC ignores. For example, IDC makes no claims about the pattern of evolutionary change, and especially avoids discussion of such basic scientific principles as the age of the Earth. Whenever possible, it even avoids the question of whether common ancestry occurred, though the vast majority of ID proponents reject even theistic evolution. This is clear in the statements of prominent ID theoreticians such as Phillip Johnson and William Dembski, the latter of whom has remarked, "Design theorists are no friends of theistic evolution."[5]

What little science there is in IDC concentrates on the *process* part of evolutionary biology, especially, the mechanism of natural selection. Proponents accept that natural selection, influenced by environmental pressures, can produce large or small beaks in Galapagos finches, or pesticide resistance in insects, but they deny that natural selection can produce body plans such as the phylum-level differences that appeared in the Cambrian explosion over 500 million years ago. As such, IDC is much more about what evolution (or science) *cannot* do than it is a scientific research program presenting a new approach to explaining nature.

This "Creationism Lite" makes the minimal claim that it is possible to detect those complex structures in nature that are produced by intelligence, and to distinguish them from those that were produced by natural causes. It is a restatement of William Paley's argument to design: [6] that some things are so complex that they could not be the result of chance. A watch, for example, has many interacting parts, which working together accomplish the purpose of telling time. Because of a watch's complexity, there had to have been a watchmaker: the myriad components of a watch could not have randomly assembled into a time-keeping artifact. Therefore, argued Paley, whenever one encountered a highly complex *natural* structure composed of many parts such as the vertebrate eye; it too had to have been produced by an intelligent agent: its complex interacting parts could not have come together by chance.

Modern IDCs tend to use molecular and cellular structures as their examples of complexity, rather than anatomical structures such as the vertebrate eye. Mathematician William Dembski contends that what he calls "Complex Specified Information" identifies intelligently-designed phenomena, including biological phenomena. Biochemist Michael Behe in his book,[7] *Darwin's Black Box,* contends that the identification of what he calls "irreducible complexity" in a biochemical machine like the bacterial flagellum is sufficient to conclude that it requires intelligence for its origin: it had to have been intelligently designed. Yet in the mid-nineteenth century, Darwin showed that complex structures could indeed be the result of natural processes: his theory of natural selection solved Paley's problem by providing a natural mechanism to explain complex biological structures.

By undermining Paley, Darwin made it difficult for literalist Christian clergy to rely upon Paley's argument for direct creation. It is probably not mere coincidence that the Christian Modernist movement, stressing the historical roots of the Bible and its interpretation, began in the late nineteenth century a few decades after Darwin's *On the Origin of Species.*

But the ID perspective, in requiring the direct hand of God to produce complex molecular structures and processes such as the

bacterial flagellum or the blood clotting mechanism, again con-
verges with the Special Creationists of the YEC tradition. Instead of
the YEC view that God created the full range of whole organisms
("kinds") all at one time, ID proponents require God to intervene
sequentially through time, creating microscopic "irreducibly complex" structures that supposedly could not have evolved through
natural mechanisms. God thus intervenes to create, say, the first
DNA, and then the first replicating structure ("life"), and then perhaps the bacterial flagellum, and maybe later in time, the eukaryote
flagellum. Perhaps later in time, God specially created the vertebrate blood clotting mechanism—and so on—intervening every
time an irreducibly complex structure is needed. This means that
ID is really a disguised form of "progressive creationism," a sort of
"creation on the installment plan" where God creates sequentially
through time. Intelligent Design Creationism is distinguished from
classical progressive creationism in that God creates only parts of
animals rather than whole organisms. The exception to the usual
restriction of God's creativity to complex molecular structures is the
Cambrian Explosion, a period of rapid evolution about 500 million years ago when the basic body plans of most invertebrates first
appear in the fossil record. IDCs as well as YECs enthusiastically cite
the Cambrian Explosion as a major special creation event, claiming
(incorrectly) that the body plans of the various invertebrate "kinds"
cannot be derived from one another and thus must have been specially created.

Is the ID point of view consistent with what we know of nature
today? It's hard to say. ID makes almost no claims of fact, concentrating more on philosophy of science—on how to identify intelligently-
designed phenomena. I don't think we need to concern ourselves
with ID as the source of a new mythology, perhaps replacing YEC
or—as they intend— replacing secularism and evolution. First, IDC
stakes out such a minimalist position, that there is scarcely anything
to base a mythology upon. What values or cultural metaphors could
build on a position whose central claim is "evolution can't explain
X, so God did it"? What scientific claims it *does* make are largely
incoherent. I think it is safe for us to dismiss ID in the context of
our discussion today of myths and nature; it's not going to take us
anywhere. As a religious or philosophical idea, it is far too thin to
provide the necessary substrate to support robust mythology.

Evolution as Myth

So neither YEC nor IDC are good candidates for mythmaking, the
former because its claims about empirical reality (Grand Canyon
being cut by Noah's Flood, for example) are simply incompatible

with our modern understanding of nature, and the latter because
it makes so *few* claims about nature that it is vacuous. What about
evolution as myth? Surely, we hear all the time that "evolution is
the myth of our day." But considering my definition of myth for
this presentation, can we really take evolution and see in it symbolic
representations of ideas and values that are important to us in our
day and age? In the same sense as Genesis symbolized what was
important for either the urban/agricultural or pastoral/nomadic
Israelites?

My contention is that evolution does not make very good myth,
as myths go. Only part of it can express cultural values, and that
not very well. Recall that evolution is subdivided into the big idea
of common descent, plus pattern, plus process. All can be—and
are—studied independently of one another, so we should consider
each independently in the context of myth.

Let's first consider *Patterns* of evolution; I suggest that there is
not much mythological purchase here. Whether pandas are bears or
raccoons has little effect on our views of ourselves or our relationship with God! It's quite intellectually fascinating to imagine the
Thanksgiving day turkey as a living representative of creatures that
shook the earth when they walked—but whether or not birds are
dinosaurs isn't going to be of much use to us in helping symbolize
cultural values or norms. The *process* of evolution has more potential: natural selection is considered the main engine of evolutionary
change, and indeed, natural selection has inspired—or been incorporated into—many ideological views from social Darwinism and
laissez faire capitalism to some versions of socialism (recall that Marx
dedicated *Das Kapital* to Darwin—although Darwin was not very
impressed). Given the wide range of sometimes conflicting ideologies claiming natural selection as their basis, it is perhaps more accurate to say that *aspects* of natural selection were selected by different
ideologues to support their point of view. Laissez faire capitalists
seized on the competition aspect of natural selection—the "nature
red in tooth and claw" part—and the socialists seized on the possibility of the environment producing positive change, which they
visualized as occurring in society as well as in the organism.

Similarly, natural selection theory was claimed to support the
eugenic movement of the early twentieth century; today, modern
evolutionary theory, based on the synthesis of natural selection with
genetics, is used to fight racism because it shows the overwhelming
unity of humankind. Given current knowledge about the operation
of heredity and the nature of populations and species, racism can
no longer be justified through biological evolution. It appears then,
that evolution by natural selection does not compel any particular

ideological view; natural selection is an equal opportunity substratum for even conflicting ideologies.

But natural selection is not the only evolutionary process; descent
with modification can also take place as a result of chance. The term
"chance" in this context means something rather different from its
everyday usage, in which "chance" often connotes "randomness,"
or purposelessness—as in "random violence."[8] When we talk of
chance in evolutionary biology, we mean chance in the sense of
mathematical probability—in which results actually are predictable
in a stochastic sense. For example, if we know the frequency of the
sickle cell gene, we can predict (over a large number of families) the
percentage of children that will be born with the homozygous sickle
cell disease and the percentage that will be born with the less dangerous heterozygous condition, known as sickle cell trait. Though
we can't predict any particular pregnancy outcome—which child will
have what condition—by applying the laws of probability (chance),
we can make predictions about total outcomes for the group.

Chance comes into evolution through the probabilistic nature
of the generation of genetic variation, upon which natural selection
operates. There are chance, or probabilistic factors at work in the
recombination of genes and gametes, and in the generation of muta-
tions, which add new information to the genetic material. Natural
selection itself, however, is not a chance process: natural selection is
the opposite of chance, causing changes because of the adaptiveness
of genetic characteristics in a particular environment.

Chance can also affect evolution through events unrelated to a
population's or species' adaptiveness: when a meteor crashed into
the area north of the Yucatan peninsula at the beginning of the
Cretaceous, it set into play great climatic changes, and a consequent
major die-off of terrestrial fauna. That the meteor hit at that precise time was a good deal for mammals, but if it had hit a hundred
million years earlier, some non-mammalian group of animals might
have emerged to replace the dinosaurs. The Cretaceous meteor
impact was truly a chance event for mammalian evolution.

That evolution can come about through either adaptation or
chance has been recognized by theologians like Arthur Peacocke
who speak of God working through both chance and law:

> The interplay of chance and law is the basis of the inherent cre-
> ativity of the natural order, its ability to generate new forms, pat-
> terns and organizations of matter and energy. . . . A theist must
> then see God as acting rather like a composer extemporizing
> a fugue to create in the world through what we call "chance"
> operating within the created order, each stage of which consti-

tutes the launching pad of the next. The Creator, it now seems, is unfolding the divinely endowed potentialities of the universe, in and through a process in which these creative possibilities and propensities become actualized within created time.[9]

This is getting closer to what I have been talking about as a *mythic* understanding, in the anthropological sense of the symbolic representation of culturally-important values. But although a liberal theologian like Peacocke can look at the mechanisms of evolution and see a symbolic representation of how God works with nature, it cannot be said that the existence of chance working with law to produce evolutionary change *compels* Peacocke's view.

The ID and YEC proponents, for example, look at this mix of chance and law with horror. To them, a God who works through chance and law, rather than purposefully and directly, is a God who has withdrawn Himself from the world. It is a Deistic God at best, and possibly even a callous and uncaring God, which would be worse. The main concern of IDCs, in fact, is that science, by being able to explain so much by reference only to natural cause, is somehow proof that only natural cause is operant in the universe; that indeed, there is no Creator, and thus no ultimate purpose in the universe. Evolution by natural selection epitomizes this IDC and YEC fear: it is the foundation for philosophical naturalism.

But natural selection doesn't explain only the diversity of living things, it also accounts for the adaptation of species to their environments. It's possible for creationists to dismiss common descent, but it's impossible to dismiss natural selection: bacteria undeniably become resistant to antibiotics, plants undeniably become resistant to herbicides. Whether in an evolutionary context or an adaptational one, natural selection results in pain and suffering, death and waste. Can this pain and suffering be the direct action of a benevolent Creator? IDCs don't address the issue; Young-earth Creationists explain that suffering and evil exist because of the Fall, including natural selection. God is off the hook: natural selection and other evils came into the world with Adam and Eve's disobedience; it's our fault, not His.

Small scale natural selection and other mechanisms of evolution operating at the level of the species are considered "microevolution" and are viewed similarly by antievolutionists and theistic evolutionists. Both accept that adaptive change occurs at the species (or "kind") level, but theistic evolutionists accept that descent with modification—evolution—can also occur, and that species can give rise to new species and new varieties of life. Yet despite this general similarity in the acceptance of the mechanisms of evolution, YECs,

IDCs and theistic evolutionists have developed radically different theological views from them. For this reason, it doesn't appear as if the mechanisms of evolution work very well as producers of myth—or alternately, because such different values or pictures of reality can be derived from them, that these mechanisms fail to provide *consistent* myths, and thereby fail as sources of myth.

The third component of evolution, the *big idea* (common descent) has some profound consequences for how we see one another, and even how we see nature. Perhaps it is only in this aspect of evolution that we might be able to see some possibilities for myth making. The concept of common descent implies that all living things are related; human beings are kin to all other life forms. Because we are kin to—inseparable from—all other life, we might conclude that we have a responsibility to cherish and preserve our fellow living things, beings that share with us this most precious quality of life. Evolution can thus provide a very different perspective from the human dominion interpretation of Genesis, but there are other possible interpretations. The idea of common descent is also compatible with the conclusion that because we as human beings are cognitively superior to all other creatures—intellectually we have descended the farthest from our common ancestor—we can do as we wish with them! Rather than dominion being granted by a Higher Power, we may choose to grant it to ourselves—over the less-endowed species with which we share the planet.

I would argue that the perspective of kinship with all living things and the responsibility to husband nature that many of us would draw from the fact of evolution is very reasonable and very supportable, but it is not *compelled* by the concept of evolution nor any other scientific theory or data. Science, remember, is a limited way of knowing: it is merely trying to explain the natural world, restricting itself to natural causes. It doesn't in itself provide the answer to "What is the meaning of life?" or even "What is my relationship with nature?" Although some religious interpretations, such as Young-Earth Creationism, are incompatible with evolution, many religious interpretations can and are compatible with evolution; evolution *allows* but does not *compel* any particular religious or philosophical view.

And this is true for those who accept that there is an ultimate or transcendent reality, and for those who do not. Science is equally poor at compelling the conclusions arrived at by fundamentalist Christians or humanists. To borrow from Bob Funk's talk delivered previous to mine, citing Moynihan: we're all entitled to our own opinions, but not to our own facts. Science can give us the facts, but what we do with them is often governed much more by ideologies and needs with which we interpret science than by the mere facts and theories themselves.

To return to the themes of this session: there are of course, many myths of nature. Science, however, makes lousy myth. Given the symbolic and enculturative role of myth, which is to pass on values from generation to generation—science is not up to the job. Even though science is conservative, facts change too quickly, and theories, though they take longer to build, are constantly being tinkered with. For proper mythic power, you need continuity and stability, which science cannot promise. Ashley Montagu said, "The scientist believes in proof without certainty, the bigot in certainty without proof."[10] If we wish to build an environmental ethic, it needs to be brutally honest with the realities of the natural world—we cannot have an outlook that is inconsistent with reality. To devise a myth of nature, we absolutely require nature. We *must* understand nature, and have a mythology that is concordant with what science tells us. Alas, what science tells us can only *inform* our discussion, it cannot make that decision for us. We have to be brutally honest and admit that the reality of the natural world does not *compel* any particular perspectives, and, perhaps unfortunately, is compatible with many that we would not like to see. However inspiring science can be, it cannot in itself provide culturally-sustaining myths. Neither, in my opinion, can the various forms of creationism. We must look for other sources to generate meaningful symbolic representations of values and ideas, to religion and philosophy.

The Age of Ecology

Anne Primavesi

W here does the Age of Ecology belong in relation to
the Axial Ages? In a book entitled *Nature's Economy:
A History of Ecological Ideas*, historian of ideas Donald Worster
writes:

> The Age of Ecology began on the desert outside Alamogordo,
> New Mexico, on July 16, 1945, with a dazzling fireball of light
> and a swelling mushroom cloud of radioactive gases. As that first
> nuclear fission bomb went off and the color of the early morning
> sky changed abruptly from pale blue to blinding white, project
> leader J. Robert Oppenheimer felt at first a surge of elated rever-
> ence; then a sombre phrase from the Bhagavad-Gita flashed into
> his mind: "I am become Death, the shatterer of worlds". . . . For
> the first time in some two million years of human history, there
> existed a force, [created by us] capable of destroying the entire
> fabric of life on the planet.[1]

While that was certainly a defining moment in the Age of Ecology,
it did not begin then. It did not, in other words, follow on from the
Second Axial Age. In fact it *preceded* not only the Second Axial Age
but the First one too. For without what we now call "ecology" there
would have been no human history to divide into "Ages."

Therefore the Age of Ecology has historic priority over all others.
To see it in this way, however, is radically subversive. For it subverts
the accepted view of world history that is concerned almost entirely
with human cultural, political and religious activities. This usually
portrays the advance of culture and technology as releasing humans
from dependence on the natural world and providing them with
the means to manage it for their own ends. It positively celebrates
human mastery over other forms of life and expects technological
improvement and economic growth to continue to accelerate, even

if, as Oppenheimer suggested, that "improved" technology could destroy the entire fabric of life on the planet[2].

Ecology, however, subverts this view of ourselves by showing that while we may destroy large portions of it, including those that directly support us, we did not create it and cannot recreate it. That was and is beyond human power. For the fabric of life was created over the four and a half billion years that is ecology's real "Age": an age encompassing earth's history and evolution from the emergence of life on the planet up to the present moment. This ecological history takes priority in every sense over human history as it was and is essential to our existence.

To see ourselves within the framework of that history is religiously subversive too, because it challenges a fundamentalist view of ourselves as specially created by God; created, that is, outside of general evolutionary processes and the constraints of ecological principles. This challenge to our self-image, implicit in James Lovelock's scientific theory of Gaia, completes the ideological revolution set in motion by Copernicus and Darwin. For it forces us to face the fact that, like all other living species, we have always been and still are dependent on the life support systems that evolved throughout earth's history and made earth habitable for us. The pages of that history are bound into the structure of the planet; rocks are its written words; geological periods its punctuation marks; it is illustrated by the lives of microorganisms, mighty trees and human families. All these evolved and are maintained according to the ecological principle that the ability of any organism (including ourselves) to emerge, increase or maintain its numbers and to spread geographically, is limited by and dependent on environmental factors, in particular availability of resources and energy capacity.

Our past, then, is literally inconceivable without the Age of Ecology. So too is our present and also our future. Indeed there will be no future, for us, or for our faith, unless we understand and respect the myriad ways in which our planetary environment has both affected human activities and been affected by them. For human economies, cultures, politics and religion ultimately depend, whether we wish it or not, whether we are conscious of it or not, on the availability, location and limits of what are called "natural resources." Yet who could guess that from reading the *Wall Street Journal* or from listening to politicians—or church leaders?

Instead, every day we see that states act to prevent environmental degradation only when their narrow economic interests are shown to be directly threatened. Philosophical and religious ideas, scientific findings, the plight of indigenous peoples and threats to species are not, unfortunately, enough to precipitate such action. One major reason for this is that multinational corporations, which almost by definition prioritize economic growth in monetary terms alone, are often more powerful than governments. An allied reason is the fact that throughout our recorded history all the major decision-makers, political, economic, cultural and religious, have worked out of cities. The city is the locus of political, economic and religious power. Is that not why we're here in New York City rather than in Santa Rosa?

What difference has this made to our understanding of ecological history? A seminal religious narrative, the Epic of Gilgamesh, records the rise of Uruk, a city state in Mesopotamia c. 2800 BCE, well before the First Axial Age. Gilgamesh enclosed the city and its sacred sanctuary within a circuit of walls estimated at six miles in length, with 900 towers. This created a physical and psychological barrier between what happened outside the walls and what happened inside them. Inside were urban workers insulated from the land outside as they no longer shared living space with its animals and plants. Perceptually and symbolically the city walls breached the integrity of the household of life.

I say symbolically because the work done inside the walls created demand for building materials and fuels brought in from outside, most obviously earth clay for bricks and forest timber for building construction. The workers' food too was obtained through trade with an external agrarian base that could produce a food surplus through the expansion of cultivated land at the expense of forests, wetlands and arid country. The large households attached to rulers, priests, traders, military commanders and scribes did not produce food either. Nor did the soldiers who manned the towers. Their job, then as now, involved readiness to destroy the supportive fabric of life.

This readiness to destroy is vividly portrayed in the Epic when its heroes, Gilgamesh and Enkidu, go outside the walls and enter the great Cedar Forest. They are filled with awe at the sight of trees "seventy-two cubits high." Yet Gilgamesh begins to cut them down and so rouses the anger of the forest guardian, the giant Humbaba. He is captured and, in spite of his pleas and his offer to give Gilgamesh the Forest, killed by them. Then the forest too, and the species within it, begins to die. And the process of desertification begins. All that can now be seen of Uruk are some baked clay bricks from the city wall in the Pergamon Museum in Berlin and an abandoned mound in the Iraqi desert.

For whether before or after the First or Second Axial Age, a city cannot be properly understood unless it is seen as functioning within a complex series of ecological processes that impact on the city and affect its inhabitants. But the obvious fact that city-dwellers too depend on natural systems for their survival is less immediately obvious when feedback from those systems is less instantaneous. We go to the tap for water, not to a river or a well. Food comes from a supermarket, not a field. Cities now draw resources from ecosystems the other side of the globe and export their waste there too. And as food supply and work within the city increase, so population expands and demands on external natural resources rise proportionately.

These supply and demand factors have been quantified and are now popularly known as a city's ecological footprint: an area far greater than that physically occupied. London's ecological footprint is 120 times greater than its geographical boundaries. The ecological footprint of a typical North American represents at least three times his/her share of the earth's resources. It is also the case that our footprints continue to grow while our individual "earthshares" shrink.

But—behind city walls, real or metaphorical, it is all too easy to ignore the size of the footprint and the ecological principle behind it: that growth of population and economy is limited by the least available environmental resource factor, and that no resource, such as fresh water, is infinite.[3] And in economic terms as usually understood, it is all too easy to ignore the fact that human economies can only exist within an ecology: that without an ecology there can be no economy.

What exactly then, do I mean by ecology? The word was first coined and then used in 1866 by a German biologist, Ernst Haeckel, to describe the study of all the environmental conditions that make the existence of living things possible. The prefix "eco" derives from the Greek term *oikos*, meaning the family home and household. In coining the term "ecology" Haeckel relied on a prior understanding and use of "eco" in the term *oikonomia* or "economy." There it meant (and still does) the way in which a household (or a country) organizes itself in order to ensure the supply, distribution and consumption of resources for those living there.

Haeckel relied on this common understanding of a household economy when he said that ecology is the study of the economy of Nature; of a common life system that sustains a community of living and interdependent beings through naturally occurring transfers of matter and energy within it and through dynamic exchanges between that community and all the physical factors in its environment: exchanges that in turn affect the evolution of both community and environment. Cities like Uruk are now abandoned mounds in a desert environment not just as a result of changes in rainfall and temperature but through overuse of resources and eventual exhaustion of the land. Haeckel wanted to highlight the complexity and necessity of these interactions between communities and environment and to draw attention to the necessary supply of natural resources on which all species' evolution and survival depend—including our own. Earth directly provides three of those essential resources: fertile soil, clean air and fresh water. The fourth one, heat or energy, comes to us ultimately from the sun. When we touch our skin, we touch air, water, soil and heat within us. But they are sourced outside us. Rarely do we think about their primary sources or about the fact, as I stress in *Gaia's Gift*, that we are gifted with them through Nature's economy; one that sustains and regulates the ecological lifeworld of the Earth household to which we belong.

This planetary understanding of the term "ecology" and its implicit acceptance of different scales of interaction between the personal, the local and the global was summed up in the opening statement from a declaration at a conference in Amsterdam in 2001 attended by more than a thousand delegates from scientific global climate change research programmes. They declared: "The Earth System behaves as a single self-regulating system comprised of physical, chemical, biological and human components."

The ecologically important point here is that no being, human or nonhuman, can live independently of that community or without affecting it through constant exchanges of matter and energy *from within it*. There is no question of human life being external to or independent of the earth system's self-regulatory functioning; or being independent of its common environmental resources, climatic variables or ecosystem constraints. That self-understanding (which I explore at length in *Sacred Gaia*) lies behind microbiologist Lynn Margulis's remark that "independence is a political, not a biological concept."

Independence is not a religious concept either. The original idea behind Haeckel's concept of ecology, that of an economy based on mutually fruitful and interrelated exchanges of energy, was used by early Christians to describe the mystery of relationships within God's being made visible in the world. Ephesians 3:2, 9 describes those relationships as "the *oikonomia tes Xaritos tou Theou* (the economy of the love of God) and the *oikonomia tou musteriou* (the economy of the mystery) hidden for all ages in the God in whom all is created." Irenaeus of Lyon used the term "economy" to describe the ways in which Jesus showed God to men in visible form through his many dealings with them, lest we should think ourselves to be "utterly remote from God." Tertullian used the analogy of a tree, its shoot and the fruit from it to describe the "economy" of living relationships between Father, Son and Spirit.[4] In the twentieth century Karl Rahner used the term "economic Trinity" to describe the living relationships between God and the world that are indissoluble from those within the Trinity.

I agree with Bob Miller that this makes the doctrine of the Trinity no less incomprehensible. But that makes my point here. For wherever the term "economy" was used religiously by Christians, it denoted a mysterious, living relationship or set of relationships that could not be confined within the limits of an individual existence [or a definition] but extended not only to all those from whom it emanated but encompassed and ultimately affected the lives of all. It referred not only to the mystery of relationships of love within God, and of God toward the world, but also to divine government of the natural world; to God's awesome talent for so managing the cosmos that each constituent part can perform its work with stunning efficiency. In today's terms, this reflects the ecological principle that *there is no human economy independent of a global (or divine) ecology.*

However, as I found in my study of these texts, the Greek concept of 'divine economy', with its connotations of mysterious, interlinked and all-encompassing relationships that emerge and develop organically, was translated into Latin and thence into English by such "comprehensible" terms as "dispensation," "disposition," "management" and, from the eleventh century on, "stewardship." These terms cut the mystery of the divine economy down to human size; they reduce it to the level of a series of human transactions, at best overseen by God, but in effect, carried out by God's human surrogates supposedly operating by divine authority. They, it is assumed, are in charge of dispensing, controlling and managing all natural resources; supervising and regulating them for human benefit alone and now, overwhelmingly, for financial profit.

All this has reduced the notion of the divine, mysterious economy within which the Earth household belongs and functions to a human, supposedly manageable enterprise in which we use earth's natural resources solely for our benefit. As I write, there is a report that Alaska's Tongrass temperate rainforest, untouched up to now, is to be logged. And the resources of Antarctica, the last relatively untouched natural resource base on the planet, are being targeted for exploitation by biotech companies on the apparently unassailable grounds that its resources can be exploited for our benefit and for profit share.

The original notion of divine economy, however, implied a total, relational, natural and supernatural life support system mysterious beyond words, as God is: one that cannot ever be fully expressed in human terms, controlled by human power or managed by human agency. For it encompasses and is intended to benefit the whole household of life within which we belong. No aspect or feature of that, whether microcosm or macrocosm, can be separated out by us in any absolute sense from what is deemed sacred or holy. Nor can what I call the sacredness of Gaia be enclosed by church walls or divorced from the environment that supports life. Nor can the mystery of divine presence be separated from the interactions in which each being is connected with all others and, I would say, with God. In the words attributed to Jesus in the Gospel of Thomas: "From me all has come forth and to me all has reached. Split a piece of wood, I am there; Lift up the stone; there you will find me" (Thom 77).

But the concept of Nature's economy had already lost these earlier Christian overtones when Haeckel defined the word "ecology." The religious vision of Nature's economy as God's gift to the whole household of life had been reduced to one of ourselves as its stewards. More worrying still was the theological assumption, taken up without question by many scientists, that God had devised Nature's economy *so that we can use it for our own advantage.* So botanist Carl Linnaeus, a devout Christian, wrote in the eighteenth century:

> All these treasures of Nature, so artfully contrived, so wonderfully propagated, so providentially supported throughout her three kingdoms, seem intended by the Creator for the sake of man. Everything may be made subservient to his use; if not immediately, yet mediately, not so to that of other animals. By this help of reason man tames the fiercest animals, pursues and catches the swiftest, nay he is able to reach even those which lie hidden in the bottom of the sea. . . .[5]

This explicit authorization to utilize our fellow species and all earth's natural resources to our own advantage extends, it is supposed, to eliminating those we think undesirable (as Gilgamesh destroyed Humbaba) and multiplying those we find useful. Part of my response to the unbridled arrogance evident in such claims is to stress the ecologically correct and religiously subversive final command to Adam and Eve from God in Genesis 3:38: "Serve the earth from which you were taken!" However to see ourselves as Earth's servants rather than all things on earth, indeed earth itself being there to serve us and our ends, requires a revolution in religious self-perception.

In *Making God Laugh* I tease out yet another pertinent religious thread in the concept of ecology. The Greek term *oikoumene* (ecumene), again derived from the word *oikos* meaning home or household, had the expanded sense of "the whole civilized world" or "the global community of life on earth." The Christian religious use of "ecumenism," however, while it derived its sense from the notion of the global community of life, has confined it to members of different Churches. Although not to all of them and practically to no other faith communities.

Christian ecumenism has, then, lost its implicit links with the global community of life on earth and with the all-encompassing mystery of the 'divine economy' revealed within all God has created throughout ecological history. The "Great Ecumene" is now confined to an exclusive human community rather than one embracing the "more-than-human" world. This phrase of David Abram's presupposes what ecology teaches: that we are human only in contact with and by sharing the natural resources of the larger family of life on earth. And that that includes, along with the human, the multiple nonhuman entities that constitute the ecological life-world of our personal and global environment.

This summary account of the religious and scientific insights that have fed into the concept of ecology gives us, I hope, some insight into what "The Age of Ecology" has to do with previous ages in human history. Doing so it also offers, I hope, a rather different, expansive paradigm for the future of faith. Einstein said that one can't solve a problem within the paradigm in which it was created: in our case, the traditional Christian paradigm of human salvation history. It has become a problem by confining religious faith and hope within the bounds of a fall/redemption theology in which all living beings are presumed fallen, but (relatively few) humans alone are saved. Its exclusion clauses have been and are used to justify violence, in the name of God, against various categories of people and against all other beings. All on the basis of the theological claim not only to speak to God, and about God, but for God.

An ecological paradigm counters this theological arrogance by consciously recentering us within the religious and scientific dimensions of the household of life. It expands our vision of the mystery of God's all-encompassing relationship with the whole world beyond the narrow confines of salvation history and so necessarily enlarges the framework for what we say about God beyond that of divine-human relations recorded within the Bible or in traditional teaching. It encourages a positively critical and properly humble questioning of the human-centredness of major Christian doctrines by taking full account of our ecological history.

This exposes the arrogance behind the oft-repeated liturgical phrases *pro nobis* and *propter nos*, meaning both "for us" and "because of us." "For us" assumes that God's mysterious relationship with the world throughout ecological history has been centred on us alone and that earth's creatures and resources exist solely for our use and benefit. "Because of us" assumes that because one man sinned, death entered the world as a punishment inflicted by God on all members of the household of life; except for those later saved from death through Jesus's death. Ecological history, however, teaches us that death is and has always been an evolutionary necessity in and for the life of every being.

Last, but by no means least, there is the arrogance that assumes the revelation of God is fully contained in certain human words addressed to and clearly understood by certain humans; but not others. And certainly not by the more-than-human members of the family of life. But the Gospel of Thomas credits Jesus with saying:

> When your leaders tell you
> Look, the kingdom of God is in the skies!
> The birds who fly there have known this all along.
> When they say
> Look, the kingdom of heaven is in the depths of the sea!
> The fish and the dolphins who swim there have known this all along. (Thom 3)

And how do we compare with them? Again, the Gospel of Thomas has something pertinent to say:

> The kingdom will not come by watching for it.
> You cannot say: *Look, here it is!* Or *Look, it's over there!*
> Rather the father's kingdom is spread out upon the earth,
> and people just do not see it. (Thom 113)

This is the fundamental religious vision taught us by ecological history, by indigenous peoples and by those groups and communities who now relate their own stories, in every sense, within the context of Earth's story. And the future of faith may depend on how well we learn from them to see the divine economy spread out upon the earth.

Part IV

The Moral Imperative: Sources and Sanctions

Can We Still Teach Biblical Moral Values?

Robert M. Price

From the 1963 Friends Home Service Committee report, *Towards a Quaker View of Sex,* up to 1991's Presbyterian working document, *Keeping Body and Soul Together: Sexuality, Spirituality, and Social Justice,* Protestant denominations have been agonizing like Hamlet over what course of action (or inaction) they should urge on their members—if indeed that is the point of such encyclicals. Are they perhaps public relations documents? To show how relevant the church is to those who might not otherwise consider joining up? "Here's what we do and do not stand for." In this case they are descriptive documents. But then of course they are not what they're supposed to be, since every one of these liberalizing charters of sexual ethics is hotly contested, fiercely disputed by majority or large minority caucuses who start planning a schism. No one can draft a statement that speaks for all factions on a question like sex.

But if not descriptive, are such statements after all prescriptive? Are they supposed to provide a basis on which clergy are dutifully to catechize their flocks, like a new sauce formula handed down to the franchises by the head office of a fast food chain? Personally, I do not relish the role of clergyman as party hack, as dutiful flunky. Nor do I relish the notion of a congregation as a flock of docile sheep who will imbibe a pastor's or a denominational committee's opinions without a bleat. If we think Christian education is a matter of telling church members what to think, we are giving them the most pernicious miseducation they could get: indoctrination and the stifling of moral autonomy. But the issues the denominational commissions are wrestling with are quite real and deserve some serious attention.

Biblical Morality

Conservative spokespersons in churchly debates over sexual morality are in the habit of saying, as one Presbyterian did, "What's at stake is the very identity and character of [our] church, which from the beginning has held the Scriptures as the sole authority of our faith and practice." They see the proposals of their more liberal coreligionists as a dangerous slippage from what they regard as the "eternal verities" of God's Word. The whole problem we face is that we are surfing, precariously balanced, on the crest of a wave of cultural change. But the Bible provides no fixed lighthouse for us because we can trace a similar process of change within it. In the early stages polygamy and casual divorce were all right. Later these allowances are qualified. The Patriarch Abraham could marry his half-sister. Leviticus outlaws this. The adultery ban did not exclude having concubines, or possibly, even visiting prostitutes. It just meant not having sex with one's neighbor's spouse. This has changed in the New Testament period. Unlike the Old Testament legislators, Jesus seems to have considered divorce illicit, though whether he was just saying it was tragic or actually trying to put a stop to it, New Testament interpreters cannot agree. Besides, Matthew (6:32; 19:3–9) differs from Mark (10:2–9) and Luke (16:18) as to just what Jesus said on the issue. So we have both change and exegetical ambiguity in the text. Where, pray tell, are the eternal verities?

One might contend that there are eternal, transcultural norms floating somewhere above the text of the Bible, that they are manifest in the text only in culturally-conditioned forms, and that it is the job of the biblical interpreter to sniff out the transcultural principles and apply them in our day, in appropriate, culturally adapted garb. Charles Kraft, missionary anthropologist at Fuller Seminary, makes a good go of it in his *Christianity in Culture*. But note that, this way, it's actually some supposed conceptual entity *outside* the text, not the text itself, that wears the mantle of "biblical authority" (a perfect example of the "logocentric fallacy" attacked by Derrida).

And there is a further irony. If one goes this route, the route of sophisticated and casuistical hermeneutics, one will be playing precisely the game the liberal caucuses are playing. Once one goes this route, there simply can be no more talk about having the "clear teaching of the Bible" on one's side. A case in point: I marvel at the arrogance or the naiveté of some Pro-Life advocates who shout that the Bible condemns abortion, a claim some Pro-Choicers must accept, since a group of them burned some Bibles in a recent demonstration. But in fact the issue never even comes up in the Bible! One may think it is a valid inference from "Thou shalt do no murder," but then one is doing cross-cultural hermeneutics—in other words, fancy footwork. Just like one's "Bible-twisting" opponents.

Property Rights and Wrongs

Another factor, even more important, is that biblical sexual norms are based on quite different assumptions than the bases of our moral reasoning, whether we are fundamentalists or liberals. It seems that the biblical concern for virginity before marriage and fidelity within marriage, the cornerstones of the traditional Christian sex ethic, was mainly a matter of male property rights. Note that Exodus 20:17 includes a man's wife with his property inventory as that which must not be coveted by another man, the commandments being issued only to men. For David to commit adultery with Bathsheba is to steal Uriah's property. As if I were to sneak into your den and use your VCR every time I saw you leave your house.

In Exodus 22:16–17 we read these edifying words: "If a man seduces a virgin who is not betrothed, and lies with her, he shall give the marriage present for her, and make her his wife. If her father utterly refuses to give her to him, he shall pay money equivalent to the marriage present for virgins." Just whom is this law meant to protect? Not the hapless woman, but her father, who must not be cheated out of the bride price he was entitled to for the commodity of his virgin daughter. The seducer is not entitled to free sexual favors. He must pay for the virginity he has taken—*from the woman's father!* He is not to be left holding the bag: deprived of the bride price he had hoped to receive and stuck now with unsalable "used goods"!

In the New Testament period the sexual property idea had been extended to both partners: "The husband should give to her wife her conjugal rights, and likewise the wife to her husband. For the wife does not rule over her own body, but the husband does; likewise the husband does not rule over his own body, but the wife does" (1 Corinthians 7:3–4). Whether this egalitarian balance had been struck already in Judaism or whether it was a Christian innovation, I do not think anyone knows.

Moral and Ritual Purity

Another presupposition of biblical (i.e., ancient Israelite and Christian) sex mores was the notion of purity and defilement. This is a difficult thing to explain. It is not really moral, but rather ritual degradation. As anthropologist Mary Douglas ("The Abominations of Leviticus," in her *Purity and Danger*) has ably shown, the purity laws of Leviticus, like those of other cultures, are attempts to safe-

guard the categorical boundary-markers set up by the society. The
categories of reality set up long ago by a society dictate what is
pure and impure, in terms of food, sex, intermarriage, worship, etc.
Douglas argues, quite cogently I think, that this is why the ancient
Israelite laws forbade pork. They had never heard of Trichinosis; the
trouble with pigs was that they were not *true cattle* since they did
not chew the cud, even though they had cloven hooves. True cattle,
which one could eat, did both. Why no shellfish? They were neither
fish nor fowl. Well, not real fish anyway; there was something weird
about them: they lived in the sea, but they lacked fins and scales.
They were not true to type, fell between the cracks, and thus they
were off limits.

Similarly, there could not be crossings of lines between groups of
potential sexual partners unless they were legitimated (made pure)
with appropriate rites of passage. Marriage allowed for the crossing
into sexual life, but even so, sexual intercourse rendered one tem-
porarily "unclean." This did not mean it was immoral, as some early
Christian theologians thought. Quite the contrary. *It had nothing to
do with morality.* The biblical people had a pretty robust approval of
sexuality. *Ritual impurity* was the issue.

And some lines between potential sexual partners could never be
crossed: that between human and animal, and, in some historical
periods, that between Israelite and non-Israelite. On the other hand,
sexual contact did have to be a crossing of lines: hence the prohibition
of incest (within the lines of the family circle) and homosexuality
(within the same gender).

Some degrees of impurity were fairly trivial; they did not count
any more when the sun set. Others were so weighty that they
incurred capital punishment. Was it *immoral* for a man to lie with a
beast? No, it was rather an "abomination," literally, a mixing, a gross
defilement that could not be harbored within Israel.

Early Christianity reshuffled the categories of purity and impurity,
mainly because it rapidly became a Gentile movement, shedding
traditional Jewish mores as it assimilated new Hellenistic ones. But
they seem not to have eliminated purity rules *per se*. Mark says Jesus
eliminated food purity laws (7:19). Matthew thought he hadn't and
so eliminated this statement from Mark (Matthew 15:17), but even
Matthew dropped the rule that eating without washing one's hands
incurred ritual impurity (15:20). Does the story of Jesus blessing
the (impure) woman with the issue of blood (Mark 6:24–34) mean
he rejected sexual purity laws? Hardly! No more than his allowing the hungry to glean on the Sabbath meant he disdained the
Sabbath (Mark 2:23–27). His point rather seems to have been that
human need takes precedence over such laws in individual cases.

Also, note the anxiety of Corinthian spouses with pagan partners over whether their children were "holy" (1 Corinthians 7:14). Paul replies that they are, and so is the pagan spouse, thanks to his or her attachment to the Christian. He is far from throwing out the whole distinction.

These categories seem strange to us, but I think it is safe to say that we have our own culturally defined categories of purity and defilement as well. For instance, why is it a joke that certain restaurants might chop up *cat meat* for supper? Why would you be disgusted to find *dog* on the menu? Why do most Americans think it is revolting to eat bugs, though grubs and chocolate-covered ants are a delicacy in some cultures? Why will you eat a lobster as a rare treat yet turn green (and not with envy) if you see someone eat a roach? Isn't that lobster pretty much a kissing cousin of the loathsome bug you spray to death? What counts as food varies from culture to culture, and we all regard the animals not considered food in our culture as somehow disgusting to eat. It is degrading to eat them but hardly immoral.

Why is it that anything that comes out of the body is repugnant once it's out? It has crossed a boundary it cannot recross. If it does one will be defiled. But has one done anything immoral? Of course not. Moral guilt or outrage is not the source of the disgust one feels. It is impurity that one cringes from. What I am getting at is that in the Bible sexual transgressions are at least as much and as often purity transgressions as moral ones.

Honor and Shame
Thirdly, biblical sex laws have more to do with honor and shame than with good and evil, morality and guilt. Studies of Mediterranean peasant sociology tell us that it was incumbent upon an ancient Mediterranean man to prove his virility by fathering many children, and probably also by deflowering as many virgins as he could get away with. Also by having as many wives as he could afford (hence the great honor attached to Solomon's 700 wives and 300 concubines; they attested, supposedly, his great sexual prowess). The more wives, children, sexual conquests a man could boast, the greater the esteem or honor he had earned in the eyes of his fellows.

This business of male honor also explains, I think, why the woman was always blamed for a childless marriage. For the man to be at fault was unthinkable. In some cultures a shaman or itinerant holy man was brought in to miraculously grant the "barren" woman fertility. Probably in such cases, like Sarah and other recipients of angelic annunciations, what really happened was that the woman was simply impregnated by a man (the holy man or "angel") who was not sterile like her husband. (See M. J. Field, *Angels and Ministers of Grace.*)

The honorable behavior of the woman was just the reverse of the man's. It was her duty to remain sexually inviolate except for her husband—because he *owned* her! He had to be on the watch for sly rogues (like himself!) who could score honor points by seducing his virgin daughter or sister (remember the vengeance Simeon and Levi exacted on Shechem for the rape of Dinah!) or his wife.

Hence the double standard. Only they perceived no inconsistency: it was a single standard designed around the male competition for honor. The sexual purity of women was a "limited good" in the society, and so competition for male honor was like a game of Capture the Flag, with the sexual honor and chastity of the women as the flag. (On all this, see Bruce J. Malina, *The New Testament World: Insights From Cultural Anthropology* and L. William Countryman, *Dirt, Greed & Sex.*) The honor of the woman was itself simply a function of her value as her husband's or father's property: she was a more valuable commodity if her honor were intact, like a collectible doll still in the original box.

In all this what was at stake was by no means morality! Rather it was all a matter of *points*. Status! If one had a lot of it, one had honor. If a man had lost the limited good of his wife's chastity or if a woman lost it, he or she was shamed. But that's not the same thing as moral guilt.

By the same token, prostitutes were not sinful; they were shameful—or rather shame*less*: so heedless of shame/honor distinctions that they were forced to the margins of society. They did not play the game everyone else played, so they had to sit on the sidelines. (Think of Belle Watlin in *Gone With the Wind*; she is a highly moral character yet dares not show her face in public. She bears shame but not guilt.)

What are we to make of all this if we are concerned to derive sexual instruction from the Bible? We might be tempted to conclude that the Bible can be no help to us since it is not really talking about sexual morality in our sense at all. True, it isn't. But that hardly means it is of no help.

Over the years I have read and heard a good many discussions by Christian moralists on why premarital sex is supposed to be wrong, and I have always been surprised at how weak the arguments were. It seemed like the worst kind of special pleading. I now think this is because these moralists were trying to make something into an ethical matter that belonged to a completely different realm of discourse: that of property, purity, and honor. One example: readers are told that it is wrong to live together without getting married because the law requires a marriage license; thus, since Christians are supposed to obey the secular authorities (Romans 13), premarital sex is immoral! Pretty contrived, to my way of thinking. But what *has* been dimly perceived here is that, far from being a moral matter, it is really a question of honor, of having one's sexual union legitimated by public recognition.

It ought to go without saying that some premarital sexual encounters would be immoral in the full sense, say, if they involved deception ("Sure, I'll marry you, baby!"), manipulation, or exploitation. But it would be the dishonesty, not the sexuality, of the act that would make it immoral. Similarly, we have a strong moral reason for not committing adultery. Insofar as spouses have pledged their exclusive sexual fidelity to each other, adultery is the violation of a trust. Thus it is wrong, morally wrong in the full sense. (The ambiguous situation of so-called "open marriages," on the other hand, is a more difficult matter. We seem there to be verging on a multiple-spouse marriage, such as is practiced in some cultures.)

"Sin" Versus "Wrong"

I believe we have traditionally been talking about shame and honor, purity and impurity, and even property rights, when we imagined we were talking about morality. Before the cultural revolution of the 60s it worked pretty well, and it still may work. Really, the offensive thing about the biblical mores I have just discussed was the one-sidedness of them. They were all outrageously biased toward the man. But the notions of sexual *property*, *purity*, and *honor* are in their own right by no means to be despised, nor sexist.

Mothers still warn daughters that they should not give away their sexual favors for free. They should not come to be known as "cheap," a significant choice of words. They should hold out for a commitment to marriage to test the professions of love on the part of a teenage Lothario in heat. Here is the use of the property analogy, but note that the woman's sexuality is her own property. By being taught chastity, she is being taught to value her own property. Not a bad idea. And not oppressive. Parents tell daughters not to have sex casually lest they be regarded as "sluts," "'ho's," "bad girls," etc. If she heeds mom's advice she will have given up easy popularity (= esteem without honor) with boys in exchange for the superior good of honor among her peers. This still seems not a bad way of looking at it.

What about young men? Of course their peers still deem wide sexual activity as a badge of honor. Nothing has changed in that respect. But as Christians trying to educate our youth, we must urge upon our young men the Pauline maxim of not causing one's brother, or in this case one's sister, to stumble into sin (1 Corinthians 8:9–13; Romans 14:13–15). That is, if one's honor in the eyes of one's male peers requires one's dishonoring women by initiating premarital sex with them, then as a Christian one will resolve to trade honor "before men" for honor unseen by them but visible to one's Father in heaven who sees what is in secret. Of course this is exactly the trade-off Jesus commends in the Sermon on the Mount: honor is good, but honor from God is more valuable than honor from men, and so it is worth having less of the latter if in exchange one will gain more of the former (Matthew 6:1–6, 16–18; John 5:44). And again, in all this we are still talking in terms of honor, not morality!

I have now tried to show how sexual conduct remains as it was, a matter of property and honor. But what about purity? Here is perhaps my most controversial proposal. I think that premarital sex, viewed within traditional Christian values, counts not really as a wrong, but rather as a sin. It is a ritual transgression, not a moral one. Let us remind ourselves again of the difference. There are some biblical boundaries which one transgresses without moral stain, such as food laws, but with ritual consequences. If unclean food rendered one impure, one could not approach the altar for the duration. Paul very clearly states that there is nothing immoral about eating meat offered to idols (unless one knows it will scandalize someone else), but as a ritual offense it may be deadly! He says that such eating at the altar of demons bars one from the Table of Christ (1 Corinthians 10:14–21)—just like in Leviticus! Ritual impurity, not moral, is in question.

Why, after all, do we have two different words, "sin" and "wrong"? What is the difference? A wrong may be done to a fellow human being, but a sin is perpetrated uniquely God-ward. One cannot injure God or wrong him. But certain acts cut one off from his holy presence. They are ritual in nature, and we call them sins. The great insight of the Prophets was that morally wrong acts against men and women are *also* counted as sins. This was the great moralization of the Holy that Rudolf Otto chronicled (*The Idea of the Holy*). But that hardly means immoral acts are simply the same thing as sins. It means that moral transgressions separate their doer from God as surely as ritual transgressions.

But the conversion does not work both ways: though God counts all moral wrongs as unholy, he does not necessarily count all ritually unclean acts as morally wrong. Otherwise, how could Paul have declared many of the ancient scriptural taboos defunct in the new dispensation of Christ? He certainly did not think morality had

changed! He still quotes scripture with enthusiasm when it comes
to morality. But kosher laws? Circumcision? Holy days? Take them
or leave them, says the Apostle to the Gentiles.

Back to sex. I believe that the hushed tones of condemnation and
all the talk of "stain" with which Christians have surrounded premarital sex shows that something other than morality was involved.
There is a sense of defilement, of ritual uncleanness. Notice that
Paul compares sexual transgressions to defiling a temple, a ritual
infraction, in 1 Corinthians 6:16–19 (the word "immorality" in the
Revised Standard Version begs the question; the Greek is *porneia*,
"prostitution").

Once a friend told me that he taught Sunday School in the strict
fundamentalist church he attended, but would do nothing of a
more pastoral nature. He felt he could not bring himself to control
his sexual behavior. He slept around. He felt that this behavior
barred him from any form of ministry other than strict information
dispensing. Why did he not flee the church with a bad conscience?
Or, if he felt he was in the right, why did he not feel such a deep
moral contradiction that he rejected the Christian ethic? For this
reason, many gay Christians have felt they had to leave the church.
I think my friend had implicitly understood that he was rendered
not morally guilty but ritually unclean. He could not approach the
altar as a priest, so to speak, as long as he engaged in ritually impure
behavior. But he felt generally that he belonged, because he felt no
real *moral* conflict.

And one often hears of evangelical singles who quietly disre-
gard the ban on premarital sex just as Catholic couples disdain the
decrees of their church not to use birth control. Deep down they
feel it is not wrong, but neither would they repudiate the teaching
of their church. They have committed a sin but done nothing morally wrong. Some years ago a group of Protestant seminarians sent a
letter to *Playboy* admitting, apparently without much guilt, that, yes,
they and their fiancés had engaged in premarital sex. Oh, sure, it was
sin, but it wasn't wrong. I am making explicit what was implicit in
the actions of these people. As in the Bible, premarital sex is a ritual
purity issue, not a moral one. Transgression is sin, and sin ought to
be avoided. Sin is no light matter, but it can be forgiven.

Practically speaking, what difference does this distinction make?
Just this: as long as we make premarital sex a moral wrong, we can
put forth no cogent reason to avoid it. And then people will think
there is no reason to avoid it. But if we come clean and admit there
is nothing immoral about it, that it is not in the same league with
stealing or lying, but that it is ritually, religiously wrong, like blas-

phemy or approaching the eucharist without a meditative spirit, we can inculcate among Christian youth an appropriate and honest conscience about it.

Brazen New World

I have argued that the strange-seeming mores of the Bible, stripped of their male chauvinism, can still provide a workable guide for Christian sexual conduct. But even in this moment, I am aware of the flood waters of cultural change eroding the ground beneath my feet. The writers of the denominational ethics reports I mentioned at the start may be saying precisely that cultural change is happening so fast that the very social conventions which give categories of shame, boundary transgression, etc., their meaning are rapidly fading, to be replaced by others.

Many people are coming to see sexuality not as a thing one possesses and must guard, but rather simply as a pleasant biological action, like kissing. For them it is simply not a question of property. That seems as absurd to them as when we used to warn young men that if they masturbated they would prematurely expend their energy and virility, as if they had only so much of it. (See Vern Bullough and Bonnie Bullough, *Sin, Sickness, and Sanity: A History of Sexual Attitudes.*)

If no one any more believes that sex is more than recreational, then no one is going to look down on you for your sexual escapades during Spring Break. It is apparently no longer regarded as shameful behavior. And in our rationalistic, bare-bones Protestantism which, as Weber said, has "disenchanted the world," where no one believes in any wrong but moral wrong, where holiness has become a synonym for morality, if we cannot show premarital sex is wrong, we cannot say it is sin either. The distinction I have argued will just go out the window.

Our sexual mores are in many ways just reflections of social convention and consensus. This was no less true in the Bible, as we have seen. Social assumptions move beneath us like the tectonic plates. Their motion is slow but irresistible. We have to live on the continents that are shifting; there are no others that stand still. Maybe the framers of the Quaker, Presbyterian, and other documents have seen that. Maybe they are looking further ahead than I am.

I suspect that before long it will become apparent that the only way to maintain more traditional Christian sex mores in a society indifferent to them is to construct a religious ghetto-existence like the Amish or the Hasidim or the Catholic Charismatics in Ann Arbor. Our ethic will be an increasingly cultic one, not a matter of "doing what is right in the sight of all" (Romans 12:17). One day shunning premarital sex is going to seem as esoteric a rule as the Jehovah's Witnesses' banning of blood transfusions. Perhaps that day has come. That's what the writers of those denominational sex-creeds are telling us.

Christianity changes as culture changes. This must be so even if we view our religion as counter-cultural. It must move with the culture to some extent if it is to be in a position to counter it! The Amish make little impact on the world around them; the Quakers, in their quiet way, do. The Amish are not willing to budge; the Quakers are. These are our options.

I have tried to show how the biblical values of sexual property, honor, and purity may be carried over into Christian sexuality today, but those values are inherently no more eternal than the various biblical laws based on them, many of which we reject. Who knows what Christian sexual mores will look like in the brave new world that is ever around the corner? The writer of Leviticus could never have anticipated Paul, nor could Paul have foreseen the evangelical sex manuals like *Intended for Pleasure*, much less Bishop Spong's *Living in Sin?* and Joseph Fletcher's *Situation Ethics.*

Maybe our faith should be less a fearful clinging to the taboos of the past than a trust that future generations of Christians will use the same creative wisdom Christians have (sometimes) used in the past. "Who are you to pass judgment on the servant of another? It is before his own master that he stands or falls. And the Master is able to make him stand" (Romans 14:4).

The Boy Scout and the Mafia Boss

Is There a Future for Christian Ethics in America?

Jack A. Hill

Introduction

T hinking about moral experience in our times reminds me of the ancient Buddhist story of the blind men who are asked to describe an elephant.[1]

> The one who feels the trunk says the elephant is like a tree branch. The one grasping a leg argues that an elephant is like a pillar. The one feeling the ear asserts that an elephant is like a fan. The one grasping the tail insists that an elephant is like a rope. And the one who encounters the side of the elephant argues that the others are all wrong; an elephant is like a wall.[2]

While the story teaches a lesson about the relativity of our individual vantage points, it is important to stress that each person *does* have a partial grasp of something. That is, based on their respective experiences of the elephant, they each form understandings that are true to their experiences. Albeit in a very limited way, elephants are like ropes, branches, fans, etc.

Taking the analogy one step further, we could imagine that after arguing vociferously the blind man who touched the tail takes the blind man who touched the ear over to the tail and places his hand on the tail. "See," he might say, "the elephant is like a rope after all!" We could also imagine the surprised blind man taking his self-assured colleague over to the ear, placing his hand on the ear, and replying, "Yes, but the elephant is *also* like a fan!" We could then imagine the development of intense debate about whether "tail-ness" or "earness" is really the defining characteristic of "elephant-ness," with each side arguing that the object of the other's point of reference was more of an appendage.

This scenario strikes me as analogous to the predicament of ethics in America today. The nation's moral ethos is, like the elephant, an amalgam of different textures, feels, shapes and sizes. Like the blind men catching hold of different parts of the beast, each of us adheres to certain patches or strands of the ethos, and builds up, consciously or unconsciously, what become conventional understandings based on our perception of the patches.[3] We may even be challenged to experience what another patch is like, but we inevitably do so from the vantage point of our own patch. Try as we may, we seem irretrievably captive to the perspectives embedded in our worlds of experience. Even the post-modernist's contention, that it is naïve to posit any underlining unity, is itself a patch of another sort.

Given this predicament, we need to acknowledge the ambiguity of the American moral landscape.[4] There is no one authoritative moral tradition. While there are adherents to traditions, such as absolutist ethics,[5] who claim that they have access to absolute moral truths, they would not claim that all or even most Americans concur in that claim. But given this moral pluralism, it is important to grant the reality and potential legitimacy of each ongoing patch or strand in the landscape. That is to say, if a moral perspective is rooted in an enduring experience of life, then it should not be easily or presumptively dismissed, even if it is frequently used for purposes of self-delusion.[6]

Finally, in order to gain a "sense of the whole" we will have to do more than simply view the different parts of the moral landscape in relation to each other. Referring back to our elephant story, let's imagine that all five blind men eventually introduce each other to each other's experience of the elephant. What then? They would still be at a loss to "see" the creature that is not identical with either the tail or the trunk, or with the tail, the trunk and the other three parts all meshed together. My thesis is that they will need to experience a whole different gestalt or what Thomas Kuhn calls a "paradigm shift."[7] In religious language, they will need to undergo a "conversion" of perspective. I submit that the process of interacting with these traditions—of living self-consciously in today's pluralistic and multi-faceted American village—prepares the experiential ground for prompting such a new, radical way of seeing ethics. And because the moral teachings of the historical Jesus represented an alternative, subversive wisdom for his time and place, they may constitute matchsticks that can ignite the flame of a paradigm shift in ethics for us today.[8]

In the following analysis I will therefore first sketch what I take to be popular moral traditions in American life. Then I will view these traditions in relation to fragments of Jesus' wisdom concerning who we are, where we are headed as a people, and rules of thumb for everyday life.[9] In a dialectical mode, I will both read Jesus' wisdom through the lens of American moral motifs and critique the motifs in the light of Jesus' wisdom. In the process, I will seek not to provide yet another moral perspective, but to evoke an alternative way of talking about our common moral life.

Briefly, the hallmarks of my approach include an emphasis on (1) *beginning where we are*, in all its diversity, confusion and divisiveness; (2) *honoring the validity of personal and social experience*, with all the epistemological problems empiricism entails;[10] (3) *encountering the otherness* implicit in the moral worldview of Jesus, all the hermeneutical problems notwithstanding; and (4) *formulating new ways* to articulate the base points of ethics in America in relation to the Jesus tradition. Or, recalling our elephant story; we're standing in front of the elephant; we have valid, though partial, experiences of it; we encounter a stranger who speaks with an odd, yet compelling voice about it; and in dialoguing with the stranger we begin to see the elephant in ways that prompt us to re-discover who we are, re-envision where we are going, and re-consider what we need to do to get there. To ask whether or not the elephant really exists "out there" independent of us is to become drawn into a philosophical discussion that is pointless. What we do have are our experiences and to those I now turn.

Born in the U.S.A.

The Vietnam War represented something of a watershed in American history. For many veterans and war resisters, to be "born in the U.S.A.," suddenly became, in the lyrics of Bruce Springsteen, to be "Born down in dead man's town . . . down in the shadow of the penitentiary," where there is "Nowhere to run" and "Nowhere to go."[11] But this sentiment was not universally shared by baby boomers, some of whom felt a burst of patriotic pride when they heard Lee Greenwood sing, "I'm proud to be an Amer-i-can."[12] Commentators tended to take up sides in what became known as the "culture wars" in American social and political life. The apparent unity of moral resolve and purpose associated with WWII and life in the 50s had been rent asunder. To confound the matter, religion didn't seem to be much help. There were Christians and Jews on each side, and liberals and conservatives were equally adamant that Scripture supported their respective points of view. How could we find any ethical mooring, much less re-establish moral authority in our lives together?

The motifs in the title of this essay, "The Boy Scout and the Mafia Boss," reflect polar moral identifications that lie beneath the language of culture wars and, I think, more adequately reflect deep-seated tensions in the American psyche. On the one hand, there is the ideal of the Boy Scout—the reliable and self-disciplined young man who is always prepared to take care of himself and to help people in need. The Scout motto is "Be Prepared," and the Scout Law is "A Scout is trustworthy, loyal, helpful, friendly, courteous, kind, obedient, cheerful, thrifty, brave, clean (and) reverent."[13] In the U.S. context, the Boy Scout is the "American boy," a junior citizen who will become an "American Man."[14] Scouts join local patrols and troops, train and have adventures in the great outdoors and become part of a world brotherhood of scouts.[15] The Boy Scout is the good boy, the paragon of virtue, and the "right stuff."

On the other hand, there is America's fascination with the shadowy underworld of the mafia boss.[16] The Godfather is also "trustworthy," indeed a self-styled "man of honor"—a family man par excellence who can be counted on to aid those in difficulty, especially from one's own immigrant community. But he is no Boy Scout. Rather, he bends people to his will by force or threat of force. Like a god unto himself, he is judge, prosecutor and jury—acting above the law to achieve his own sense of justice. Indeed, by doing our dirty work for us, he removes the sources of our guilt. We are enamored by his wanton uses of power and influence. He represents the collective embodiment, in a modern urban setting, of the medieval warlord and frontier bandit. Why are we drawn to him? There is something in the American spirit that secretly revels in the extraordinary bank heist, the rampage of the outlaw and the escape of the prisoner.[17] The mafia boss is that part of us that not only rebels against the sanctimonious, nationalistic excesses of the Boy Scout, but who does so with a dramatic flare that takes our breath away. He is the bad boy, the scion of vice, and the benign "terminator."[18]

The Boy Scout and mafia boss are related to many other popular motifs in America today, such as the contrasting images of the Lone Ranger and the suburban professional. The Lone Ranger—that masked man who rode off into the sunset on his horse Silver—pushes the Boy Scout metaphor in the direction of a radical, self-reliant and socially disengaged individualism. The suburban professional, what William May has called the "beleaguered ruler,"[19] refines and hones the mafia motif as a "highly credentialed" power broker in an occupational subculture. While such images may seem far removed from what we normally think of as moral teachings, they all recapitulate core moral traditions in the American experience. In the ensuing analysis I will suggest how this is the case by correlating the Boy Scout and mafia boss motifs with four basic stories or "narratives" in American culture: the Biblical covenant, the mission of America, the Enlightenment vision of progress and the human potential movement.[20] It should then become clear how our motifs from popular culture express enduring moral sentiments about God, country, work and self.

The New Israel and
the Eagle Scout

The Biblical Covenant

The Pilgrims who landed in New England in the 1600s intended to build what H. Richard Niebuhr has called "the Kingdom of God in America."[21] They viewed themselves as obedient servants in a covenant relationship with the Judeo-Christian God. Like their Israelite predecessors, they also understood themselves to be the elect or chosen among all peoples. In covenant relation with God, the Pilgrims were stewards, not owners, of God's creation. But as covenantal partners with God, they were obliged "to be faithful to Jesus' command that they love both God and neighbor, for faithfulness was the appropriate response to God's gift of the covenant."[22]

Loving God and neighbor in the family of God entailed submitting to the will of the common good, generating an ethos of voluntary self-sacrifice.[23] This ethos extended to warfare, for according to the Biblical story, God gives the gift of land to Israel, in part at least, to punish the present inhabitants of the land.[24] And receiving the gift entails obeying all of God's laws, including having no other gods before "him," Sabbath keeping, treating workers fairly, and caring for orphans, the poor, strangers, and widows.

For Christians, the Biblical story is further developed in the life and teachings of Jesus. Jesus, viewed as the Christ of faith, is the Son of God who is sent into the world to reconcile it with God. Jesus proclaims the reign of God by teaching in metaphors and parables that often suggest a reversal of ordinary expectations; for example, that the rich shall be sent away empty and that the lowly shall be exalted.[25] He also lived a self-sacrificial life, so you and I are likewise called to give sacrificially of ourselves. But in the Biblical covenant narrative, the primary significance of Jesus is that by dying on the cross he fulfills the covenant by reconciling us to God.

The Mission of America

In the American colonies, the Biblical story quickly became intertwined with the story of the mission of America when the Pilgrims joined hands with—and sometimes morphed into—the patriots of an emerging world power. This mission of America story was twofold. First, Americans began to view themselves as having a special worldwide destiny to be an example of God's plan for a free and democratic nation. Second, they had a responsibility to encourage the spread of these values, by force if necessary, to all people everywhere, "leading them toward a future world state of . . . liberty yet unknown."[26] Like the Israelites of old, Americans had experienced an exodus—fleeing Europe and traversing the Atlantic—and had been given a new land. And this was just the beginning. The first Great Awakening (1730–60) and the American Revolution (1776) were viewed as harbingers of a coming millennial age.[27] The former united the many different denominations on the frontier by enabling individual Americans to see themselves as part of a corporate nation state on a mission. The Revolution birthed a nation of free people with unalienable rights—a government that, in principle, would no longer oppress people unjustly.[28] America would become the first and premier nation of the millennial age.

The Biblical story's image of the faithful self was now combined with the Mission of America's image of the faithful nation.[29] The second Great Awakening (1800–1830) gave rise to a host of schools, religious education programs, associations and movements for temperance and world peace—all calling on America to be an example to the world.[30] In addition, Americans began to believe that America had its own unique Manifest Destiny. Herman Melville spoke of the political Messiah as having "come to *us* (Americans)."[31] Josiah Strong stretched manifest destiny into an ethnic, global doctrine when he argued that, "God was training the Anglo-Saxon race in America for a mission to the whole world."[32] Although the "mission of America story" has since undergone reformulations—as anticommunist crusade in the Vietnam and Cold War eras and more recently as the worldwide anti-terrorist campaign since 9/11—it is still alive and well in the American moral landscape.

The Boy Scout: Pilgrim and Patriot?

The ideal of the Boy Scout reflects many of the core themes of the Biblical Story and the mission of America. The covenantal character of the Scout Oath is explicit in the inclusion of the word "promise" in the title of the oath—"The Scout Oath or Promise." The oath states that, ". . . I will do my best to do my duty to God and my country and to obey the Scout Law; to help other people at all times. . . ."[33] Subsections on duty to God and duty to country are featured in the 1959 *Handbook* table of contents. In the 1990 *Handbook*, reference to God is no longer included in the contents, but there are mini sections which explicate what being reverent to God means, including two pages on religious emblems. The later *Handbook* adds pages celebrating democracy and the history of the American flag, the national anthem, and the Bill of Rights.

Obeying the Scout Law entails being trustworthy, loyal and obedient to the Scoutmaster and "all other duly constituted authorities," as well as befriending others; "not receiving tips for courtesies or good turns," "not hurting any living creature needlessly," and being "reverent toward God," "faithful in his religious duties," and respectful of "the convictions of others in matters of custom and religion."[34] The covenant's preoccupation with the metaphor of the "land" is paralleled in the Scout focus on wilderness training, and adventuring in and caring for the great outdoors. Teamwork is also stressed and a scout's identity as a member of a patrol, troop and worldwide brotherhood echoes the "family" ethos of the covenant. The Scout should play his part in promoting the common good. The Scout's special status, over and against non-scouts, as exemplified in his uniform and merit badges, evokes the theme of election in the Biblical story.

But there are also subtle divergences from the covenant and mission stories. The sense in which the land and the promise of prosperity (in return for obedience to the covenant's requirements) are *gifts* is not stressed in the Boy Scout ideal. The great outdoors and the expectation of success in life are presented more as birthrights than as gifts.[35] In fact the *Handbook* presents God as a more or less distant benign creator being who sets things in motion, and who should be thanked and acknowledged, but who is otherwise not integral to daily life. There is no emphasis on "not having other gods before Him," because God is seen to be such a perfect fit with the other sources of loyalty in the Boy Scout world, such as parents, patrol leaders and scoutmasters. For the Boy Scout, the struggle is not one of choosing between competing goods. The struggle is one of methodically progressing on the path of scouting—to do all the things required to become an Eagle Scout.

A major divergence from the Covenant story is the Scouting emphasis on charitable acts rather than on doing justice. Indeed, to read the *Handbook* is to enter a world in which virtually everyone is middle-class and living in safe, secure home environments.[36] There is no reference to challenging an unjust authority within one's patrol or troop or nation, apparently, because it simply does not arise as an issue. Moral development is a matter of performing a good deed everyday, being ready to apply first aid and rescue skills, assisting people who are physically challenged, helping out in roadside emergencies and performing community service.

Finally, the Scout virtues do not include references to forgiveness, self-sacrifice or turning the other cheek. Scouts are to be friendly, kind and courteous, but are not instructed about what to do when wronged, other than maintain a stiff upper lip. Helping others does not translate into giving up something valuable to oneself. According to the oath, Scouts should be prepared "to take care of themselves and help people in need" (*Handbook*, 19). Scouting is about adventure and fun, not self-denial. Neither is it about fighting or not fighting, though reference is made to growing into a citizen who is ready to defend his country. Scouts never quarrel in the *Handbook*, so fights simply will not occur.

Rags-to-Riches, Finding Yourself and the Mafia Boss

The Enlightenment Story of Progress

During the first century of the American experiment, a public or civil religion emerged alongside the Biblical covenant and mission of America narratives. For men like Benjamin Franklin and Thomas Jefferson, Enlightenment notions of reason, progress and natural law began to supplant Biblical notions of grace, faith and covenant.[37] God is still involved as creator and judge, but for persons of the Enlightenment, the moral life increasingly becomes something of one's own creation. Jefferson's universal gospel, *The Life and Morals of Jesus of Nazareth* abstracts Gospel passages from the Biblical narrative that express simple, non-miraculous teachings that appeal to reason. Franklin's "self-made" man in his *Autobiography* develops his moral character by acting according to a practical moral wisdom that proves useful for personal success, not by surrendering himself in obedience to God. This wisdom centered on clear, self-evident maxims, such as "time is money" and "credit is money," which when taken together, constituted an ethic of individual worldly success. To make money was to prove one's good character. In a rational, burgeoning industrial world of cause and effect, industry, thrift, self-discipline and frugality not only led to wealth and fame, but also became the pre-imminent marks of high moral stature.

In the emerging civil religion of worldly success, public virtue mattered more than private salvation. Both Franklin and Jefferson stressed the need for a common morality based on reason and a rational apprehension of the fundamental laws of the universe.[38] The Declaration of Independence articulated a public religion—sometimes called "the democratic faith"—in terms of what were taken to be universally self-evident moral values: equality, life, liberty, happiness and unalienable rights. The Constitution represented a fusing of Biblical law with natural law to form a moral law that was viewed as having God's stamp of approval. To be a responsible citizen in the New Republic meant that one took charge of one's life, exercising power responsibly according to the moral law. This meant living out one's calling, which was simultaneously to pursue personal goals that also benefited the community. The highest good was to succeed in one's calling.

During the industrial revolution of the late 1800s, this sense of a socially responsible "calling" in the pursuit of individual success becomes wedded to evolutionary notions of progress and the survival of the fittest. The good, righteous self who works hard, invests capital wisely and competes effectively in the marketplace, not only survives, but becomes an "architect" of his own future, reaping huge profits.[39] The individual's quest for unlimited economic success now becomes a single vision of life in which the best and the brightest lead the rest of us toward unparalleled progress. This "gospel of wealth" valued individualism, private property, accumulation of wealth and competition.[40] While those at the bottom of the economy may suffer, this scenario is good because it ensures the survival of the fittest. At the same time, the fittest are to be generous toward the less fortunate. Since economic growth is viewed as potentially unlimited, and jobs at the upper echelons are always being created, anyone with enough savvy and self-discipline should, in theory, be able to rise from rags to riches.

The Story of Personal Well-being

In post-World War II America, the gospel of success began to be overshadowed by a widespread concern for personal self-esteem and well-being. As the face-to-face familiarity of rural America gave way to the faceless anonymity of urban life, individuals turned inward for a sense of value, meaning and purpose. As women entered the workforce in record numbers and middle-class youth accessed unprecedented educational opportunities, the baby boomer generation migrated toward niches of relative affluence in an ever-expanding economy. Freed from fears of scarcity (which their parents had experienced in the Depression years) but culturally uprooted in a rapidly changing, pluralistic society, many boomers suddenly found themselves in a moral and spiritual vacuum. Distanced from the Biblical covenant, cynical about the mission of America, and more or less successful in professional careers, the boomers sought meaning and purpose in (1) social cause movement, (2) therapeutic or (3) techno-consumerist visions of the good life.[41]

The union, women's suffrage, civil rights, anti-war, farm worker, feminist, environmental and gay rights movements of the twentieth century all represented moral crusades for social reform. Each provided avenues to involve oneself in a cause greater than the self. As part of such a movement, one could re-capture a sense of social connectedness and moral purpose in an otherwise alien, anomic and immoral society. But, unlike the Pilgrims and many of today's super patriots, war resisters and feminists were not by and large acting in response to a biblical covenant or a notion of manifest destiny. Rather, they advocated for peace and women's full humanity out of deep-seated, humanistic convictions about justice and human rights. While many of their right-wing opponents frequently appealed to biblical or patriotic worldviews, the leftists appealed to humanistic concepts such as equality, distributive justice, mutuality and sustainability. By identifying with a social cause, the activist created a purpose in life in an otherwise godless, parochial, chauvinistic and homophobic world.

However, once the sixties generation began to settle into America's suburban enclaves, many turned to therapeutic models of the good life. Although the majority may not have sought psychological counseling, they nonetheless found meaning and direction in life by developing quality interpersonal relationships.[42] Magazines entitled *Self* and *Psychology Today* reflected the new emphasis on personality, sharing feelings, authenticity ("being real") and integrity ("being whole"). "Pulling yourself together," letting go of "hang-ups," and having meaningful relationships with "significant others" became the by-words of this story.[43] A critical element in this story is that the relationship in question is evaluated in terms of its potential to enable each person to "do his or her own thing." The movie, *Looking for Mr. Goodbar*—in which a woman leads a double life as a conventional teacher by day and as a seductive siren by night—epitomized the shadow side of the new ethos, where making fleeting romantic connections becomes the *raison d'etre* of existence.

Finally, extraordinary technological innovations, combined with a growth economy, have given rise to the techno-consumerist story of well-being. In this narrative, the good life is achieved through increasing use of, and engagement with, the latest technological gadget or system. It is a story of the computer geek, the perpetual tourist, and the inveterate shopper. It is achieving well-being through "international patterns of consumption," that is, through purchasing the products of transnational corporations sold by means of mass advertising. It frequently entails a submersion in mass entertainment.

Since the dawn of the cinema, invention of the television, and introduction of hundreds of cable and satellite channels, Americans are spending more and more time gratifying desires to be entertained. For fanatical sports fans, bored housewives and underemployed senior citizens, watching television has become a way of entering another life of sports heroes, sit-coms, and game shows.

For generation X'ers and Y'ers, surfing, chatting and purchasing on the Internet have become major aspects of one's lifestyle. Unlike the Pilgrims, today's consumerist sees well-being as dependent not on obedience to a covenant with God, but on possessing or at least utilizing the latest entertainment system or computer technology. While the story of the mission of America evokes a heritage of military and political heroism with strong links to natural and international communities, the story of the consumerist celebrates the individual's own private quest for happiness in the pursuit of purely personal interests and relationships. And, in counter distinction to the story of success, the story of personal well-being through technology is a narrative of self-gratification and pleasure, rather than self-denial and hard work. Although it usually entails holding down a job of some sort, it is primarily a "living for the now" centered on the leisure activities which the job's income make possible.

The Boss: C.E.O. and Playboy?

Whereas the image of the Boy Scout embodies many of the moral themes associated with the biblical covenant and mission of America narratives, the Mafia boss image evokes a number of the themes connected with the stories of personal success and well-being.[44] First, he is the self-made man *par excellence*. As Frank Sinatra crooned, he does it "my way." He is the master of his fate, and the originator of his value system. Moreover, as a member of an economically subordinate, immigrant community, he embodies the Horatio Alger story, rising from rags to riches.[45] By sheer tenacity and will, he exemplifies the fittest survivor in an arena of bloodshed and lawlessness.

In concert with the gospel of wealth narrative, the mafia boss values individualism, private property, the accumulation of wealth and competition. Due to his business acumen and capacity to innovate,[46] he seems to be living "the American dream," typifying "the American values of individualism and hard work in the pursuit of upward social mobility."[47] Gay Talese's novel about the Bonanno family, *Honor Thy Father*, portrays the family as "just another middle-class family."[48] As C.E.O. of a mob organization, the mafia boss exercises savvy and self-discipline. His wealth is not only indicative of his power, but because it is also a means of expressing his generosity and capacity to aid others in distress, it becomes a mark of a magnanimous character. He rewards favors and holds others accountable for reciprocal favors. At his best, he can be trusted to fulfill promises and commitments. And, as the chosen one in a family of contenders for the top job, there is a sense in which he is "called" into his vocation. Protected by bodyguards, respected by friends and enemies alike, driven to and fro in his limo from his lavish estate, the boss is the quintessential, if nefarious, symbol of success in America.

Although the mafia motif does not evoke the story of well-being to the same degree that it reflects the story of success, there are a few parallels with the former. The "Don" cultivates, and in turn thrives upon, a celebrity status. In this sense he reflects the story of well-being's emphasis on personality. Although he is not known for his authenticity or integrity, and keeps his feelings to himself, he still moves in a field of significant others and respects the other's rights to do their own thing (as long as it does not negatively impact on his own operations). He also "lives for the now," although romantic connections are secondary to the success of his enterprise; and in his ostentatious displays of wealth, he is an unabashed consumer. Finally, the mafia boss was historically linked to mass entertainment; including casinos, prostitution, cigarette bootlegging, illicit drug sales, and sports activities, such as horse racing and boxing.[49]

As with the image of the Boy Scout, there are several ways in which the mafia boss motif does not express the narratives of personal success and well-being.[50] Clearly, while the Don is rational and works with the legal system, he uses the law to circumvent the law. He pays off judges and prosecutors, and when charged with crimes, abuses the Fifth Amendment. He also becomes a law unto himself, judging and executing others for disloyalty or wrongdoing. By violently intimidating, assaulting, maiming or murdering those who threaten his interests, the mafia boss disregards the inviolability of unalienable rights such as life, liberty and pursuit of happiness.[51]

Moreover, in his lifestyle he is not particularly frugal or thrifty, nor is he concerned for social justice or reform. Although he promotes his own and his community's interests, he is not a revolutionary. He does not advocate fundamental systemic changes. He is parochial and chauvinistic. As noted above, he is not a "touchy feely" kind of guy. In fact, because he must act as ruthless terminator to maintain his power, his marriage and family life suffer because he distances himself from his emotions.

The Boss, the Scout and Jesus

To sum up the argument thus far, while the Boy Scout and mafia boss motifs do not evoke the full terrain of America's moral landscape, they are expressive of core themes of the nation's classic moral narratives. The Boy Scout ideal re-capitulates the strong sense of duty, honor and reverence endemic to the biblical covenant and mission of America stories. The emphasis on trust, wilderness, lending a hand and loyalty to one's own round out a picture of the optimistic, straight-talking, square living, law abiding, God-fearing, patriotic citizen who takes care of himself and is prepared to do good deeds and perform heroic actions.

The mafia boss ideal evokes the clever, self-reliant, magnanimous individualist characteristic of the stories of personal success and well-being. His independent willingness to hold others accountable and his success in amassing wealth, power and influence epitomize the gospel of wealth theme. He is the benign, if terrifying, father figure you can trust to make things right when the dominant legal system appears irrelevant or oppressive. He is the great benefactor, the tough guy with a generous spirit for the powerless. He is also the self-made man who, embodying a subterranean value system and flouting authority, lives on the edge—freely indulging in America's "good life" of drink, sex and entertainment.

On the surface it would appear that the mafia boss, his benign qualities notwithstanding, has very little to do with the historical Jesus. He is violent, where Jesus counsels us to turn the other cheek. He extorts money, where Jesus tells us to lend without expecting returns. He ruthlessly punishes disobedience, while Jesus forgives the repentant. And, on the other hand, it would seem that the Boy Scout has a lot in common with Jesus. Like Jesus, he strives to be obedient and reverent toward God. Like the Good Samaritan, the Scout is always prepared to help someone who is injured, and he doesn't expect payment for good deeds. And like Jesus, he appears to be kind to children, the elderly and animals.

But beneath the surface this black and white moral dichotomy begins to break down, especially if we view some of the more enigmatic of Jesus' teachings and actions in the light of these motifs. Let us therefore reconsider the moral import of Jesus by examining *The Gospel of Jesus** in the light of the mafia and Boy Scout motifs. Such an analysis yields some surprising moral insights for Christians in America today. It may also alter the way we view Jesus himself. I will organize these reflections in terms of Jesus' teachings about three foci of the moral life: (a) a sense of who we are, (b) practical rules of thumb for everyday life, and (c) a vision of where we are going.

Being Wandering Disciples

While the Boy Scout is firmly rooted in a patrol, troop, family, community, religious institution and country, Jesus recommends that

---

* In the subsequent analysis, unless otherwise indicated, all scripture references will be drawn from Funk, *The Gospel of Jesus According to the Jesus Seminar.*

we "Be passersby" (3:19; Thom 42).[52] Following Jesus necessitates moving into a nomadic mode: "And Jesus said, 'Foxes have dens, and birds of the sky have nests, but this mother's child has nowhere to rest his head'" (3:12; Luke 9:58). We are to lead a "liminal"[53] existence in which we are disengaged from attachments to hearth and home, social status, or institutional approbation. As liminal selves, we live in transition, betwixt and between the lives we led before "going along the road" with Jesus and the outcome of the journey. This existence has an anti-structural quality. Conventional understandings of what counts as good moral character are called into question.

In the parable of "the Pharisee and the tax collector," Jesus appears to have fewer scruples with the toll collector, who is at least sincere in his plea for mercy, than he does with the Pharisee who promotes his own self-righteousness (13:5–10; Luke 18:9–14). In this parable, it is interesting to note that the sins enumerated by the Pharisee, which include "thieving" and "being like that toll collector over there" (13:7), are precisely the types of activities and ways of being that one might associate with the mafia boss motif. Jesus points out that the toll collector went home "acquitted" and the Pharisee did not (13:10).[54] One way to read this passage is that both the Pharisee and the toll collector stood under judgment, but that the Pharisee wasn't conscious of his need for acquittal. That is, that he had a false consciousness (or arrogance) about being beyond moral judgment. In this instance, Jesus' teaching about the need for humility stands as a corrective to the Boy Scout's implicit self-congratulatory preoccupation with doing good deeds and achieving merit.

Viewing the parable in the light of liminality, a further implication is that the Pharisee errs in equating his moral worth with an established moral character that has been built up over time. The liminal self is in transition from the past and is in some sense "not yet." This is not to argue that building up a good moral character is not important for Jesus or anyone else, but rather that it is a "project-in-process." In the parable, the Pharisee goes home "not acquitted" not because he has done anything wrong, but because he thinks his well-established moral character ("I fast twice a week, I give tithes of everything that I acquire" [13:8]) somehow distinguishes him as more morally praiseworthy than "that toll collector over there"(13:7).

Jesus' statement that, "What goes into you can't defile you; what comes out of you can" (14:7; Mark 7:15–16), appears not only to challenge pollution and purity laws, but also puts the stress on active responses to prior actions. To a certain extent, we cannot undo what has already happened to us. But, for liminal selves who are projects-in-process, what has happened to us is never the last word. What goes into us can't defile us because, in part, our moral characters are already compromised; but also, because they are fluid, not static. However, what comes out of us—what we do in response to all our received moral traditions—is what is really at stake in the moral life.

The wild and wooly John the Baptist, who allegedly sported "a mantle of camel hair"[55] and lived on locusts and raw honey, is an affront to the clean-cut, relatively affluent Boy Scout. The Jesus who is portrayed as allowing his disciples to eat without washing their hands (14:1–5; Mark 7:1–5) gather grain on the Sabbath (10:1–4; Mark 2:23) and heal on the Sabbath (10:5–11; Mark 3:1–5), subverts not only an ethic of cleanliness, but in so doing raises questions about the moral propriety of being overly preoccupied with religious rituals such as Sabbath observance.

Moreover, just as John the Baptist is not interested in hearing about the blue blood or ethnocentric character of our family lineage ("Don't even start saying to yourselves, 'We have Abraham for our father" [1:6; Luke 3:8]), Jesus is not inordinately attached to his biological family. As a "passerby" he instructs, "If any of you comes to me and does not hate your own father and mother and wife and children and brothers and sisters—yes, even your own life—you're no disciple of mine" (11:11; Luke 14:26). And as a prophet, he can't get respect "on his home turf and among his relatives and at home" (11:17; Mark 6:4)! Clearly, such a message runs counter to both the Scout and the mafia boss's celebration of family ties and values.

John the Baptist's message and vulnerability to arrest would also represent checks on the mafia boss's self-image as a sly criminal who can literally get away with murder. John demands an end to price gouging ("Charge nothing above the official rates" [1:11; Luke 3:13]) and extortion ("No more shakedowns! No more frame-ups either!" [1:13; Luke 3:14]). Unlike the Don, John is not beholden to political figures, and therefore is free to criticize king Herod's marriage to Herodias. But, lacking the political connections of the boss, he is especially vulnerable to arrest, imprisonment and execution.

In the Shadow of God's Imperial Rule

While both the Scout and the boss are headed toward clearly envisioned personal destinies, Jesus preaches about an endgame that is mysterious and only indirectly described.[56] Like the elephant in the Buddhist story, the Father's imperial rule is "spread out upon the earth, and people don't see it" (15:7; Thom 113:4). It's not something we'll be able to observe coming within our sights in a matter-of-fact way and say, "Look, here it is!" or "Over there!" And yet, Jesus says, "God's imperial rule is right there in your presence" (15:8–10; Luke 17:20–21).

Positively, it is like a "treasure hidden in a field" that one "sells every last possession" to obtain (9:11–12; Matt 13:44),[57] or a "single pearl" that is purchased by the sale of a "supply of merchandise" (9:13–14; Thom 76:1–2). It is of uttermost value, yet it can be compared with quite insignificant, ordinary things: "It's like a mustard seed. It's the smallest of seeds, but when it falls on prepared soil, it produces a large plant, which becomes a shelter for birds of the sky" (2:19–20; Thom 20:1–4). The tiny seed grows into a large plant, which freely provides a habitat for the birds. What was originally small is transformed into the big.[58] This transformation theme is reiterated in the parable of the yeast: "When speaking of the kingdom, Jesus would say: . . . It is like leaven that a woman took and concealed in fifty pounds of flour until it was all leavened" (2:21–22; Luke 13:20–21).[59]

Accordingly, in God's imperial rule there is growth and expansion, buoyancy, a sprouting forth. There is a subtle, but significant "creation of space." In the parable of the empty jar, the kingdom is compared to the empty space that results from the spilling of the meal from a jar (2:23–26; Thom 97:1–4). Also, like the mustard seed slowly taking root in the soil and the leaven concealed in the flour, the spilling of the meal goes unnoticed. Thus, God's imperial rule is a "behind-the-scenes" creating of space which makes room for something to happen.[60] That "something" may include human efforts—in the parable of the growing seed, Jesus refers to a "harvest time" when the "farmer sends for the sickle" (12:10–13; Mark 4:26–29)—but it may have much more to do with the way God graciously works through nature.

Indeed, Jesus bears witness to a God who not only "gives good things to those who ask him" (18:5–7; Matt 7:9–11), but who also "causes the sun to rise on both the bad and the good, and sends rain on both the just and the unjust" (7:5; Matt 5:45). Which is to say, counter to the *de facto* beliefs of many devotees of the Biblical covenant story, that God doesn't play favorites with law abiding, church-going, responsible citizens. Striving to become an Eagle Scout may be a worthwhile pursuit, but it doesn't guarantee any special privileges or blessings. In fact, God may rain on the Scout's parade while shining on the mafia bosses' killing.

In this connection, it is intriguing to interpret the parable of the assassin with the mafia motif in mind. In the parable, God's imperial rule is associated with "a person who wanted to kill someone powerful" and, after practicing beforehand, does the deed (12:39–41; Thom 98:1–3).[61] Is God therefore cold-hearted? According to Luke, Jesus says that God is "generous to the ungrateful and wicked" (7:5; Luke 6:35). The generous character of God's imperial rule is revealed in the parable of "the prodigal son" (9:15–46; Luke 15:11–32), where the Father celebrates the return of his errant son; and in the parable of "the laborers in the vineyard" (4:4–21; Matt 20:1–15), where the proprietor pays each laborer the same amount, although some have worked longer hours than others. The tension in both parables is rooted in perfectly reasonable concerns about the fairness of the protagonists' actions. While the older son in the prodigal parable may have a just grievance—that is, his father may have taken him for granted ("You have never once provided me with so much as a kid goat" [9:42])— the son is fixated on this hurt to such an extent that it constrains him from being glad about his brother's return. Because he is not living as a passerby ("See here, all these years I have slaved for you. I never once disobeyed your orders" [9:41]) he cannot appreciate his father's graciousness to his wayward brother.

In an analogous way, the master in the vineyard parable, when viewed in terms of the story of success, seems manifestly unjust. It doesn't seem fair that those who worked a full day should get the same as those who worked the last hour only. In the Scout world, for example, it would be unfair to give each laborer an equal amount of credit toward a merit badge. But Jesus is utilizing an entirely different frame of reference. We are nomadic selves, laboring in a liminal existence, detached from a "punch the clock" mentality (even if we have to punch it for a living)—thankful for the bread we receive, and positively disposed to welcoming latecomers. Again, in response to God's graciousness, the liminal self does not elevate the part she/he plays above the parts others play.[62]

Finally, the graciousness of God's imperial rule is associated with children, those exorcised of demons and the poor. After calling for the children, Jesus says, "God's domain belongs to people like that" (2:7–8; Mark 10:14). He says that we have to be able to accept God's domain "the way a child would" (2:8; Mark 10:15). The child's vulnerability and ready acceptance of attentive entreaty represent correctives to the calculating and defensive postures associated with the mafia boss metaphor and the mission in America theme, respectively. God's domain is also connected with attacks on demons: "But if by God's finger I drive out demons, then for you God's imperial rule has arrived" (5:17; Luke 11:20). Although demons were formerly associated with a wide range of ailments and afflictions, it could be argued that, in our times, the demons could be equated more broadly with self-delusions—such as greed, envy and jealously—which hamper our ability to live out the moral conventions we espouse.

But perhaps especially, Jesus stresses the centrality of the poor in the kingdom: "Congratulations, you poor! God's domain belongs to you" (2:3; Luke 6:20). The message for the rich is not so good: "I swear to you, it is very difficult for the rich to enter Heaven's domain" and "it's easier for a camel to squeeze through a needle's eye than for a wealthy person to get into God's domain" (17:6–7; Matt 19:23–24).[63] We "can't be enslaved to both God and a bank account" (17:9; Luke 16:13), and rich persons who think that they can invest their money and thereby "lack nothing" are in for a rude awakening (17:10–13; Thom 63:1–4). Jesus' assurances to the poor (and bleak appraisal of the future outlook for the rich) subvert the stories of success and well-being, which are central to both the Boy Scout and the mafia boss.

In Search of Moral Wisdom

As a number of scholars have argued, Jesus' teachings often reverse our conventional expectations of what is or should be the case.[64] Because, as wandering disciples we are liminal beings, it is not surprising that our journey on the road to God's Imperial Rule should be littered with reversals. In contrast to the one-dimensional stories of success and well-being, we are embarking upon a path with a teacher who says paradoxical things such as, "Whoever tries to hang on to life will forfeit it, but whoever forfeits life will preserve it" (17:14; Luke 17:33). In the exaggerated and surprising spirit of Jesus' dictum, "The last shall be first and the first last," (4:3; Matt 20:16), we are supposed to be ready to do the unexpected; including, love our enemies (7:2; Luke 6:27), leave "the dead" to bury our own father (3:13–14; Luke 9:59–60); when conscripted for one mile of service, volunteer for a second mile (3:17; Matt 5:41)[65] and in these and other ways "Struggle to get in through the narrow door," which "many will try to get in, but won't be able" (3:20; Luke 13:24). For companions on the journey we should be on the look out for ordinary folks, such as fishermen, toll collectors, "sinners," and women (3:1–5, 8–10; 8:1–3; 21:10–11; Mark 1:16–20; Luke 8:1–3; Mark 2:15–16; 15:40–41).[66]

Clearly, although there may be some areas of congruence, these are not the guidelines of a Boy Scout civil religion. In fact, on close examination, Jesus begins to look less and less like a Boy Scout. Although Jesus appears to sound very much like a Scout when he says, "When you pray, say, Our Father, your name *be revered*" (13:2–4; Luke 11:2), he may be speaking tongue-in-cheek. In this utterance he combines the informal, familiar address "Abba" with the admonition to revere the Holy Name, which he then doesn't mention.[67] Jesus' words about visiting homes while traveling ("Stay at one house" and "eat whatever is set before you" [18:8–10; Luke 10:5, 7, 8]) would resonate well with a Scout's code of civil behavior, except that for Jesus' Jewish followers, the injunction to eat whatever is served, even if it were non-kosher, would have been a radical demand.[68] Finally, although the Scout is to offer service without any desire for favors—suggesting Jesus' saying, "when you give to charity, don't let your left hand know what your right hand is doing" (13:16; Matt 6:3)—there is no hint in the Scout *Handbook* about the paradox that "one cannot keep the activities of the right hand secret from the left."[69]

At the same time, although Jesus frequently appears to be a tough, irascible character, he advocates a moral consciousness that we would not normally associate with the mafia boss. He charges us to hold our friends accountable in ways that invite us to deal with our own arrogance and self-delusion ("When you take the timber out of your own eye, then you will see well enough to remove the sliver from your friend's eye" [13:12; Thom 26:2]).[70] He resists stock answers about how to cope with violence ("When someone slaps you on the right cheek, turn the other as well" [3:15; Matt 5:39]).[71] Unlike the mafia boss—who would aggressively utilize a legal system in which he had bribed the judge, hired the best defense attorney, and blackmailed witnesses—Jesus urges his follow-ers not to rely on human courts ("If someone is determined to sue you for your coat, give that person the shirt off your back to go with it" [3:16; Matt 5:40]).[72] In counter distinction to the boss—who strives to honor and maintain strong family ties—Jesus challenges us to recognize altruism outside our own families and ethnic groups in the parable of the Good Samaritan (18:11–18; Luke 10:30–35). Jesus also wants to see genuine sacrificial giving rather than meager acts of charity. The Samaritan who comes to the aid of the roadside victim not only acts as a medic and gets him to the inn, but he offers to pay his expenses during recovery.[73]

But what more can be said? Perhaps if we read some of the more enigmatic and disturbing parables of Jesus through the lens of the mafia motif, we can see Jesus and his moral exemplars in surprising ways. For example, the parable of the talents (Matt 25:14–28; Luke 19:12–24) has generally been interpreted as encouraging "patient and trustworthy service while waiting for the kingdom."[74] It seems to fit well with the story of success. The slaves who make good on their investments (read "entrepreneurs") are labeled "competent" and "reliable." The slave who buries his money (read "lazy" or "irresponsible") is "incompetent and timid." But if, for the sake of experimentation, we read the parable thinking of "the master" as a mafia boss, interesting nuances emerge.

First, as a boss, the master is in the business of making money. He also has a pretty good hunch about who can be trusted with his wealth. Because the first slave is a good bet, he gets 30,000.[75] The second slave has great promise, so he gets 12,000. The third slave is a bit of a risk, but he is willing to put him to the test, so he gives him 6,000. The crux of the story centers on the third slave, who is afraid of the master because, as he states, "I know that you drive a hard bargain, reaping where you didn't sow and gathering where you didn't scatter (4:34)." Rather than deny the accusation, the master replies that if the slave knew he was a crooked dealer then why didn't he at least take the money to bankers (that is, to the legitimate financiers?). Presumably, that way the slave would not have had to risk what the other two slaves were willing to risk, and the master would get interest on his capital. But because the slave simply buried the money in fear, the master has the 6,000 taken from him and entrusts it to the slave who doubled the 30,000 given to him.

Viewed in terms of the mafia motif, the third slave gets what's coming to him. He knew with whom he was dealing with and what was expected of him when he took the 6,000, so his failure to act is reprehensible. His failure of nerve, his timidity, is particularly blameworthy; although, given the master's intimidating power, it is understandable. But, the fact that the master is apparently willing to dispense with any punishment could be interpreted as a sign of his magnanimous character.[76] In this light, Jesus' saying, "Those who have something in hand will be given more, and those who have nothing will be deprived of even the little they have," (4:22–23) could be read as more a matter of fact statement about a business decision of a "hard" master. Interpreted in this way, the third slave actually gets off easy because he wasn't punished for his reprehensible behavior.[77]

Taking the interpretation one step further, if we imagine Jesus as identifying with the master quo mafia boss, it is clear that Jesus does not suffer sanctimonious pretenders or fools lightly.[78] He gives us resources that are morally tainted to begin with, but if we're going to accept those resources, we had better not fear the negative repercussions that utilizing them may entail. At the very least, we cannot cop-out by claiming a kind of moral purity. Rather than simply "encouraging patient and trustworthy service," the parable would appear to be suggesting that Jesus, like the master, is a tough guy who not only expects us to make good on what he gives us, but has no patience for those who shirk from the task with lame excuses, such as that they are afraid of him or that what he has provided is morally tainted. On the other hand, the first two slaves should not maintain any illusions about being morally pure. They have played the system as it should be played, but they agreed to work with a corrupt boss and they have done what they had to do to double his money. Like the third slave, they may also have been partially motivated by fear. They are competent and reliable, yes, but they are no Boy Scouts.

Again, if we reflect on the parable of "the dishonest manager" (12:14–26; Luke 16:1–8) with the mafia motif in mind, we gain clues about how we are to get along in a morally compromised world. In the parable, Jesus says that a rich man praises a manager who has squandered his estate. Why would he do this? One possible explanation is that he praises him because, under extreme duress, the manager salvages something positive from a bad situation. Jesus' rejoinder, "for the children of this world exhibit better sense in dealing with their own kind than do the children of light"(12:26; Luke 16:8),[79] would then suggest a keen appreciation for practical expertise, even among wheeler dealers. By calling attention to the way in which the children of darkness successfully deal with their own kind, Jesus is portrayed as stressing the importance of engaging one another, warts and all, and figuring out ways to move forward together. When all is said and done, mafia bosses are pretty good at this. In this light, Jesus' observations about the powerful man ("No one can enter a powerful man's house to steal his belongings unless he first ties him up. Only then does he loot his house" [5:18; Mark 3:27]) could be interpreted as a tidy bit of basic instruction from a mafia boss. Similarly, the parable of the widow and the unjust judge (12:27–31; Luke 18:2–5) could be read as a Don's advice to underlings; namely, keep pestering the hell out of the judges and eventually you're wear them down.

In some cases, we may simply have to deal with the fact that big men use coercion to get what they want, but that doesn't necessarily mean that there are no morally redeeming aspects to such courses of action. For example, if we read Jesus' parable of the great dinner (2:9–18; Luke 14:16–23) as if the host of the dinner is a spurned mafia boss, it is easier to make sense out of the master's order to "force people" to come into his house. We are not told why all the invited guests are making excuses, but perhaps they don't want to socialize with the master because he is mean spirited or danger-ous. In any event, viewed as a boss, he can't throw a banquet and have nobody come, so he orders his slave to bring in some bodies, "the poor, crippled, the blind and the lame." It makes for a motley crowd, but it is one way of sticking it to his reluctant invitees, and even a mafia boss has a heart for the dregs of the earth. When it turns out that there is still more room, the slave is instructed to force people to come. The boss thereby saves face by filling the house by any means necessary.

In an analogous way, the secular ruler Jesus describes in the parable of "the unforgiving servant" (7:8–19; Matt 18:23–34) could be read as exemplifying a big-hearted, yet no nonsense, mafia boss. The slave who owes him a fortune is entirely at his mercy, but the boss is compassionate, lets him go and cancels his debt. As might be expected, however, his generosity has limits, so when the slave who has just been forgiven refuses to forgive his fellow slave in turn, the ruler is angered and has the slave punished. Like the ruler, we are to exude a magnanimous spirit; and, like the slave, we are to expect serious repercussions if we don't act accordingly. As in the parable of the talents, the slave is held to account by the boss, and we can trust the boss to do that.

These points not withstanding, Jesus' moral teachings do suggest that there is more than the world of the boss. In Jesus' gang, where ostentatious displays of clothes, haughty uses of professional titles, and demonstrations of pride of place in public gatherings are decidedly un-cool (13:14–15; Luke 20:45–46), the flashy lifestyle of the mafia boss would be out of place. We won't be siding up to "those who wear fancy clothes," because they are found "in regal quarters" (6:13–14; Matt 11:7–8). In fact, in a provocative and outlandish way, Jesus counsels us not even to worry about material necessities (2:29–35; Luke 12:22–28) and promises that if we but ask, seek and knock that we'll receive, find and be granted entrance (2:27–28; Matt 7:7–8). While this promise is no doubt a gross exaggeration, it points to a dimension of faithful living that contrasts with both the Scout's and the boss's willful, and often anxious, pursuits of personal success and well-being. Perhaps we could say that for wandering disciples situated at the periphery of the powers and principalities, that the promise evokes a subterranean, countervailing optimism.

Conclusion

Who We Are

As wandering disciples in twenty-first century America, we are liminal beings poised for creative responses in a rapidly changing moral arena. We have a heritage of moral conventions, rooted in core moral traditions, which are expressed in contemporary moral motifs. But as "passersby" we must view those conventions with a wary and discerning eye, being both "sly as snakes and as simple as doves" (3:18;

Thom 39:3). As liminal selves, with one foot in the past and one in the future, we do not equate moral worth with a static conception of moral character built up over time. In transition, we are guided as much by expectations of what the future will bring as we are by what the past has wrought. Our ethics will therefore be pulled in the direction of our various notions of the imperial rule of God. This means, at the very least, that we will resist a too steadfast or ironclad identification with any currently existing established institution, corporate body or political party. While we can appreciate the Scout's patriotism and the Boss's loyalty to extended family interests, we will be alert to how any patriotism or family loyalty may become a self-delusion or roadblock to God's domain. Vulnerable but undaunted, we will not fear blowing the whistle, while listening for voices from the wilderness which both exasperate and surprise us.

Where We Are Headed

The Boy Scout and mafia boss motifs suggest idealized and relatively static models of the future. They promise either a house in the suburbs in a secure nation that is a beacon for freedom and is blessed by God; or, a get rich quickly fast life, where we have a lot of fun, and flout the authorities. But as nomadic disciples, we are beckoned toward a domain that is much more mysterious and fluid, and less comfortable, than those evoked by our popular American moral motifs. Although we can't picture it, it's right under our noses. The rule of God is aliveness, an uplifting movement that is creating spaces for extraordinary happenings. It is a shroud of amazing grace, poured out over good and bad alike, such that grudges, envy and jealousy are not the last word. It is a domain where a childlike acceptance and vulnerability rules the day, demonic self-delusions are brought out into the open, the poor are the proprietors and the rich are struggling to get in.

Rules of Thumb Along the Way

As wandering liminal disciples we are on a road littered with reversals. We need to be prepared to "let go" of all our cherished understandings so that we can leave dead rituals, institutions and relationships behind. As part of a rag-tag movement we will join hands with unlikely—and in some cases, unkempt and un-cool—persons in our paths in order to figure out ways to move forward as a community. We will need to avoid confusing a self-sacrificing love with timidity and escapism. While the Boy Scout is confident about the inherent righteousness of his values, we will need to be less naïve about our inevitable entanglement in corrupt practices and institutions. While the mafia boss freely indulges in violent intimidation, we are called to respond to violence in unscripted ways. While acknowledging that tough, aggressive action may sometimes be the most fitting recourse of a magnanimous leader, we will also be alert to how such action can be a cover for self-delusion. We will not put a lot of faith in legal solutions to social problems, and we will be prepared to turn away from familial and ethnic ties that unduly constrict us. Buoyed by the countervailing optimism of the poor and the outsider, we will be open to creative new ways of responding to poverty, anonymity and fear in the post 9/11 world. If we can begin to do this, ethics has a future in America.

Notes

Robert W. Funk, Enlightened Faith

1. Borg, *Jesus a New Vision*, 41.
2. Bloom, *Omens of Millennium*, 19.
3. Greene, "The Time We Thought We Knew."
4. Quoted by Howard Margolis, *It Started with Copernicus*, 113.
5. Margolis, *It Started with Copernicus*, 114.
6. Greene, *The Elegant Universe*, 108.

Joe Bessler-Northcutt, Hard Questions

1. See Nicholas Kristof's "God, Satan and the Media" (March 4, 2003) and "Believe It, or Not," (August 15, 2003). In the March 4 article Kristof reported, "A new Gallup poll shows that 48 percent of Americans believe in creationism, and only 28 percent in evolution (most of the rest aren't sure or lean toward creationism). According to recent Gallup Tuesday briefings, Americans are more than twice as likely to believe in the devil (68 percent) as in evolution." On August 15, Nicholas Kristof reported that according to a recent Gallup poll that Americans "are three times as likely to believe in the Virgin Birth of Jesus (83 percent) as in evolution (28 percent)." "Not only do 91 percent of Christians say they believe in the Virgin Birth, but so do an astonishing 47 percent of U.S. non-Christians."
2. See, for example, Lloyd Geering's recent book *Christianity Without God*.
3. Sallie McFague's *The Body of God*, is an example of a text that locates the mystery of God through the lenses of nature and ecology. So also Gordon Kaufman's *In the Face of Mystery* takes something of a wider view. He writes of God as "the serendipitous movement which we discern in the cosmic evolutionary and historical processes that have created human existence" (342).
4. Bhabha, *The Location of Culture*, 5.
5. Bessler-Northcutt, "Truth as Empire."
6. See also Lakoff and Johnson, *Metaphors We Live By.*
7. McFague, *Models of God*, 28.
8. Don Cupitt's recent book *Emptiness and Brightness* helpfully argues against claims to "religious experience." "Religious *experience* as a way of knowing is a dead duck. Why? Because we are the only users of language. Only *we* describe the world and theorize the world. . . . The flying saucer, the Virgin Mary, the heavenly Voice don't come to us *from outside.* They are the projected conclusions of a largely or wholly unconscious process of religious thought that was going on inside *us*" (79).
9. Keller, *Face of the Deep*, 83.
10. Over twenty years ago, Johann Baptist Metz in *Followers of Christ* called for an *ars moriendi*, an art of dying on the part of the now old religious orders, precisely in order to make room for new charisms needed to respond to the spiritual and cultural crises of the contemporary world.

11. See especially, SteinhoffSmith, *The Mutuality of Care.*
12. See the background document for John Paul II's quite remarkable service of March 12, 2000, "Memory and Reconciliation: The Church and the Faults of the Past," released on March 7ᵗʰ by the Vatican's International Theological Commission. Located at http://www.vatican.va/roman_ cur.../rc_con_cfaith_doc_20000307_memory-reconc-itc_en.htm. Visited April 4, 2002. For a strong critique of the intellectual and moral dishonesty of the Vatican, see Garry Wills, *Papal Sin.*

Stephen J. Patterson, Killing Jesus

1. Koester, "Jesus the Victim."
2. See, e.g., Williams, *Jesus' Death as Saving Event;* Hengel, *The Atonement;* Seeley, *The Noble Death.*
3. Stowers, "Greeks Who Sacrifice." Stowers follows the analysis of Detienne and Vernant in *The Cuisine of Sacrifice* which also informs my own approach.
4. Patterson, "'Why Did Christians Say'?"
5. Esp. Nickelsburg, *Resurrection, Immortality, and Eternal Life.*

Robert J. Miller, Literal Incarnation

1. My thinking on this and related topics is heavily indebted to Hick's *The Metaphor of God Incarnate,* a book I strongly recommend.
2. Hick, *Metaphor,* p. 48.
3. Hick, *Metaphor,* p. 45.
4. Hick, *Metaphor,* p. 154.
5. Hick, *Metaphor,* p. 155.
6. These are more fully analyzed by Hick, *Metaphor,* on pp. 155–58.
7. Hick, *Metaphor,* pp. 158–59.
8. Hick, *Metaphor,* p. 163.
9. The preceding formulation is adapted from Hick, *Metaphor,* p. 167.

Roy W. Hoover, Tradition and Faith

1. Tarnas, *The Passion of the Western Mind,* 416.
2. Cupitt, *Reforming Christianity,* 1.
3. Smith, *The World's Religions,* 387.
4. Cited by Rowan Williams in his essay, "*Honest to God* in Great Britain," 167. Compare the remark of theologian Gordon Kaufman that "religious rituals and symbol-systems . . . can function effectively . . . only if they are believed 'true,' that is, only if they are taken to represent (more or less adequately) . . . 'how things really are' with humanity, the world roundabout, and God (or the gods or other resources of life and meaning)," *In Face of Mystery,* 432.
5. Oden, *The Rebirth of Orthodoxy,* 84–85.
6. Oden, *Rebirth,* 162. Italics in the original.
7. Oden, *Rebirth,* 156, 188. The personal odyssey which Oden narrates in the book can be briefly characterized as a journey from an immersion in youthful revolutionary fervor in the 1960s to an embrace of authoritarian religious traditionalism in his own 60s.
8. Oden defines orthodoxy as "ancient consensual scriptural teaching," *Rebirth,* 29. More amply stated this is teaching that is grounded in "apostolic antiquity" [and is thus canonical]; universal [across the generations,

nor merely regional or held only by some or only for a time]; and has
"conciliar consent"—has been "confirmed by an ecumenical council or by
the broad consensus of the ancient Christian writers" 162–63.

9. Hauerwas, *With the Grain of the Universe*, 140.
10. Hauerwas, *With the Grain*, 190–91.
11. Barth, *Dogmatics in Outline*, 5; cited in Hauerwas, *With the Grain*,
179. Cp. the remark of Paul Tillich that "the famous 'No' of Karl Barth
against any kind of natural theology, even of man's [*sic*] ability to ask
the question of God, in the last analysis is a self-deception, as the use of
human language in speaking of revelation shows" (*Systematic Theology*, II,
14).
12. Cp. Tillich's remark that in Barth's theology the doctrine of the Trinity
"falls from heaven, the heaven of an unmediated biblicism and ecclesiastical authority" (*Systematic Theology*, III, 285).
13. Hauerwas, *With the Grain*, 206.
14. Kaufman, *Mystery*, xi–xii.
15. Tillich, *The Religious Situation*, 35.

Richard Holloway, Church Organist

1. Nietzsche, *Human, All-Too-Human*, pp. 54–55 in Kaufmann, *The
Portable Nietzsche*.

Daryl D. Schmidt, Veritas

1. Monroe, *Finding God at Harvard*.
2. Köstenberger, "Review."
3. Borg notes this as well (*God*, 3).
4. See www.gc.cuny.edu/studies/key_findings.htm. The Newhouse News
Service carried a story (Nov. 25, 2003) by Mark O'Keefe with personal-
ized vignettes, "Number of 'Nones,' Those Who Claim No Religion,
Swells in U.S."
5. Sheler, "Way of Worship," 8.
6. Titles by Pinnock and Sanders suggest the emphasis: *Wideness in God's
Mercy; Unbounded Love; The Openness of God; God Who Risks; Most Moved
Mover*. See update in *Chronicle of Higher Education*, Nov. 26, 2004, "Can
God See the Future?" (A11–12, 14), which reports that Huntington
College recently fired Sanders.
7. All the ETS documents are posted on their website: etsjets.org. The
vote required 2/3 majority, with Sanders coming closest at 62.7%, but
Pinnock getting only 32.9% for dismissal. Geisler's statement is posted
on his homepage: normgeisler.com. Geisler is president of Southern
Evangelical Seminary, in Charlotte, NC, which includes the Veritas
Graduate School of Apologetics and Counter-Cult Ministry.
8. A classic case is the healing of Hezekiah, after God said, "You will not
recover" (2 Kgs 20:1), but then sent Isaiah with the message that "I have
heard your prayer . . . ; I will add 15 years to your life" (vv. 5–6).
9. From an online interview (modernreformation.org/mr98/novdec/
mr9806freespace.html).
10. The authors, Phillip Gulley and James Mulholland, are identified as
pastoring Quaker meetings, although Mulholland is ordained Baptist.
They met as students at Christian Theological Seminary (Disciples),
Indianapolis.
11. Borg, *Heart*, xii.

12. Borg, *Heart*, 15, 14.
13. Borg, *Heart*, 37–38.
14. Borg, *Heart*, 63.
15. For his fuller treatment of this argument see Borg, *God*.
16. Borg, *Heart*, 64. He cites his fuller discussion in *God*, 37–44.
17. Borg, *Heart*, 216, 218.
18. Borg, *Heart*, 212. See also Rodney Stark's critique of the reductionism of social science approaches to religion in "Why Gods Should Matter in Social Science."
19. Borg, *Heart*, 213–14 (emphasis in Borg). Kaufman's recent reflections on the nature of theology continue to develop his focus on God as serendipitous creativity (*In the Beginning . . . Creativity*).
20. Klaassen, *Anabaptism*. He identifies five "radical" dimensions in Anabaptism: religion, discipleship, freedom, theology, and politics. Its "radical religion" lies in the claim that "Anabaptism testifies uniformly that sacredness or holiness does not attach to special words, objects, places, persons, or days" (11). In the middle of the sixteenth century (former Catholic priest) Menno Simons described a long list of "papist" practices as "nothing but human invention" (15).
21. Grant, *Theology of God's Grace*. At the time this article was written Grant's book was as yet unpublished so it was impossible to give precise references. For a similar critique of postmodern theology, see Bessler-Northcutt, "Theological Risks."
22. Borg, *Heart*, 212.
23. Sharf, "Experience," 95, 96.
24. A corollary to pursue in another context is the theory that Indo-European cultures share a common tripartite mythic and social structure, inherited from their common linguistic ancestry (see Appendix).
25. My emphasis.
26. The literature is both vast and beyond my comprehension, but highly intriguing. One example is the electronic journal, "Behavioral and Brain Sciences" (bbsonline.org); see, e.g., Mueller, "Innateness, Autonomy, Universality? Neurobiological Approaches to Language" (with extensive bibliography). Other suggestive titles include: Deacon, *Symbolic Species*; Hurford, *Approaches to the Evolution of Language*; Christiansen, *Language Evolution*.
27. See, e.g., Chomsky, *Language and Mind; Language and Responsibility*.
28. Searle, "Problem."
29. The development of memory is also associated with similar processes, e.g., De Haan and Johnson, *Cognitive Neuroscience of Development*.
30. Borg, *Heart*, 40 (see Smith, *Belief and History*).
31. See Cupitt, *Life, Life*, chap. 15.
32. Borg also emphasizes the centrality of grace in Christian faith (e.g., *Heart*, 220; *God*, 168).
33. The analogy of "speech act" is suggestive here: To say "I commit" is the speech act of making a promise. The actual act of "trust" ("I entrust myself") is not contained in any speech about trust or loyalty, but only in lived-out acts of trusting and being loyal.
34. See chapter 12 in Cupitt, *Life, Life*.
35. Schmidt, "Making Sense of Paul," 10.
36. Grant, *Believing God's Grace* (chap. 4).
37. Grant, *Believing God's Grace* (end of chap. 4).
38. Grant, *Believing God's Grace* (chap. 5).

39. Funk, *Credible Jesus*, 17, 22, 31, 38.
40. See Schmidt, "Making Sense." Note how the Scholars Version translation renders the traditional "justification through faith" language.
41. Littleton, *New Comparative Mythology*, 6, 17.
42. Littleton, *New Comparative Mythology*, 5.
43. See Porter and Hobbs, "Trinity and Indo-European Tripartite Worldview." They describe the three functions as (1) concerned with order, (2) concerned with action, and (3) concerned with sustenance (1–2).
44. Geering, "Secular Trinity," which identifies (1) self-creating physical universe, (2) self-evolving human species, and (3) emerging global consciousness.

Don Cupitt, Beginning All Over

1. Address: "The Price of Free World Victory." Wallace's book, *The Century of the Common Man* was published the next year, in 1943.
2. "Live options"—a term introduced by William James—are choices that are momentous and unavoidable. Some choices are not urgent, because the issues involved are no longer "alive." They can be deferred. But a live option confronts us daily, and calls for a decision.
3. *The New Religion of Life; Life, Life.*
4. *Philosophy's Own Religion.*
5. *Reforming Christianity.*
6. *Emptiness and Brightness.*
7. *Emptiness and Brightness.*

John C. Kelly, Anti-Realism

1. Meeks, *Origins*, 92–96.
2. *Origins*, 101.
3. This is the major thesis of Nancey Murphy's *Beyond Liberalism and Fundamentalism*.
4. Leaves, *Odyssey*, 91–100.
5. Cupitt, *Philosophy's Own Religion*, 59.
6. *Mysticism*, 74.
7. *Philosophy's Own Religion*, 27–29.
8. *Philosophy's Own Religion*, 34–35.
9. *Philosophy's Own Religion*, 59.
10. *Philosophy's Own Religion*, 87.
11. "Idealism," 142–43.
12. The idea that language is world making is the major theme of Cupitt's aptly titled *Creation Out of Nothing*. In particular, see the concluding pages for a summary of the application of this idea to religion (194–203).
13. *Philosophy's Own Religion*, 41.
14. *Religion of Being*, 88.
15. *Dynamics of Faith*, 41–43.
16. Borg, for example, recognizes that there are different religious world views each having a different vocabulary, but he sees them as attempts to get at something "more" beyond the ordinary world of space, time, and material objects (*Heart of Christianity*, 63–65). Thus, for Borg faith is inherently relational (36). Similarly, John Shelby Spong, while rejecting what might be called classical theism, nonetheless insists on the reality of something answering to the name "God" (*New Christianity*, 75).

17. This way of characterizing Christian non-realism might appear to be unfair to Cupitt who does accept the results of the critical, historical study of the New Testament and Christian origins. But, I think this illustrates that Cupitt, like Rorty and other anti-realists, often slips into a realist mode of discourse, particularly when discussing concrete questions.
18. See, for example, his discussion of the etiology of the belief in realism and of the gains to be made by coming to recognize its illusory character in *Philosophy's Own Religion* (120–26).
19. *Life, Life*, 3.
20. "Rorty on Knowledge," 75.
21. I have benefited enormously from Michael Williams' discussion of Hume's "biperspectival solution" to skepticism, and of the general relationship between skepticism and anti-realism in "Rorty on Knowledge" (73–75).
22. "Rorty on Knowledge," 75.

Darren J. N. Middleton, Relational Theology

1. A former Dean of Emmanuel College and Lecturer in the Philosophy of Religion at The University of Cambridge, Cupitt has written numerous books and articles. For an introduction to his life and career to date, see Don Cupitt, "The Wandering Philosopher." Readers interested in book-length commentaries on Cupitt's work should consult Scott Cowdell's *Atheist Priest?* which is a somewhat dated but still helpful assessment of Cupitt's early writings. Also see Nigel Leaves's two-volume assessment, *Odyssey on the Sea of Faith* and *Surfing on the Sea of Faith*. Having followed Cupitt's work for almost twenty years, I think his most important book is *The Sea of Faith*. Readers interested in sampling his different writings should consult Don Cupitt, *Is Nothing Sacred*.
2. I take my percentage figure from Nicholas D. Kristof's fascinating article in the *New York Times*. See http://www.nytimes.com/2003/03/04/opinion/04KRIS.html?ex=1074854464&ei=1&en=bbbe9d2db2ecf5fa I also recommend George Gallup, Jr. and D. Michael Lindsey, editors, *Surveying the Religious Landscape*, 68.
3. I have been helped by reading Sebastian Bakare's *The Drumbeat of Life*. Bakare's work was written to accompany the 1998 jubilee assembly of the World Council of Churches. Talking drums are powerful features of African life. And here Bakare uses them as a metaphor for Christianity's future. I advocate adding "drumbeat of life" to Cupitt's growing list of idioms, or popular expressions, that inform the Second Axial Age's religion, even if we would do well to reflect on the *different* meaning it carries for Africans and Westerners alike. See Don Cupitt, *Life, Life*, 143–47.
4. See Don Cupitt, *Life, Life*: "Living is not a matter of applied *knowledge*," he says, "but rather of applied *stories*." And the kind of people who live this way are "life people," women and men who would "like to have more poetical power, and a bigger lexicon of good stories for building their lives with" (11–12). Related ideas may be found in Don Cupitt, *Emptiness and Brightness*, 26–28, 48, 58–63, 84.
5. I propose to concentrate on Cupitt's last two books only. Both are highly readable, even if his *Philosophy's Own Religion* strikes me as more philosophically precise.
6. Cupitt, *Emptiness*, 3, 7–10, 12–15, 18, 22.

7. *Emptiness*, 25.

8. *Emptiness*, 37–42. Also see Cupitt, *Life, Life*, 13–17, 30, 36, 84.

9. Cupitt, *Emptiness*, 26.

10. *Emptiness*, 44. Also see Cupitt, *Life, Life*, 84.

11. Cupitt, *Emptiness*, 103–12. Also see Cupitt, *Life, Life*, 47–50, 91–94, 115–17.

12. There is no question that Cupitt's observations hold true for Great Britain, where Christianity is not so much in decline as it is in free fall. See Callum Brown, *The Death of Christian Britain*. To my mind, however, applying his remarks to North America, much less the rest of the world, is stretching the point. See Christian Smith, *American Evangelicalism*. On the subject of Christianity in postcolonial nations, I can think of no better introduction than two recent books by Andrew F. Walls. See *The Missionary Movement in Christian History* and *The Cross-Cultural Process in Christian History*.

13. Numerous books record this development. I recommend Mark A. Noll, *American Evangelical Christianity*. Also see Stephen Prothero, *American Jesus*.

14. Cupitt, *Emptiness*, 7–15.

15. *Emptiness*, 28.

16. *Emptiness*, 34.

17. Western writers who use this story-cycle include (to name but a few of the many): Wendell Berry, Carol Bly, Frederick Buechner, Annie Dillard, Louise Erdrich, Tess Gallagher, Gail Godwin, Patrica Hampl, Oscar Hijuelos, Garrison Keilor, Kathleen Norris, Reynolds Price, Anne Tyler, and John Updike. Recent films that make full use of this story-cycle include *The Lord of the Rings* and *The Matrix* trilogies, two of the most successful movie franchises in worldwide cinematic history. For additional information on films in this genre, see the online journal of religion and film: http://www.unomaha.edu/~wwwjrf/ Interested readers should also see David S. Cunningham, *Reading is Believing*; David Dark, *Everyday Apocalypse*; Robert Jewett, *Saint Paul at the Movies*; Robert K. Johnston, *Reel Spirituality*; Larry J. Krietzer, *Gospel Images in Fiction and Film*; and, finally, Bernard Brandon Scott, *Hollywood Dreams and Biblical Stories*.

18. I have in mind writers such as Mongo Beti, Ayi Kwei Armah, Assia Djebar, Alex La Guma, Anthonia C. Kalu, and Leila Sebbar, to name but a few.

19. I have learned much from Margo Jefferson, the *New York Times Book Review* critic: "Why has there been such an insistent call for an expanded vision of literature, from the Western world to the East, South and North, including oral as well as written work? Because so many of the West's literary custodians failed to do what they taught us literature demands. They failed to extend their intellectual and imaginative capacities past familiar boundaries, to study worlds so unfamiliar at first they were confusing or forbidding and perhaps demanded new kinds of study. It is only human to feel nervous and suspicious at first. Can you trust these finely honed judgments and instincts you are so proud of? How do you make your presence felt? All readers are tourists. We want to make sense of what we see and hear, to find the balance between what is unknown and what we can call ours." See Margo Jefferson, "We Are All Tourists," p. 27. Let me suggest that it is possible to make a similar case for studying

Christianity in its global contexts: We must become good student-tourists of Christianity's cultural and demographic transformation.

20. Cupitt, *Life, Life*, 1–7, 33–38. Also see Cupitt, *Philosophy's Own Religion*, 15–32.

21. See Philip Jenkins, *The Next Christendom*. This book has some obvious weaknesses, not the least of which concerns the unfortunate use of "Christendom" to describe the rise of Christian communities outside the West, but it is a good place to begin thinking about Christianity's future. My own research focus concerns African Christianity. And here I recommend Kwame Bediako, *Christianity in Africa* and Mercy Amba Oduyoye, *Hearing and Knowing*.

22. Cupitt, *Emptiness*, 120. Also see Cupitt, *Life, Life*, 52–53.

23. In this sense, I am not sure our task is to "develop a new and *single* global moral and religious vocabulary." Cupitt, *Emptiness*, 90.

24. As I see it, this is the main point in Cupitt, *Life, Life*, 75–79.

25. We have not always recognized this diversity, what we might call the faith's local expressions, which are born of Christianity's inherent vernacularizing tendencies. But we underestimate Christianity's particular incarnations at our peril. Locality shapes Christian history completely. I suspect that the Ecumenical Creeds are ecumenical failures, for example, because local ideas were not allowed to prevail—it is no secret that the Armenian churches were not invited to sit at the Ephesus table and talk theologically.

26. http://www.fox.com/kingofthehill/ For Cupitt's comments, see his chapter in the present volume.

27. I have learned much on this issue from Thomas C. Fox, *Pentecost in Asia*.

28. See Bakare, *The Drumbeat of Life*, 30–34.

29. Arun Jones, "Learning to Live as Christians," 5.

30. See Gianni Vattimo, *After Christianity*, 15. Also: "Hospitality . . . is not realized if not as a placement of oneself in the hands of one's guest, that is, an entrustment of oneself to him. In intercultural or interreligious dialogue, this signifies acknowledging that the other might be right. If Christian identity, applying the principle of charity, takes the shape of hospitality in the dialogue between religions and cultures, it must limit itself almost entirely to listening, and thus giving voice to the guests" (100–01).

31. While postmodernists have recently turned to the theme of hospitality, I have learned that it is crucial to the stories and ethics of many African communities of faith. Feminist theologians also draw attention to the hospitality ethic as essential to many Western women's spiritualities. It goes without saying that the New Testament upholds hospitality. See Luke 14:16–23; Romans 12:13; 1 Timothy 3:2, 5:10; Titus, 1:8; Hebrews 13:2; and 1 Peter 4:9. Finally, see Robert W. Funk, *A Credible Jesus*, 35–40.

32. Expressed philosophically: If we reconfigure Be-ing as event, as Cupitt does, rather than as Indubitable Foundation, then Be-ing weakens thought. Here 'weakening' entails that hegemonic structures collapse, stories proliferate, and endlessly hospitable readings of such stories emerge as the way forward. I have been helped in this way of thinking by Vattimo, *After Christianity*, 20–24, 41–56. Also see Cupitt, *Life, Life*, 19–22. Hospitable readings of others' stories, or reading with tact, intrigues me. See Valentine Cunningham, *Reading After Theory*.

Eugenie C. Scott, Evolution

1. Lamont, *Philosophy of Humanism*, xi.
2. Jacob, "Evolution and Tinkering."
3. Hyers, "Comparing Biblical and Scientific Maps," 22–23.
4. Hyers, "Comparing Biblical and Scientific Maps," 23.
5. Dembski, "What Every Theologican Should Know," 3.
6. Paley, "Natural Theology."
7. Behe, *Darwin's Black Box*.
8. Scott, "Problem Concepts in Evolution."
9. Peacocke, "Biology and a Theology of Evolution," 704.
10. Montagu, *Science and Creationism*, 9.

Anne Primavesi, Ecology

1. Worster, *Nature's Economy*, 339.
2. Hughes, *Environmental History*, 30–38.
3. Bettenson, *Early Christian Fathers*, 103, 126, 166.
4. Worster, *Nature's Economy*, 36.

Jack A. Hill, Boy Scout

1. The story is found in Pali Buddhist literature. It also appears in Jacob, *A Second Handful of Popular Maxims*, iv–v, 63, and in other publications. I am indebted to Andrew Fort for linking me to listserve correspondence with Amod Lele concerning the origins of this story. Amod Lele attributes her information to Katherine Ulrich at DePauw University.
2. Mary Fisher, *Living Religions*, 134.
3. To the extent that we *consciously* build up our storehouses of moral conventions, we give "consent" to some conventions and reject others. In this sense, we can be said to be participating in what Richard Holloway describes as "our new lightweight moral tradition" (see his *Godless Morality*, 156).
4. Throughout the essay, I use the expression "American" to refer to citizens of the United States, and not the rest of the Americas.
5. Robertson McQuilkin would represent this school of thought. See his *An Introduction to Biblical Ethics.*
6. Here I am not adopting a realist position about the "elephant" under discussion. Rather, I am saying that we do have "conventions" which persons take to have moral force, and therefore, which have practical validity. To the degree that I am concerned to ground ethics in experiences of life itself, I share Don Cupitt's focus on "life" (see his *Life, Life*).
7. Thomas Kuhn, *The Structure of Scientific Revolutions*. See especially, chapter ten, "Revolutions as Changes of World View," 111–35.
8. Given the pre-eminence of the Judeo-Christian tradition in the American experience, the Jesus tradition represents the most practical, available instrument for pressuring ethical progress in the U.S. context. Similarly, the teachings of the Buddha (in many areas of South East Asia) or Lao-Tzu (in China) might equally represent practical instruments for igniting parallel paradigm shifts in their respective contexts.
9. These categories—of the self, our social destinies and criteria for action—represent modifications of James Gustafson's three base points of ethics in *Christ and the Moral Life*, 1–2.

10. In this regard, my approach has affinities with Anglo-American pragmatism, and rejects the ontological assumptions implicit in Paul Tillich's rationalistic-progressive approach, which still posits the existence of eternal principles and what he termed "the natural law of morals" (see his essay, "Ethics in a Changing World," 695).

11. Bruce Springsteen, "Born in the U.S.A."

12. In *God Bless the U.S.A.*, by Lee Greenwood.

13. See *Boy Scout Handbook*, 19, 84. The Girl Scout phenomenon represents a parallel development that would be important to consider in a longer work. Here I am simply utilizing the Boy Scout metaphor as a way of talking about the moral ambiguity implicit in the country, and do therefore provide a male perspective on a moral paradigm which has a clear male bias.

14. *Boy Scout Handbook*, 11.

15. While the international dimension of the Boy Scout organization has evolved in recent years, I am primarily concerned with its American manifestation. The eagle with the shield on the Boy Scout badge is the national emblem of the United States.

16. Dwight C. Smith, Jr. describes this popular image of mafia in *The Mafia Mystique*. I use the term "mafia" here as a heuristic term to describe this popular image, not to specify gangsters associated with particular Italian American families. As an indication of the level of our fascination with the mafia it is interesting to note that the film, "The Godfather," was the greatest money-making movie of its time (Conklin, "Organized Crime and American Society," 1).

17. As cases in point, consider the cinematic portrayals of each of these deeds in The Thomas Crown Affair, Butch Cassidy and the Sundance Kid, and Cool Hand Luke, respectively.

18. It is interesting to note how much political mileage the current governor of California derived from playing upon his movie identification as "terminator."

19. In *Beleaguered Rulers*.

20. "Cultural narratives" are the stories a culture tells us about itself. Roger Betsworth sketches the four narratives above in his *Social Ethics*. I draw heavily, though not exclusively, on Betsworth's typology.

21. See Niebuhr, *The Kingdom of God in America*. In a sermon on board the *Arbella* before landing in America, John Winthrop elaborated how the Puritans were to establish the Massachusetts Bay Colony as the New Israel. See Winthrop, "A Model of Christian Charity," 83.

22. Betsworth, *Social Ethics*, 16.

23. Betsworth, *Social Ethics*, 26.

24. See Deut 9:15.

25. See Luke 1:52–53.

26. Betsworth, *Social Ethics*, 17, 109.

27. Betsworth, *Social Ethics*, 110.

28. See Jonathan Edwards' sermon, "The Latter-Day Glory is Probably to Begin in America."

29. Betsworth, *Social Ethics*, 111.

30. Hudson, *Religion in America*, 60–194.

31. *White Jacket*, 157.

32. Betsworth, *Social Ethics*, 124–25.

33. *Handbook*, 83.

34. *Handbook*, 84–85. An international dimension is added in the 1990

Handbook, which now states the loyalty requirement as, "A Scout is true to his family, friends, Scout leaders, school, nation, and world community" (7).

35. For example, there is a reference to thanking God for the abilities he has given **you**, where the emphasis is on one's own development rather than on the fact that God equipped you for such development (see *Handbook,* 381).

36. The 1959 edition of the *Handbook* presents all of its scouts as white except for one dark face in the world brotherhood section (25). On the other hand, the 1990 edition pictures five white and two black children on its cover, and includes numerous pictures of non-white children throughout. There are references to Martin Luther King, Harriet Tubman and the civil rights movement and even a mention of AIDS, but no explicit reference to poor Americans, let alone to any class conflict.

37. See Betsworth, *Social Ethics,* 53–80. The following account draws on Betsworth's key points regarding the Gospel of success in America.

38. See Mead, *The Nation with the Soul of a Church.*

39. See McGuffey, *McGuffey's Fifth Eclectic Reader,* 231.

40. Carnegie, "Wealth."

41. These value orientations have affinities with the non-traditional ways of being religious in Streng, Lloyd, and Allen, eds., *Ways of Being Religious.* I have combined the seventh and eighth modes of religiosity in my "techno-consumerist" moral orientation. I also draw heavily on Betsworth's account of the story of well-being, *Social Ethics,* 81–106.

42. Christopher Lasch describes the heavy demands modern Americans place on personal relationships in *The Culture of Narcissism.*

43. Betsworth, *Social Ethics,* cites Nena and George O'Neill's *Open Marriage* as an example of this moral orientation.

44. As with the Boy Scout image, I focus on the Mafia boss image as a shared "mental construct" or "ideal type" in the popular imagination. For a detailed discussion of the "mafia mystique" as "pictures in our heads" see Smith, *The Mafia Mystique* , 8–16.

45. In the late 1920s, Italian-Americans became dominant among mobsters in America and were still the major ethnic group in large-scale criminal syndicates in the 1970s. See Conklin, *The Crime Establishment,* 9.

46. Conklin, *The Crime Establishment,* cites one observer who viewed the Mafia as a "model of management" for all businessmen to emulate ("Mafia as a Model of Management"). Citing the article, Conklin says that the mafia syndicate is characterized by "the small number of levels of management, the quality of information flow, the control over subordinates, and organizational sensitivity to changing social conditions" (3).

47. Conklin, *The Crime Establishment,* 2–3. For an illustration of such mobility, Conklin refers readers to Ianni, *A Family Business,* 83.

48. Conklin, *The Crime Establishment,* 4.

49. While some of these activities may be viewed as essentially "crimes without victims," the sale of narcotics, loan sharking, extortion, embezzlement, the corruption of public officials, and murder clearly victimize others.

50. According to Conklin, there are several senses in which the mafia motif evokes a "subterranean" value system, including a get rich quickly mentality, spending money in ostentatious ways and challenging authority (3). However, some sources argue that the bosses of organized crime

generally live more modest and unostentatious lifestyles. See Chamber of Commerce of the United States, *Deskbook on Organized Crime*, 8.

51. However, there is a popular perception that the gangster directs his violence only against rival mobsters or petty criminals who thus get "what they deserve." While this is not in fact the case, there is a sense in which the mafia's violence represents a very carefully constructed and surgically executed weapon against the greediest and hard-hearted among us. See Conklin, *The Crime Establishment*, 1–2.

52. While this passage is open to a variety of interpretations, and the Fellows of the Jesus Seminar were evenly divided on its authenticity, I have utilized it as a point of departure because I want to emphasize Jesus' identity as a follower of John the Baptist, and this passage reflects what was apparently John's fluid, counter-cultural lifestyle. It also serves as a bridge to the concept of the "liminal" self who is in transition from one established place, stage or identity to another place, stage or identity that is yet to materialize. In the following section, where there are two chapter and verse citations provided for a passage of scripture, the first citation is drawn from Funk and the Jesus Seminar, *Gospel of Jesus*. Where only one citation is provided, it is also from *Gospel of Jesus*.

53. Arnold Van Gennep defined the "liminal" as "all the ceremonial patterns which accompany a passage from one situation to another" (*The Rites of Passage*, 10). Victor Turner expanded the concept to include persons in movements and larger social processes in which "the past has lost its grip and the future has not yet taken definitive shape" ("Liminality and Morality," Firestone Lecture delivered at the University of Southern California, Los Angeles, 1980). Such periods are marked by "hitherto unprecedented modes of ordering relations between ideas and people" (*Image and Pilgrim in Christian Culture*, 2).

54. It should be noted that this is the only time the term "acquitted" or "justified" is used in the gospels with reference to an individual, while it is prominently employed in Paul's letters. Therefore, its inclusion may be more reflective of the early Christian movement than it is of the historical Jesus' utterances. But, since it is a key element in explicating the sense in which the parable points to a stunning reversal, it is legitimate to emphasize the term here. See the commentary in *Five Gospels*, 369.

55. The Fellows of the Jesus Seminar viewed this depiction of John with skepticism because it used a commonplace description of a prophet's attire. See "Notes" to *The Gospel of Jesus*, 90–91.

56. For a synopsis of the Seminar's thinking regarding Jesus and an apocalyptic view of history, see the essay, "God's Imperial Rule," in the *Five Gospels*, 136–37.

57. In the passage, by covering up the treasure and buying the field without telling the owner, the person acts with a level of deception. Perhaps Jesus uses this questionable moral example as a way of suggesting that even God's imperial rule is not immune to corrupt human behavior (see, in this connection, the discussion of the parable of the dishonest manager below).

58. As described in Thomas, the fact that the mustard seed grows only into a large plant, rather than into a tree, would suggest that the growth from small to large should not be overstated. Here Jesus may well be making light of established expectations that the kingdom would be compared to something truly great.

59. Since leaven was traditionally viewed as a symbol of corruption and evil, Jesus' use of it to describe the kingdom is all the more shocking.

60. The film *Babette's Feast,* in which a French chef converts a lottery win into an elaborate celebrative meal for guests, who themselves experience "changes of heart" in the process of eating the meal, is illustrative of these themes.

61. Because this parable has only been known since the discovery of the Gospel of Thomas, and there are no parallels with other gospels, there was some reluctance on the part of the Jesus Seminar scholars to view it as authentic to Jesus (See Funk, *The Five Gospels,* 524–25). While it is reminiscent of parables that focus on one's capability to perform an action, or may represent a reversal where the little guy takes out the big guy, it may also reflect Jesus' provocative way of symbolizing how the kingdom is creating a space. The assassination of the evil one may be the act of a gracious god. That is, it may be an embodiment of love that maintains and saves life.

62. Both the latecomers and the early arrivals are surprised in the parable, and the graciousness shown to the latecomers parallels God's reversal of expectations for the poor. See the commentary (Funk, *Five Gospels,* 225).

63. Although it would be erroneous to take the passage literally—it evokes comic imagery of a camel being wedged through a narrow passage—it does resonate with a "context where wealth functioned as an impediment to entering God's domain" (see commentary, Funk, *Five Gospels,* 223).

64. See Funk, *Honest to Jesus,* and Borg, *Meeting Jesus Again for the First Time.*

65. This passage is a "case parody" (like the dictums to turn the other cheek and give the shirt off one's back) or an exaggerated admonition that, because of its extreme nature, prompts fresh kinds of reactions. See commentary, *Five Gospels,* 144–45.

66. While Jesus probably didn't recruit any followers, he certainly had them.

67. See the comparison of Jesus' mode of addressing God with the regulation found in one of the Dead Sea Scrolls in the "Notes" to *The Gospel of Jesus,* 99–100.

68. See commentary in *Five Gospels,* 318–20.

69. See commentary in *Five Gospels,* 148.

70. There is a parallel teaching in the story of the woman caught in adultery, where Jesus says, "Whoever in this crowd has never committed a sin should go ahead and throw the first stone at her" (7:20–30; John 8:3–11).

71. As a case parody (see note 65 above), this aphorism would function to prompt listeners to "react differently to events of aggression" (see commentary, *Five Gospels,* 144–45). Thus, while it is perhaps erroneous to read it—as some Pacifists do—as a literal call for non-violent responses, the aphorism does call into question the kind of knee jerk resorts to violence that we would associate with the mafia motif.

72. This passage, like the preceding one, is an example of a case parody and therefore could serve as a catalyst for imaginative thinking, even though it might conjure up an image of defendants walking around naked. Elsewhere, Jesus appears to stress the importance of trying to mediate disputes or settle out of court (3:21–22; Luke 12:58–59).

73. When it comes to helping out folks in distress, the gospel writers portray a Jesus who challenges us to go the whole nine yards ("Whoever has two

shirts should share with someone who has none; whoever has food should do the same" [1:9; Luke 3:11]).

74. Footnote 19.11–27 in *The New English Bible*, 97–98.

75. The wildly exaggerated amounts of money signal the hearers of the parable that it is not intended as a simple matter-of-fact tale.

76. It is interesting to note that in conventional versions of this parable Jesus is also portrayed as having his enemies killed on the spot. In *The New English* Bible, just after Jesus finishes telling this parable he is reported as exclaiming, "I tell you, the man who has will always be given more; but the man who has not will forfeit even what he has. But as for those enemies of mine who did not want me for their king, bring them here and slaughter them in my presence." (Luke 19:26–27).

77. This is at least a plausible reading, even if the listeners to the parable would probably have thought that burying the money was the "safe" thing to do.

78. Nor does Jesus refrain from aggressive action against crooks. Whether or not he chased vendors and shoppers out, and/or upended bankers' tables and the chairs of the pigeon merchants, he was certainly angry in the temple (20:1–2; Mark 11:15, 17).

79. Although this passage was not authentic to Jesus, and appears to represent a moralizing by Luke, it coheres well with the kind of sharp, unsentimental moral insight Jesus might have intended but not expressed in such a prosaic fashion (see commentary, Funk, *Five Gospels*, 358–59).

Works Consulted

Robert W. Funk, Enlightened Faith

Berger, Peter L. and Thomas Luckman. *The Social Construction of Reality: A Treatise in the Sociology of Knowledge.* Garden City, NY: Doubleday, 1966.

Bloom, Harold. *Omens of Millennium: The Gnosis of Angels, Dreams, and Resurrection.* New York: Riverhead Books, 1996.

Borg, Marcus J. *Jesus a New Vision: Spirit, Culture, and the Life of Discipleship.* HarperSanFrancisco, 1987.

Greene, Brian. *The Elegant Universe: Superstrings, Hidden Dimensions, and the Quest for the Ultimate Theory.* New York: Vintage Books, 1999.

_____, "The Time We Thought We Knew." Op ed. *New York Times.* January 1, 2004.

Margolis, Howard. *It Started with Copernicus: How Turning the World Inside Out Led to the Scientific Revolution.* New York: McGraw-Hill, 2002.

Robinson, John A. T. *Honest to God.* Philadelphia: The Westminster Press, 1963.

Wilson, Edward O. *Consilience: The Unity of Knowledge.* New York: Vintage Books, 1998.

Joe Bessler-Northcutt, Hard Questions

Arendt, Hannah. *The Human Condition.* Chicago: University of Chicago Press, 1958.

Bhabha, Homi K. *The Location of Culture.* New York: Routledge, 1994.

Bessler-Northcutt, Joe. "Truth as Empire: A Troubling Metaphor in Christian Theology," *Encounter* 65, 2 (2004), 137–62.

Cupitt, Don. *Emptiness and Brightness.* Santa Rosa, CA: Polebridge Press, 2001.

Geering, Lloyd. *Christianity Without God.* Santa Rosa, CA: Polebridge Press, 2002.

Heiffetz, Ronald. *Leadership Without Easy Answers.* Cambridge, MA: Belknap/Harvard University Press, 1994.

Kristoff, Nicholas. "God, Satan and the Media." *New York Times* , March 4, 2003, A27.

_____, "Believe It, or Not." *New York Times,* August 15, 2003, A29.

Kaufman, Gordon. *In the Face of Mystery.* Cambridge, MA: Harvard University Press, 1993.

Keller, Catherine. *Face of the Deep: A Theology of Becoming.* New York: Routledge, 2003.

Lakoff, George and Mark Johnson. *Metaphors We Live By.* Chicago: University of Chicago Press, 1984.

McFague, Sallie. *The Body of God.* Minneapolis: Augsburg Fortress Press, 1993.

_____, *Models of God.* Philadelphia: Fortress Press, 1987.

Metz, Johann Baptist. *Followers of Christ: The Religious Life and the Church.* New York: Paulist Press, 1978.

SteinhoffSmith, Roy. *The Mutuality of Care.* St. Louis: Chalice Press, 2000.

Wills, Garry. *Papal Sin: Structures of Deceit.* New York: Image Books, 2001.

Arthur J. Dewey, Ecclesial Tectonics

Jenkins, Philip. *The Next Christendom: The Coming of Global Christianit,.* Oxford: Oxford University Press, 2002.

Stephen J. Patterson, Killing Jesus

Detienne, Marcel and Jean-Pierre Vernant. *The Cuisine of Sacrifice Among the Greeks.* Trans. by Paula Wissing. Chicago: University of Chicago Press, 1989.

Hengel, Martin. *The Atonement: The Origins of the Doctrine in the New Testament.* Philadelphia: Fortress, 1981.

Koester, Helmut. "Jesus the Victim." *Journal of Biblical Literature* 111 (1992): 3–15.

Nickelsburg, George. *Resurrection, Immortality, and Eternal Life in Intertestamental Judaism.* Harvard Theological Studies 26. Cambridge, MA: Harvard University Press, 1972.

Patterson, Stephen. *Beyond the Passion: Rethinking the Death and Life of Jesus .* Minneapolis: Fortress, 2004.

Patterson, Stephen J. 'Why Did Christians Say: 'God Raised Jesus from the Dead'? 1 Cor 15 and the Origins of the Resurrection Tradition," *Forum* 10 (1994): 135–60.

Seeley, David. *The Noble Death: Greco-Roman Martyrology and Paul's Concept of Salvation.* Journal for the Study of the New Testament, Supplement Series 28. Sheffield: JSOT Press, 1990.

Stowers, Stanley. "Greeks Who Sacrifice and Those Who Do Not: Toward an Anthropology of Greek Religion." Pp. 293–333 in L. Michael White and O. Larry Yarbrough, *The Social World of the First Christians: Essays in Honor of Wayne A. Meeks.* Minneapolis: Fortress, 1995.

Williams, Sam. *Jesus' Death as Saving Event: The Background and Origin of a Concept.* Missoula, MT: Scholars Press, 1975.

Robert J. Miller, Literal Incarnation

Hick, John. *The Metaphor of God Incarnate.* Louisville: Westminster John Knox, 1993.

Roy W. Hoover, Tradition and Faith

Cupitt, Don. *Reforming Christianity.* Santa Rosa, CA: Polebridge Press, 2001.

Kaufman, Gordon. *In Face of Mystery: A Constructive Theology.* Cambridge, MA: Harvard University Press, 1993.

Oden, Thomas C. *The Rebirth of Orthodoxy.* HarperSanFrancisco, 2003.

Smith, Huston. *The World's Religions.* HarperSanFrancisco, 1991.

Tarnas, Richard. *The Passion of the Western Mind: Understanding the Ideas That Have Shaped Our World View.* New York: Ballantine Books, 1993.

Tillich, Paul. *Systematic Theology.* Vol. II. Chicago: University of Chicago Press, 1957.

_____, *Systematic Theology.* Vol. III. Chicago: University of Chicago Press, 1963.

_____, *The Religious Situation*. Trans. by H. Richard Niebuhr. New York: Meridian Books, 1956.

Williams, Rowan. "*Honest to God* in Great Britain." Pp. 153–83 in John A. T. Robinson, *Honest to God*. Fortieth anniversary edition. Louisville and London: Westminster John Knox Press, 2002.

Richard Holloway, Church Organist

Friedrich Nietzsche. *Human, All-Too-Human*, section 224. *The Portable Nietzsche*, selected and translated, with an introduction, prefaces, and notes by Walter Kaufmann. New York: Penguin Books, 1976.

Daryl D. Schmidt, Veritas

Bessler-Northcutt, Joe. "The Theological Risks of Taking Jesus Seriously." *Forum* N.S. 4,2 (forthcoming).

Borg, Marcus. *The God We Never Knew: Beyond Dogmatic Religion to a More Authentic Contemporary Faith*. San Francisco: HarperSanFrancisco, 1997.

_____, *The Heart of Christianity: Rediscovering a Life of Faith*. San Francisco: HarperSanFrancisco, 2003.

_____, *Jesus, New Vision: Spirit, Culture, and the Life of Discipleship*. San Francisco: HarperSanFrancisco, 1987.

_____, *Meeting Jesus Again for the First Time: The Historical Jesus and the Heart of Contemporary Faith*. San Francisco: HarperSanFrancisco, 1994.

_____, *Reading the Bible Again for the First Time: Taking the Bible Seriously but Not Literally*. San Francisco: HarperSanFrancisco, 2001.

Chomsky, Noam. *Language and Mind*. New York: Harcourt, Brace, Jovanovich. 1968; enl. ed. 1972.

_____, *Language and Responsibility: Based on Conversations with Mitsou Ronat*. Trans. John Viertel. New York: Pantheon Books, 1977.

Christiansen, Michael H., and Simon Kirby, eds. *Language Evolution: The States of the Art*. Oxford: Oxford University Press, 2003.

Cupitt, Don *Life, Life*. Santa Rosa, CA: Polebridge Press, 2003.

Deacon, Terrence W. *The Symbolic Species: The Co-evolution of Language and the Brain*. New York: W. W. Norton, 1997.

De Haan, Michelle, and Mark H. Johnson, eds. *The Cognitive Neuroscience of Development*. New York: Psychology Press, 2003.

Funk, Robert W. *A Credible Jesus: Fragments of a Vision*. Santa Rosa, CA: Polebridge Press, 2002.

Geering, Lloyd. "The Secular Trinity." Pp. 33–50 in *The Once and Future Faith*. The Jesus Seminar. Santa Rosa, CA: Polebridge Press, 2001.

Geertz, Clifford. *The Interpretation of Cultures*. New York: Basic Books, 1973.

Goldman, Ari L. *The Search for God at Harvard*. New York: Random House, 1991.

Grant, C. David. *A Theology of God's Grace: Life, Faith, and Commitment*. St. Louis: Chalice Press, forthcoming.

_____, *God, the Center of Value: Value Theory in the Theology of H. Richard Neibuhr*. Fort Worth, TX: Texas Christian University Press, 1984.

_____, *Thinking Through Our Faith: Theology for 21ˢᵗ Century Christians*. Nashville: Abingdon Press, 1998.

Gulley, Phillip, and James Mulholland. *If Grace Is True: Why God Will Save Every Person*. San Francisco: HarperSanFrancisco, 2003.

Hurford, J. R., M. Studdert-Kennedy, and C. Knight, eds. *Approaches to the Evolution of Language: Social and Cognitive Bases*. Cambridge: Cambridge University Press, 1998.

Kaufman, Gordon D. *In the Beginning . . . Creativity.* Minneapolis: Fortress Press, 2004.

Klaassen, Walter. *Anabaptism: Neither Catholic nor Protestant.* Waterloo, Ontario: Conrad Press, 1973.

Köstenberger, Andreas. "Review of The Search for God at Harvard." *Trinity Journal* 13 (1992): 249.

Littleton, C. Scott. *The New Comparative Mythology: An Anthropological Assessment of the Theories of Georges Dumézil.* 3d. ed. Berkeley: University of California Press, 1982.

Monroe, Kelly, ed. *Finding God at Harvard: Spiritual Journeys of Thinking Christians.* Grand Rapids, MI: Zondervan Publishing House, 1996.

Mueller, Ralph-Axel. "Innateness, Autonomy, Universality? Neurobiological Approaches to Language." www.bbsonline.org/documents/a/00/00/05/16/bbs00000516/bbs.mueller.html.

Porter, Andrew P., and Edward C. Hobbs. "The Trinity and the Indo-European Tripartite Worldview." *Budhi* 3,2–3 (1999): 1–28; www.jedp.com/trinity.html.

Pinnock, Clark H. *Most Moved Mover: A Theology of God's Openness.* Grand Rapids, MI: Baker Books, 2001.

_____, *Unbounded Love: A Good News Theology for the 21ˢᵗ Century.* Downers Grove, IL: InterVarsity Press, 1994.

_____, *A Wideness in God's Mercy: The Finality of Jesus Christ in a World of Religions.* Grand Rapids, MI: Zondervan, 1992.

_____, et al., *The Openness of God: A Biblical Challenge to the Traditional Understanding of God.* Downers Grove, IL: InterVarsity Press, 1995.

Sanders, John E. *The God Who Risks: A Theology of Providence.* Downers Grove, IL: InterVarsity Press, 1998.

Schmidt, Daryl D. "Making Sense of Paul." *The Fourth R* 15,2 (March–April 2002): 9–11, 14.

Searle, John. *Consciousness and Language.* Cambridge: Cambridge University Press, 2002.

Sharf, Robert H. "Experience." Pp. 94–116 in *Critical Terms for Religious Studies.* Ed. Mark C. Taylor. Chicago: University of Chicago Press, 1998.

_____, *The Construction of Social Reality.* New York: Free Press, 1995.

_____, *Mind, Language, and Society.* London: Weidenfield & Nicolson, 1999.

_____, *The Mystery of Consciousness.* New York: New York Review Press, 1997.

_____, "The Problem of Consciousness." Recent essay posted on: Http://cogsci.soton.ac.uk/~hamad/Papers/Py104/searle.prob.html.

_____, *Rationality in Action.* Cambridge, MA: MIT Press, 2002.

_____, *The Rediscovery of the Mind.* Cambridge, MA: MIT Press, 1992.

Sheler, Jeffery L. "The Ways of Worship." *U.S. News & World Report: Mysteries of Faith* (Special edition, 2003): 7–15.

Stark, Rodney. "Why Gods Should Matter in Social Science." *Chronicle of Higher Education* (June 6, 2003): B7–9.

Wright, G. Ernest. *The God Who Acts: Biblical Theology as Recital.* SBT 8. London: SCM Press, 1952.

Don Cupitt, Beginning All Over

Cupitt, Don. *Emptiness and Brightness.* Santa Rosa, CA: Polebridge Press, 2001.

_____, *Life, Life.* Santa Rosa, CA: Polebridge Press, 2003.

_____, *The New Religion of Life in Everyday Speech.* London: SCM Press, 1999.

_____, *Philosophy's Own Religion*. London: SCM Press, 2000.

_____, *Reforming Christianity*. Santa Rosa, CA: Polebridge Press, 2001.

Wallace, Henry A. *The Century of the Common Man*. New York: Reynal & Hitchcock, 1943.

John C. Kelly, Anti-Realism

Borg, Marcus J. *The Heart of Christianity*. New York: HarperSanFrancisco, 2003.

Cupitt, Don. *Mysticism After Modernity*. Malden, MA: Blackwell Publishers, Inc., 1998.

_____, *The Religion of Being*. London: SCM Press, 1998.

_____, *Philosophy's Own Religion*. London: SCM Press, 2000.

_____, *Life, Life*. Santa Rosa, CA: Polebridge Press, 2003.

Leaves, Nigel. *Odyssey on the Sea of Faith: The Life and Writings of Don Cupitt*. Santa Rosa, CA: Polebridge Press, 2004.

Meeks, Wayne A. *The Origins of Christian Morality: The First Two Centuries*. New Haven, CT: Yale University Press, 1993.

Murphy, Nancey. *Beyond Liberalism & Fundamentalism: How Modern and Postmodern Philosophy Set the Theological Agenda*. Edited by W. H. Kelber, *The Rockwell Lecture Series*. Harrisburg, PA: Trinity Press International, 1996.

Pagels, Elaine. *Beyond Belief*. New York: Random House, 2003.

Rorty, Richard. "Idealism and Textualism." Pp. 139–59 in *Consequences of Pragmatism*. Minneapolis: University of Minnesota Press, 1982.

Spong, John Shelby. *A New Christianity for a New World*. New York: HarperSanFrancisco, 2001.

Tillich, Paul. *Dynamics of Faith*. London: George Allen & Unwin LTD, 1957.

Williams, Michael. "Rorty on Knowledge and Truth." Pp. 61–80 in *Richard Rorty*. Edited by C. Guignon and D. R. Hiley. Cambridge: Cambridge University Press, 2003.

Darren J. N. Middleton, Relational Theology

Bakare, Sebastian. *The Drumbeat of Life: Jubilee in an African Context*. Geneva, Switzerland: WCC Publications, 1997.

Bediako, Kwame. *Christianity in Africa: The Renewal of a Non-Western Religion*. Maryknoll, NY: Orbis Books, 1995.

Brown, Callum. *The Death of Christian Britain*. London and New York: Routledge, 2002.

Cowdell, Scott. *Atheist Priest?: Don Cupitt and Christianity*. London: SCM Press, 1988.

Cunningham, David S. *Reading Is Believing: The Christian Faith Through Literature and Film*. Grand Rapids, MI: Brazos Press, 2002.

Cunningham, Valentine. *Reading After Theory*. Oxford; Malden, MA: Blackwell Publishers, 2002.

Cupitt, Don. *Emptiness and Brightness*. Santa Rosa, CA: Polebridge Press, 2001.

_____, *Is Nothing Sacred?: The Non-Realist Philosophy of Religion: Selected Essays*. Bronx, NY: Fordham University Press, 2002.

_____, *Life, Life*. Santa Rosa, CA: Polebridge Press, 2003.

_____, *Philosophy's Own Religion*. London: SCM Press, 2000.

_____, *The Sea of Faith: Christianity in Change*. London: British Broadcasting Corporation, 1984.

_____, "The Wandering Philosopher," *The Fourth R*, 14, 1 (January/February, 2001): 3–7.

Dark, David. *Everyday Apocalypse: The Sacred Revealed in Radiohead, The Simpsons, and Other Pop Culture Icons*. Grand Rapids, MI: Brazos Press, 2002.

Fox, Thomas C. *Pentecost in Asia: A New Way of Being Church*. Maryknoll, NY: Orbis Books, 2002.

Funk, Robert W. *A Credible Jesus: Fragments of a Vision*. Santa Rosa, CA: Polebridge Press, 2002.

Gallup, George, Jr. and D. Michael Lindsey, *Surveying the Religious Landscape: Trends in U. S. Beliefs*. Harrisburg, PA: Morehouse Publishing, 1999.

Jenkins, Philip, *The Next Christendom: The Coming of Global Christianity*. New York and Oxford: Oxford University Press, 2002.

Jefferson, Margo. "We Are All Tourists," *New York Times Book Review*, July 8, 2001, 27.

Jewett, Robert. *Saint Paul at the Movies: The Apostle's Dialogue with American Popular Culture*. Louisville, KY: Westminster/John Knox Press, 1993.

Jones, Arun. "Learning to Live as Christians with World Christianity," *Insights: The Faculty Journal of Austin Seminary*, 119, no. 1 (2003): 3–7, 34.

Johnston, Robert K. *Reel Spirituality: Theology and Film in Dialogue*. Grand Rapids, MI: Baker Books, 2000.

Krietzer, Larry J. *Gospel Images in Fiction and Film: On Reversing the Hermeneutical Flow*. Sheffield Academic Press/Continuum, 2002.

Küster, Volker. *The Many Faces of Jesus Christ: Intercultural Christology*. Maryknoll, NY: Orbis Books, 2001.

Leaves, Nigel. *Odyssey on the Sea of Faith: The Life and Writings of Don Cupitt*. Santa Rosa, CA: Polebridge Press, 2005.

_____, *Surfing on the Sea of Faith: The Ethics and Religion of Don Cupitt*. Santa Rosa, CA: Polebridge Press, 2005.

McGrath, Alister. *The Future of Christianity*. Oxford; Malden, MA: Blackwell Publishers, 2003.

Noll, Mark A. *American Evangelical Christianity: An Introduction*. Oxford; Malden, MA: Blackwell Publishers, 2001.

Oduyoye, Mercy Amba. *Hearing and Knowing: Reflections on Christianity in Africa*. Maryknoll, NY: Orbis Books, 1986.

Prothero, Stephen. *American Jesus: How the Son of God Became a National Icon*. New York: Farrar, Straus & Giroux, 2003.

Scott, Bernard Brandon. *Hollywood Dreams and Biblical Stories*. Minneapolis, MN: Fortress Press, 1994.

Smith, Christian. *American Evangelicalism: Embattled and Thriving*. Chicago and London: Chicago University Press, 1998.

Vattimo, Gianni. *After Christianity*. Translated by Luca D'Isanto. New York: Columbia University Press, 2002.

Walls, Andrew F. *The Cross-Cultural Process in Christian History: Studies in the Transmission and Appropriation of Faith*. Maryknoll, NY: Orbis Books, 2001.

_____, *The Missionary Movement in Christian History: Studies in the Transmission of Faith*. Maryknoll, NY: Orbis Books, 2001.

Woodward, Kenneth L. "The Changing Face of the Church." *Newsweek*, April 16, 2001, 47–52.

Wolfe, Alan. "The Opening of the Evangelical Mind." *The Atlantic Monthly*, October 2000, 55–76.

Lloyd Geering, Global Future

Metz, Johann-Baptist and Jürgen Moltmann. *Faith and the Future.* Maryknoll, NY: Orbis Books, 1995.

Teilhard de Chardin, Pierre. 'How I Believe' in *Christianity and Evolution.* Collins, 1971.

Eugenie C. Scott, Evolution

Behe, Michael. *Darwin's Black Box: The Biochemical Challenge to Evolution.* New York: The Free Press, 1996.

Dembski, William. "What Every Theologian Should Know About Creation, Evolution, and Design." *Center for Interdisciplinary Studies Transactions* 3, 2 (1995): 1–8.

Hyers, Conrad. "Comparing Biblical and Scientific Maps of Origins." In *Perspectives on an Evolving Creation.* Edited by K. B. Miller. Grand Rapids, MI: Eerdmans, 2003.

Jacob, Francois. "Evolution and Tinkering." *Science* 196, 4295 (1977): 1161–66.

Lamont, Corliss. *The Philosophy of Humanism.* Sixth ed. New York: The Continuum Publishing Company, 1988.

Montagu, M. F. Ashley. *Science and Creationism.* New York: Oxford University Press, 1984.

Peacocke, Arthur. "Biology and a Theology of Evolution." *Zygon* 343, 4 (1999): 695–712.

Paley, William. *Natural Theology: Or, Evidences of the Existence and Attributes of the Deity, Collected from the Appearances of Nature.* 5th ed. London: Faulder, 1803.

Scott, Eugenie. "Problem Concepts in Evolution: Cause, Purpose, Design, and Chance." In *The Evolution-Creation Controversy II: Perspectives on Science, Religion, and Geological Education.* Denver: Paleontological Society, 1999.

Anne Primavesi, Age of Ecology

Bettenson, H., ed. *The Early Christian Fathers.* London, Oxford University Press, 1956.

Hughes, J. D. *An Environmental History of the World.* London and New York: Routledge, 2001.

Primavesi, A. *Gaia's Gift: Earth, Ourselves and God after Copernicus.* London and New York: Routledge, 2003.

Primavesi, A. *Making God Laugh: Human Arrogance and Ecological Humility.* Santa Rosa, CA: Polebridge Press, 2004.

Worster, D. *Nature's Economy: A History of Ecological Ideas.* Cambridge: Cambridge University Press, 1977.

Robert M. Price, Biblical Moral Values

A Group of Friends. *Towards a Quaker View of Sex.* London: Friends House, 1963.

Bullough, Vern, and Bonnie Bullough. *Sin, Sickness, and Sanity: A History of Sexual Attitudes.* New York: Meridian Books/New American Library, 1977.

Campbell J. K. *Honour, Family, and Patronage: A Study of Institutions and Moral Values in a Greek Mountain Community.* New York: Oxford University Press, 1964.

Countryman, L. William. *Dirt, Greed and Sex: Sexual Ethics in the New Testament and Their Implications for Today.* Philadelphia: Fortress Press, 1988.

Douglas, Mary. "The Abominations of Leviticus." Pp. 54–72 in Mary Douglas, *Purity and Danger: An Analysis of Concepts of Pollution and Taboo.* Baltimore: Penguin Books, 1970.

Ellis, Marvin M. and Sylvia Thorson-Smith with Task Force on Human Sexuality. *Keeping Body and Soul Together: Sexuality, Spirituality, and Social Justice.* General Assembly, Presbyterian Church (USA), 1991.

Field, M. J. *Angels and Ministers of Grace: An Ethno-psychiatrist's Contribution to Biblical Criticism.* New York: Hill and Wang, 1971.

Fletcher, Joseph. *Situation Ethics: The New Morality.* Philadelphia: Westminster Press, 1966.

Kraft, Charles M. *Christianity in Culture: A Study in Dynamic Biblical Theologizing in Cross-cultural Perspective.* Maryknoll: Orbis Books, 1979.

Malina, Bruce J. *The New Testament World: Insights from Cultural Anthropology.* Atlanta: John Knox Press, 1981.

Otto, Rudolf. *The Idea of the Holy: An Inquiry into the Non-rational Factor in the Idea of the Divine and Its Relation to the Rational.* Trans. John W. Harvey. New York: Oxford University Press, 1924.

John Shelby Spong. *Living in Sin? A Bishop Rethinks Human Sexuality.* New York: HarperCollins, 1988.

Vannoy, Russell. *Sex Without Love: A Philosophical Exploration.* Buffalo: Prometheus Books, 1980.

Wheat, Ed and Gaye Wheat. *Intended for Pleasure.* Fleming H. Revell Company, 1980.

Jack A. Hill, Boy Scout

Betsworth, Roger. *Social Ethics: An Examination of American Moral Traditions.* Louisville, KY: Westminster/John Knox Press, 1990.

Borg, Marcus J. *Meeting Jesus Again for the First Time: The Historical Jesus and the Heart of Contemporary Faith.* New York: Harper Collins, 1995.

Boy Scout Handbook: A Handbook of Training for Citizenship Through Scouting. 6th ed. New Brunswick, NJ: Council of the Boy Scouts of America, 1959.

Carnegie, Andrew. "Wealth." *North American Review* 391 (June 1889): 653–64.

Chamber of Commerce of the United States, *Deskbook on Organized Crime.* Washington, DC: Chamber of Commerce of the United States, 1972.

Conklin, John E., ed. *The Crime Establishment: Organized Crime and American Society.* Englewood Cliffs, NJ: Prentice-Hall, 1973.

Conklin, John E. "Mafia as a Model of Management." *Boston Evening Globe* (8 Sept. 1972).

Cupitt, Don. *Life, Life.* Santa Rosa, CA: Polebridge Press, 2003.

Edwards, Jonathan. "The Latter-Day Glory is Probably to Begin in America." Pp. 55–60 in Conrad Cherry, ed., *God's New Israel.* Englewood Cliffs, NJ: Prentice-Hall, 1971.

Fisher, Mary. *Living Religions.* 5th ed. Upper Saddle River, NJ: Prentice-Hall, 2002.

Funk, Robert W. *Honest to Jesus: Jesus for a New Millennium.* San Francisco: Harper and Polebridge Press, 1996.

Funk, Robert W., Roy W. Hoover, and the Jesus Seminar. *The Five Gospels: The Search for the Authentic Words of Jesus.* New York: Macmillan, 1993.

Funk, Robert W., and the Jesus Seminar, *The Gospel of Jesus According to the Jesus Seminar.* Santa Rosa, CA: Polebridge Press, 1999.

Greenwood, Lee. *God Bless the U.S.A.* Music Corporation of America and Songs of Polygram International, 1984.

Gustafson, James. *Christ and the Moral Life.* Chicago: University of Chicago Press, 1968.

Holloway, Richard. *Godless Morality: Keeping Religion Out of Ethics.* Edinburgh: Canongate Books, 1999.

Hudson, Winthrop S. *Religion in America.* New York: Macmillan, 1987.

Ianni, Francis A. J., and Elizabeth Reuss-Ianni. *A Family Business: Kinship and Social Control in Organized Crime.* New York: Russell Sage Foundation, 1972.

Jacob, C. G. A. *A Second Handful of Popular Maxims Current in Sanskrit Literature.* Bombay: Nirnaya-Sagar Press, 1902.

Kuhn, Thomas. *The Structure of Scientific Revolutions.* 2nd ed., enl. Chicago: University of Chicago Press, 1970.

Lasch, Christopher. *The Culture of Narcissism.* New York: W. W. Norton, 1979.

May, William F. *Beleaguered Rulers: The Public Obligation of the Professional.* Louisville: Westminster John Knox Press, 2001.

McGuffey, William H. *McGuffey's Fifth Eclectic Reader.* Cincinnati: American Book Co., 1879.

McQuilkin, Robertson. *An Introduction to Biblical Ethics.* Rev. ed. Wheaton, IL: Tyndale House, 1989.

Mead, Sidney. *The Nation with the Soul of a Church.* New York: Harper & Row, 1975.

Melville, Herman. *White Jacket.* Quoted in Ernest L. Tuverson, *Redeemer Nation.* Chicago: University of Chicago Press, 1968.

Niebuhr, H. Richard. *The Kingdom of God in America.* Chicago, New York: Willett, Clark and Co., 1937.

O'Neill, Nena and George O'Neill. *Open Marriage.* New York: Avon Books, 1972.

Smith, Dwight C., Jr. *The Mafia Mystique.* New York: Basic Books, 1975.

Springsteen, Bruce. "Born in the U.S.A." Insert in LP record album, *Born in the U.S.A./Bruce Springsteen.* Columbia Records/CBS, 1984.

Streng, Frederick, Charles L. Lloyd and Jay T. Allen, eds. *Ways of Being Religious: Readings for a New Approach to Religion.* Englewood Cliffs, NJ: Prentice-Hall, 1973.

The New English Bible: The New Testament Oxford Study Edition. New York: Oxford University Press, 1972.

Tillich, Paul. "Ethics in a Changing World." Pp. 693–700 in Paul Tillich, *Writings in Social Philosophy and Ethics,* ed. Erdmann Sturm. Berlin, New York: De Gruyter–Evangelisches Verlagswerk GmbH, 1998.

Turner, Victor, and Edith Turner. *Image and Pilgrim in Christian Culture: An Anthropological Perspective.* New York: Columbia University Press, 1978.

Van Gennep, Arnold. *The Rites of Passage.* Translated by Monika Vizedom and Gabrielle Caffee. Chicago: University of Chicago Press, 1960.

Winthrop, John. "A Model of Christian Charity." Pp. 79–84 in Perry Miller, ed., *The American Puritans.* Garden City, NJ: Double Day, Anchor Books, 1956.

CPSIA information can be obtained
at www.ICGtesting.com
Printed in the USA
FFOW01n0116170115
10277FF

9 781598 150001